DEMOCRACY ON THE EDGE

Second Edition

★ ★ ★ ★ ★

A DISCUSSION OF POLITICAL ISSUES IN AMERICA

Terry A. AmRhein

**WITH DR. WILLIAM K. FIFIELD
ON GLOBAL WARMING AND THE ENVIRONMENT**

STRATTON
—PRESS—
Publishing Life

Democracy On The Edge
Copyright © 2020 **Terry A. AmRhein**

All rights reserved. No part of this book may be used or reproduced by any means, graphic, electronic, or mechanical, including photocopying, recording, taping or by information storage and retrieval system without the written permission of the author except in the case of brief quotations embodied in critical articles and reviews.

Stratton Press Publishing
831 N Tatnall Street Suite M #188,
Wilmington, DE 19801
www.stratton-press.com
1-888-323-7009

Because of the dynamic nature of the Internet, any web addresses or links contained in this book may have changed since publication and may no longer be valid. The views expressed in the work are solely those of the author and do not necessarily reflect the views of the publisher, and the publisher hereby disclaims any responsibility for them.

ISBN (Paperback): 978-1-64895-162-6
ISBN (Ebook): 978-1-64895-163-3

Printed in the United States of America

DEDICATION

This book is dedicated to the victims and survivors of the attack on the World Trade Center and the Pentagon on September 1, 2001. It changed my life forever. And to Jennifer, Paul, Kurt, Will, Maddie and Lucy, my children and grandchildren, who are the ultimate reason I wrote this book.

ACKNOWLEDGEMENTS

To my wife Cindy, who read my chapters even though she's not very interested in politics. To Bill Fifield who helped edit the book and also wrote the chapter on "Global Warming and the Environment". And to Amie Ruggiero and Rob Brill, my editors, who encouraged me to write the right things even though I didn't want to. And to retired teacher and fellow environmental advocate Barrie Bailey of Salisbury, Vermont for her help in the writing, editing and organization the chapter on Global Warming.

Without the assistance, of these individuals the clarity of this book would have been much diminished.

And last but not least, to Kathleen Stolle who encouraged me to write this book in the first place.

CONTENTS

Dedication 3

Acknowledgements..5

Introduction...9

Chapter 1: Citizens United, Super PACS And Nonprofits......13

Chapter 2: Gun Control In America 38

Chapter 3: Global Warming And The Environment 60

Chapter 4: Health Care In America......................................89

Chapter 5: Business In America...124

Chapter 6: The Financial Crisis 159

Chapter 7: The Tea Party, A Comedy Of Contradictions 200

Chapter 8: Debt And The Economy..................................217

Bibliography...247

Endnotes 267

Index...279

INTRODUCTION

9/11 changed my life. I remember I was at work preparing for a meeting when I heard the news. At first I thought it was an accident until the second plane hit the tower. What on earth had happened! I was totally distraught; how could anyone hate Americans so much that they would kill 3,000 people?

Over the following months and years I began to gather information to learn why Al Qaeda hates us. I read many books. One written by Sayyid Qutb, first published in 1964, called *Milestones or Sign Posts in the Road*, was particularly relevant. Qutb was an Egyptian who was educated in the United States. He was a Muslim fundamentalist who was appalled at the decadence and licentiousness of American culture. His book extracted excerpts from the Quran to prove that America is evil and that all good Muslims should fight against American culture at every turn. Osama bin Laden was a disciple of Qutb's teachings. I also read *Approaching the Quran* by Michael Sells which translated many of the suras (verses) into English and then explained their meaning. The Quran is written in poetic verse and the meanings of the suras are not always obvious. I learned that, just like the Bible, the Quran is basically a moral book that preaches moral ideas. I learned that there are many similarities between the Bible and the Quran: a belief in one God, kindness toward your neighbors and the celebration of holy days like Ramadan and Christmas. Also however, like the Bible, the Quran has passages that, if taken out of context and misinterpreted by religious fanatics, could be used to incite extreme violence and ultra-intolerance. Some Muslims extend the belief in one God to such extremes that they will follow only the teachings of God and not any other authority, such as a regional or national government or ruler. Some Muslim governments are intertwined with the Muslim faith and the practice of Islamic law called the Sharia. Obviously bin Laden believed in this "only one God" principle and was appalled at the United States' intrusion into the Muslim holy land of Arabia.

When President George W. Bush announced that Iraq and Saddam Hussein were preparing weapons of mass destruction and that Hussein had contacts with bin Laden, I knew this could not be true. Religious fanatics do not violate their most sacred laws and cooperate with a ruthless dictator. The Bush administration was perpetrating a fraud on the American public. There was never a "clear and present danger" to America from Saddam Hussein and Bush and his cronies knew it. Almost 4,500 Americans have sacrificed their lives for their country in Iraq under completely contrived pretenses from our country's leaders. Books such as *State of Denial* by Bob Woodward confirm that Bush was predisposed to attack Hussein regardless of the facts.

After the invasion, Bush declared "Mission Accomplished" and appointed J. Paul Bremer as special envoy to Iraq. Soon after his appointment, Bremer dissolved the Baath party, effectively eliminating the Iraqi government, and disbanded the Iraqi army. Bremer had just created one million enemies in a very hostile country; most of the people in the government and the entire military, the majority of them armed. It was the dumbest move I could imagine. It extended the war for years, added billions to the cost of the war and added innumerable names to the death toll.

Then came the financial crisis at the end of the Bush administration. Again, I was astounded. How could such a strong prosperous nation plunge from the height of success and prosperity into the perdition of bankruptcy, foreclosures and massive deficits in only a few months? Again I took to educating myself. Much of the information about the financial crisis was available on the internet (although not all of it is true) from sites like Wikipedia. Also National Public Radio provided valuable information about the crisis along with articles in newspaper and magazines. "The Great American Bubble Machine" by Matt Taibbi for example, is an article published in The Rolling Stone Magazine that describes how Goldman Sachs has been swindling America for decades.

By this time I was getting sick and tired of lies and half truths, of statements by members of political parties without any proof of their veracity. Republicans statements suggesting that enactment of Obamacare will lead to death panels that dole out healthcare, were patently absurd to me. Any people who believed this, as Sarah Palin apparently did, has no faith in the American system of democracy and justice. Yet many Americans believe it!

Well, I'm feed up! As an engineer and scientist, I try to make my decisions based on facts. I decided to write a book to investigate various political issues and to explain to those people willing to listen (and read), what the situation really is. I'm not a political scientist, sociologist or politician but I have learned through the years to take complex ideas and break them down into simplified terms that can be understood by non-experts. This is what I did in this book (with the help of William Fifield, MD who wrote the chapter on global warming) I broke down the sometimes complex and controversial political issues in America into easily understood and informative chapters. These chapters are sprinkled with humorous, personal experiences and entertaining interludes to help illustrate key points. I call this book *Democracy on the Edge, A Discussion of Political Issues in America*. I truly hope you enjoy it.

CHAPTER 1

Citizens United, Super PACS And Nonprofits

The First Amendment to the Constitution of the United States of America states:

> *"Congress shall make no law respecting an establishment of religion, or prohibiting the free exercise thereof; or abridging the freedom of speech, or of the press; or the right of the people peaceably to assemble, and to petition the government for a redress of grievances."*

In 2010, the Supreme Court's ruling in the case *Citizens United v. Federal Election Commission* allows corporations, unions and associations to have the same freedom of speech rights as individuals and therefore permits them to spend literally unlimited funds on political campaign advertising. Corporations, unions and associations (like the National Automobile Dealers Association) henceforth are allowed to spend millions of dollars to expound on the superior qualities and virtues of their candidate and why he or she is uniquely fit to be elected to the office of president or senator or congressman. Or corporations, unions and associations can likewise spend millions of dollars telling the voting public why a particular candidate is a lying, deceitful good- for-nothing who has fabricated and falsified all of his or her so-called achievements throughout his or her entire life and in fact is not even an American citizen.

To understand how this situation developed, we must look back into history. As far back as 1907, under a law called the Tillman Act, corporations were prevented from contributing money *directly* to candidates' political campaigns. Following in kind, in 1947 Congress enacted the Taft-Hartley Act that, among other things, prohibited labor unions from contributing directly to a candidate's campaign. Although these laws prohibited corporations and unions from contributing directly to campaigns, nothing prohibited them from acting as a fundraiser for a candidate. The Congress of Industrial Organizations, a federation of labor unions that would later merge with the American Federation of Labor to become the AFL-CIO, formed the first political action committee (PAC) to help raise funds for candidates favorable to their view. In response, corporations began their own fundraising efforts and established their own PACs. The PACs then contributed money to their candidates' campaigns. So what we had were laws forbidding corporations and unions from donating directly into a candidate's campaign fund, but they were allowed to donate to a PAC and then the PAC could make donations directly to the candidate's campaign. These shenanigans proceeded for quite a while, with corporations contributing through PACs to candidate's campaigns to help assure the candidate's election and subsequent favorable votes on legislation. Union members, likewise, contributed to their candidates in an attempt to influence votes. This practice was followed by both parties, Democrat and Republican. No one was immune to the candidate contribution fever. As elections progressed, Democratic contributions competed against Republican contributions, in true capitalistic fashion, and election campaigns became more and more costly. PACs for unions and corporations remained unregulated and influential in political campaigns until the 1970s. In 1971 Congress passed the Federal Election Campaign Act and in 1974 created the Federal Election Commission (FEC). As a result of the FEC's creation, rules were finally established to regulate how PACs were funded and how PACs could spend their money. The rules required, among other things, that:

- Corporations and unions *cannot* contribute directly to candidates or parties, (because of the Tillman and Taft Hartley acts). However, PACs are allowed to contribute directly to candidates and political parties. Labor unions and corporations were allowed to contribute to PACs although the amounts of the donations were limited (initially to $5000 per candidate per election).
- The names of most donors and the expenditures of the PAC must be disclosed in monthly or quarterly reports to the FEC.

So this is how political action committees function. These rules still apply to PACs today (the donation amounts are periodically adjusted for inflation).

From the 1970s to the beginning of the 21st century, the costs of elections continued to grow, and the influence of corporations and unions helped fund this growth. In 2002, Congress, concerned about the growth in election finances and the influence of corporations, unions and wealthy individuals, passed the Bipartisan Campaign Reform Act, better known as the McCain-Feingold Act, named after Senators John McCain, Republican from Arizona, and Russ Feingold, Democrat from Wisconsin. The law sought to reduce the influence that corporations, unions and the rich had on federal elections. As part of McCain-Feingold, "electioneering communications" were forbidden. Electioneering communications are defined as a broadcast that mentions a candidate within 60 days of a general election or 30 days of a primary.

Although the law allowed PACs and other political organizations to support their candidates, it attempted to reduce the influence of these groups by limiting media exposure in the critical time just before elections. Of course, there will always be somebody who will test the "constitutional" waters of any law they don't like. So in 2008 a conservative 501c4 nonprofit corporation (more on nonprofits and 501c4s in a minute) called *Citizens United* sought to show *"Hillary: The Movie"* on DirectTV within 30 days of the Democratic primary. The movie was critical of Hillary Clinton's campaign for the Democratic nomination for President. Fearing that showing Hillary was a violation of the "electioneering communications" law, *Citizens United* sought an injunction from the U.S. District Court of Washington D. C. on showing the movie. The District Court upheld the law saying that showing the political information within the prohibited time limits was unlawful. So, of course, Citizens United appealed that decision and the case reached the Supreme Court.

The Supreme Court decided on January 21, 2010, that it was unconstitutional to limit free speech provided by the First Amendment through restrictions on *independent* communications by corporations, unions and trade associations. The word "independent" is important. It means communications that are conducted with no coordination with the political party or candidate (i.e. the expenditures are independent of the party and candidate). The decision did not overturn the Tillman Act or the Taft-Hartley Act forbidding corporations, unions and associations from making *direct* contributions to political campaigns or parties. But it did make portions of the McCain-Feingold Act unconstitutional, and it overturned the ruling in *Austin v. Michigan Chamber of Commerce*. (In 1990, the Supreme Court ruled that it was not unconstitutional to prohibit corporations from using funds to make independent expenditures on candidates. In other words, prohibiting independent expenditures did not violate the Constitution.) *Citizens United* was a very similar case, and the court decided exactly the opposite.

The Supreme Court effectively permitted a new type of PAC, an "independent expenditure only committee" in which the PAC can expend its funds on advertisements and commercials independent of the candidate's campaign. Following the *Citizens United* decision, corporations, unions and trade associations are now allowed to make *unlimited* contributions to independent expenditure only committees. Voila! The "super PAC" is born. While the contribution limits for a traditional PAC are limited to $5,000 from individuals only, for super PACs contributions are now *unlimited*, and corporations, unions and associates are allowed to contribute. In addition, these super PACs are not limited by the amount of money they can spend on their "independent expenditures." The sky is the limit!

Following *Citizens United*, SpeechNow.org, an independent expenditure only committee, filed suit against the Federal Election Commission to allow individuals to also make unlimited contributions. The Washington, D.C., Court of Appeals decided in March 2010, based on the *Citizens United* case, that individuals' contributions to super PACs were also unlimited. Corporations, unions, trade organizations and now individuals have no limit on the amounts they can contribute to super PACs.

Why, after about 100 years (1907 to about 2007) of Congress repeatedly attempting to limit the influence of big business and big labor on the national elections, would the Supreme Court decide to open the flood gates and let the deluge of money flood into on the election process?

The Citizens United decision

The *Citizens United* case was a 5-to-4 decision. Justice Anthony Kennedy wrote the majority opinion.

— He stated that the First Amendment does not differentiate between business corporations and news corporations. Therefore the McCain-Feingold Act would allow Congress to regulate newspapers (for example,

suppressing political commentary) like it restricts some business transactions and corporate dealings in the business world.
- The majority further reasoned that the First Amendment protects associations of individuals in addition to single individuals and does not limit free speech based on the identity of the speaker.
- The question regarding the influence of "big" money was also addressed. The majority ruling stated that there is no evidence of "quid pro quo" (i.e. donors getting favors from the candidate in exchange for their contributions to a campaign) for large donations. However, large sums are required to provide information to the public, and differing opinions support the public's further knowledge of the issue. After all, the court asserted, "There is no such thing as too much speech."

The dissenting opinion was written by Justice John Paul Stevens, whose ire over the decision is evident. The decision of the court "… threatens to undermine the integrity of the elected institutions across the nation… A democracy cannot function effectively when its constituent members believe laws are being bought and sold." Justice Stevens referenced a number of First Amendment cases that argued that the court had long recognized that to deny Congress the power to safeguard against "the improper use of money to influence the result [of an election] is to deny to the nation in a vital particular the power of self-protection".

Justice Stevens addressed a number of major issues with the decision:
- Expenditures on a campaign, although they may not provide a specific quid pro quo, provide the donor access to the candidate.

- Expenditures create the appearance of corruption.
- The unique quality of corporate perpetual life (e. g. to amass large sums of money, to have limited liability, no ability to vote, no morality, no purpose other than profit making and no loyalty) makes them a danger to a democratic election. The court should allow legislators to regulate corporate participation in the political process. Legal entities are not "We the People." The First Amendment protects individuals' self-expression. Corporate spending is the farthest from the "core of political expression" protected by the Constitution. Spending on a political campaign is just a business transaction to a corporation.
- Justice Stevens attacked the idea that corporate spending allows the general public to hear all available information. Business has unfair influence because of vast sums of money which distort the debate, pushing other ideas off the prime broadcast spots and thus dominating the market. Justice Stevens added that the constitution recognizes limits on free speech, such as fighting words, obscenity restrictions and time/place utterances (you cannot shout fire in a movie theater unless there is truly a fire). Too much speech from one source drowns out other points of view.
- The idea that Congress could sensor the media as a corporation should be dealt with when and if that situation occurs and not pre-empt a decision before it happens. Justice Stevens said the new rules prohibit a law from distinguishing between a speaker and a funding source. He visualized the "press" and "corporations" as entities that are dealt with one by one. The majority view "freedom of the press" as a process or activity, applicable to all citizens and groups, people and corporations alike.

- Justice Stevens also expressed his concern that the new laws would make it very difficult for states to deal with corruption in elections.
- The new laws ignore the rights of the shareholders. Corporate officers and shareholders can contribute to PACs separately from, and possibly in opposition to, the contributions made by the corporation. In fact, the ruling provides corporate officers two voices in the political arena, one as the corporate officer and the other as an individual.

The results of the *Citizens United* case and the advent of super PACs in influencing the national elections may not have reached their full potential during the 2012 election. The Federal Election Commission reported that in the 2008 election, about $1.8 billion was spent on Presidential primary elections, general elections and conventions.[1] For the 2012 elections, the value rose to about $2.4 billion according to the Washington Post.[2] These values, however, are highly suspicious because of *slippery* campaign financing tricks and *fuzzy* regulations governing campaign finances, which will be discussed later. Nevertheless, the super PACs prevalent in 2012 are important. You will hear their names again in future elections. So here are the top 10 conservative and top 10 liberal super PACs based on expenditures in the 2012 election along with some information about each one.[3]

Top 20 super PACs based on 2012 election expenditures

Name of super PAC	Expenditures	Comments
Top 10 Conservative Super PACs		
1. Restore our Future	$142.1 million	Established to support Republican presidential candidate Mitt Romney. Largest contributor is John Paulson, billionaire hedge fund manager. Also W. Spann LLC, a dummy corporation created to cover up a $1 million donation from Edward Conard, a Bain Capital executive. Similar dealings reported by Paumanok Partners LLC and Glenbrook LLC. Contributions also from Marriott family and Melaleuca Products owned by Frank L. VanderSloot.
2. American Crossroads	$104.7 million	Founded by Karl Rove, George W. Bush's senior White House adviser. Members include Mike Duncan, former Republican National chairman; Steve Law, deputy secretary of labor, and Haley Barbour, former governor of Mississippi. Established Crossroads GPS, a 501c4, but aroused suspicion of tax-exempt status due to large sums spent on political campaigns and donations specified for election ads.
3. Freedom Works for America	$19.6 million	Founded by FreedomWorks Inc., a Tea Party 501c4 nonprofit. Ryan Hecker, founder of Contract from America, is treasurer, COO and counsel. Opposed GOP Senators Orin Hatch from Utah and Richard Lugar from Indiana. Supported Ted Cruz in his successful primary campaign against David Dewhurst for the Republican nomination for Senate. (See Texas Conservative Fund below.)

4. Winning Our Future	$17.0 million	Established to support Newt Gingrich. Sheldon Adelson, gambling magnate, contributed at least $21 million. Winning Our Future hired Rich Tyler, long time press secretary to Romney.
5. Club for Growth Action	$18.6 million	Supports limited government and conservative fiscal policies. Touts itself as the watchdog against Republicans that don't match its ideals. Affiliated with Club for Growth PAC, a 501c4 nonprofit.
6. Ending Spending Action Fund	$13.3 million	A 501c4 nonprofit backing a balanced budget and paying down the debt. Founded by Joe Ricketts, former CEO of TD Ameritrade. Current President Brian Baker was an adviser to former Republican Senator Robert Dole of Kansas.
7. Congressional Leadership Fund	$9.5 million	All funds were spent on communications opposing Democratic candidates.
8. Now or Never PAC	$7.8 million	No funds were spent in support of Democrats, but some funds were spent opposing Republicans. Spent $1 million in support of Republican Congressman Todd Akin of Missouri, who claimed women naturally reject pregnancy when raped.
9. Texas Conservative Fund	$5.9 million	Spent $5.9 million in support of David Dewhurst for Senate against Ted Cruz in the primary that Cruz won.
10. Independence Virginia PAC	$4.9 million	Spent $4.9 million is opposition to Tim Kaine, the Democratic candidate for the Senate. Tim Kaine. Kaine won the seat by defeating Republican George Allen.

Name of super PAC	Expenditures	Comments
Top 10 Liberal Super PACs		
1. Priorities USA Action	$65.2 million	Priorities USA Action is affiliated with Priorities USA, a 501c4 nonprofit. Developed to support Barack Obama's presidency. Backed by Paul Begala, political consultant, and Bill Maher, TV comedian. Founded by Bill Burton and Sean Sweeney, former Obama campaign officials.
2. Majority PAC (Now called Senate Majority PAC)	$37.5 million	Created to support Democratic majority in the Senate. Created by Jim Jordan, Senate Campaign Exe. Director, and Monica Dixon, assistant to Al Gore. Largest contributors are National Education Association, American Federation of Teachers, Service Employees International Union. Also Joshua Bekenstein, managing director of Bain Capital, billionaire George Soros, Jeffrey Katzenberg of Dream Works Animation. Supported Missouri Senator Claire McCaskill's re-election and opposed Republican candidate Josh Mandel's effort to unseat Ohio Senator Sherrod Brown.
3. House Majority PAC	$30.5 million	Formed to support Democrats in the House of Representatives. Organized by Alixandria Lapp, formerDemocratic Congressional Campaign Committee official. Contributors include billionaire George Soros and the American Federal of State, County and Municipal Employees union.

4. Independent USA PAC	$8.2 million	Formed by Mayor Michael Bloomberg of NewYork City to support moderate candidates, Republican, Democrat or independent, who support gun control, marriage equality and education reform.
5. WomensVote!	$7.7 million	A super PAC supporting Emily's List, a PAC that supports pro-choice women candidates.
6. AFL-CIO Workers Voices PAC	$67.3 million	Organized and supported by the AFL-CIO.
7. Service Employees International Union	$5.3 million	Supported by the Service Employees International Union.
8. Parenthood Planned Votes	$5.0 million	Supported by Planned Parenthood.
9. Florida Freedom PAC	$3.3 million	Supported by the Service Employees International Union. Most expenditures were on Obama's election.
10. Fair Share Action	$2.9 million	Supported job creation. Expenditures were all to Democrats.

For a more complete up-to-date listing of super PACs and expenditures go to www.opensecrets.org/pacs/superpacs.php?cycle=2014

You will remember that these PACs are "independent expenditure only committees"; their expenditures are required to be independent of a candidate's campaign. However, look at the names of people running these super PACs, both Republican and Democrat. Many of them worked with the candidates or worked in arenas closely associated with the candidates. They know the candidates well and are totally familiar with the candidates' stand on the issues. Hmm, makes you wonder what "independent" truly means, doesn't it?

Also note that total super PAC contributions to Republicans in the 2012 national elections (President, Senators and

Representatives) far outweighed the contributions to Democrats. According to the Washington Post, Republicans received $225 million compared to $92 million for the Democrats.[4] Of course, the Republicans had a national primary that helped elevate the amounts. Still, Mitt Romney received more super PAC money then Barack Obama. Of course, super PACs are not the only source of money. The Republican National Committee and the Democrat National Committee also collect and disburse huge amounts of money. Individuals are allowed to contribute up to $30,800 to a national political party each year (in 2014 this amount became $32,400) and traditional PACs are allowed to contribute $15,000. Again, according to the Washington Post, Republicans received $351 million from their national committee and Democrats received $289 million. In addition, the campaigns can also request donations from ordinary citizens (i.e. "all y'all" folks). (Remember, corporations and unions cannot contribute directly to candidates.) Individuals can donate up to $2,500 ($2,600 in 2014) per candidate per election and traditional PACs, $5,000. In this category, Romney received $479 million and Obama received $733 million. Adding all this up, and allowing for some funds not included in the above three categories, Romney received $1.18 billion and Obama received $1.2 billion.[5]

Just as important as the amount of campaign financing being raised, is the "who" that is making the contributions to the super PACs. Eighty percent of the contributions to the super PACs came from 100 to 200 individuals,[6,7] not corporations or unions. These individuals include:[8]

- Sheldon Adelson, billionaire gambling magnate, donated $10 million to Romney's super PAC *Restore Our Future* and $21.5 million to Newt Gingrich's super PAC, *Winning Our Future.*
- Harold Simmons of Contrac Corp., donated $10 to $20 million to *American Crossroads* run by Karl Rove, $2 million to *Restore Our Future.*

- Bob Perry, the late home builder and instigator in the Swiftboat Veterans for Truth that helped derail John Kerry's bid for President, gave at least $4 million (maybe $10 million) to *Restore Our Future*, $7.5 million to *American Crossroads.*
- Joseph Ricketts, founder of TD Ameritrade and head of the family that owns the Chicago Cubs, donated $12.25 million to his own super PAC, *End Spending Action Fund.*
- Bill Mariott, Marriott Hotel International, contributed $1 million to *Restore Our Future* supporting Mitt Romney. Romney served on the Marriott's board of directors. Both Romney and Marriott are members of the Mormon Church of Jesus Christ of Latter Day Saints.
- Fred Eychaner, owner of Newsweb Corp., donated $3.8 million to *Majority PAC,* $3.75 million to *House Majority PAC,* $3.5 million to *Priority USA.*
- James Simons, chairman of Renaissance Technologies, donated $3.5 million to *Priorities USA* and $3 million to *Majority PAC.*
- Peter Thiel, libertarian venture capitalist, co-founded PayPal, donated $2.6 million to *Endorse Liberty* in support of Ron Paul.
- Robert Rowling, runs TRT Holdings that owns Omni Hotels and Golds Gym, gave $5 million to *American Crossroads.*
- William Koch, energy magnate, gave $4 million to *Restore Our Future.*
- Jeffrey Katzenberg, film producer, former chairman of Walt Disney Studios and presently CEO of Dreamworks Animation, donated $3 million to *Priorities USA Action* and smaller amounts to other PACs.

- Frank VanderSloot of Melaleuca Inc. gave $1.1 million to *Restore Our Future* and $200,000 to *American Crossroads.*
- George Soros, hedge fund manager, contributed $30 million to 527 groups in 2004 to defeat George W. Bush. He contributed $1 million to *American Bridge 21st Century* and $1 million to *Priorities USA Action* for the 2012 election.
- Morgan Freeman, actor, contributed $1 million to *Priorities USA.*

All of the above individuals are part of the 100 or so donors who contributed 80% of the total funds to super PACs in the 2012 Presidential election. You can see that they work in a variety of fields. Most support Republican causes, but some support Democrats. Some are well known, but others are not. They all have one common feature though: They are all mega-rich.

Individuals are not the only ones that contribute heavily to super PACs. Unions have contributed a significant portion to the fray. Here are a few:

- United Auto Workers Union has donated a total of $10.7 million, including $8.3 million to its own super PAC, *UAW Education Fund*, as well as $1.1 million to *Priorities USA*, $800,000 to Majority PAC and $250,000 to *House Majority PAC.*
- American Federation of State, County and Municipal Employees, the largest public employee union in the country, has contributed $4.2 million to liberal-leaning super PACs.
- The National Education Association, the largest teachers union in the country, has contributed $9.7 to super PACs, including $8.3 million to its own super PAC, *NEA Advocacy Fund,* as well as $500,000 to *Moving*

Ohio Forward PAC and $440,000 to *AmericaVotes Action Fund*.
- AFL-CIO, the largest confederation of unions in the U. S., with 12 million members, donated $6.1 million to super PACs including $5.9 million to its own *AFL-CIO Workers' Voice PAC*.
- American Federation of Teachers, the second largest union in the U. S., gave $1.1 million to *AFL-CIO Workers' Voice PAC*, $1 million to Majority PAC and $1 million to *Priorities USA*.
- Service Employees International Union donated a total of $9.4 million to super PACs, including $5.8 million to *Florida Freedom PAC* and $1 million to *Priorities USA*.
- Associations and corporations can also contribute to super PACs. Here are a few:
  - National Association of Realtors donated $2.1 million to its own PAC.
  - National Association of Letter Carriers donated $2.2 million total, including $1.2 to *AFL-CIO Workers' Voice PAC*.
  - Chevron donated $2.5 million to *Congressional Leadership Fund* to elect House Republicans.
  - National Air Traffic Controllers Association donated $2.1 million, $1.25 to *Priorities USA*, $600,000 to *Majority USA* and $156,000 to *AFL-CIO Workers' Voice PAC*.

You can see a full list of 209 major contributors to super PACs on http://www.huffingtonpost.com/2012/09/27/women-vote-super-pac-female-mega-donors_n_1920518.html#slide=893705.

Surprisingly, corporate contributions to the 2012 election did not play a major role. Publicly held corporations appear to be reluctant to enter the political arena when their stockholders vary widely in political affiliation. And why should corporations get into this political funding mess? The CEOs and highest levels of management within corporations made huge contributions to super PACs, but they contributed as individuals, not as corporations. So the corporate world seems to be speaking through its executives, not as corporations. And it seems like, based on the 2012 election results, that the big players in the *Citizens United v. FEC* super PAC debacle are the mega-rich and the unions. If this trend continues into the future, and we will see in 2014 and 2016 elections, the Supreme Court may have set the stage for the greatest source of class warfare in the United States since the early 1900s.

As discussed above, the total expenditures on national elections in 2008 was $1.8 billion dollars and in 2012, total expenditures was $2.4 billion according to the Washington Post report. In the 2016 election, total expenditures on national elections totaled $1.07 billion and in 2018 expenditures totaled $822 million. Remember though that 2016 was a presidential election and therefore reaps more funds. No matter how you figure it though, to buy a congress or president is expensive.

Below is listed the top 20 PACs (top 10 conservative and top 10 liberal) donors.

Top 20 Super PACs based on 2018 Election Expenditures

Name of Super PAC	Supports/Opposes	Indepentent Expenditures
Top Conservative Super PACs		
Congressional Leadership Fund	Conservative	$138,305,427
Senate Leadership Fund	Conservative	$95,054,781
New Republican PAC	Supports Scott	$30,508,249
American First Action	Conservative	$29,251,724
Defend Arizona	Conservative	$21,966,560
Club for Growth Action	Conservative	$12,837,437
Restoration PAC	Conservative	$7,344,432
Integrity New Jersey	Conservative	$7,141,967
Americans for Prosperity Action	Conservative	$6,784,564
American PAC	Conservative	$6,174,526
Top Liberal Super PACs		
Senate Majority PAC	Liberal	$111,587,750
House Majority PAC	Liberal	$72,107,669
Independence USA PAC	Liberal	$38,123,497
Women Vote!	Liberal	$28,022,490
League of Conservaton Voters	Liberal	$16,235,957
League of Conservaton Voters	Liberal	$16,235,957
Change Now PAC	Liberal	$7,912,429
New American Jobs Fund	Liberal	$7,696,817
Highway 31	Liberal	$4,232,558
Next Generation Action	Liberal	$4,123,244

Super PACs and nonprofits

By Federal Election Commission regulations, all donations that a traditional PAC or a super PAC receives and all expenditures that are made are required to be identified in the monthly or quarterly report that each PAC must file with the FEC. The source of the donation and the purpose of the expenditure must be identified in the report. These requirements were established to provide full disclosure to the American public so we'll know who is contributing the money to whom. But suppose a multi-billionaire, Mr. Big Bucks, wanted to contribute a billion dollars secretly, without anyone knowing that he is the donor. (A billion dollars would provide a candidate enough money to run a campaign with no other donations. Add other donations and he or she could amass twice as much money as his/her opponent!) How could Mr. Big Bucks accomplish this? Welcome to the arena of the nonprofits.

Most of us are familiar with "not-for-profit" corporations. The United Way, American Red Cross, Salvation Army, Good Will, Habitat for Humanity, Boy Scouts and the SPCA are not-for-profit corporations. They are called "charitable organizations" or public charities. The Internal Revenue Service has a section in the tax code, section 501c3, defining how the organization must operate. A 501c3 corporation operates exclusively for religious, charitable, scientific, testing for public safety, literary or educational purposes, or for the prevention of cruelty to children or animals. As a 501c3, the organization is exempt from paying taxes, and contributions to the organization are tax-deductible. However, 501c3s are not political organizations. For a 501c3, no "substantial part" of its activities can go to lobbying or political campaigns, and 501c3s are prohibited from having political activities. While voter registration and voter education, for example, are permitted, they must be conducted in a non-political manner.

There are, however, more than twenty 501c, not-for-profit categories. One of these is a 501c4, called "social welfare" organizations that promote the common good and general welfare of a community. This type of nonprofit has been in existence for years. Unlike a 501c3, however, a 501c4 can lobby, campaign and otherwise participate in elections so long as the activities are in tune with the organization's purpose and are *not* the primary activity (practically interpreted as less than 50 percent of the expenditures) of the organization. A 501c4 is exempt from federal income tax, but funds spent on political activities are taxable. Contributions to 501c4 organizations are generally not tax-deductible. The most wonderful thing about 501c4s — and most 501c corporations, for that matter — in Mr. Big Buck's eyes, is that donors to 501c4s are not disclosed! Some donors to any not-for-profit organization may want to make the donation anonymously. In fact, some may not contribute if their name is disclosed. So, not-for-profits are not required to disclose donors. Do you see the huge loophole that the Supreme Court has permitted? Mr. Big Bucks can now contribute his $1 billion to a 501c4 and nobody will know who made the contribution. The 501c4 can then contribute the money to a super PAC without divulging where the $1 billion came from. Beautiful... for Mr. Big Bucks! This type of undisclosed secret money has become known as "Dark Money,"

That's not the only way the game can be played though. Suppose the marketing team for the 501c4 places an ad on TV with an irate elderly man emphatically stating "The Affordable Care Act will not work. It will cost participants 15 percent to 25 percent more in health insurance. It will result in patients seeing unfamiliar doctors that they have not chosen and will reduce the amount of care you will receive. There will be 'Death Squads' working in America." Is this a political ad? Some will say it's not a political ad, it's an "issues ad" designed to educate the public. They are promoting the public good and are, therefore, not political. While some may say these *are* political ads and some may say they are *not*, it's not up to us. It's up to the 501c4 not- for-profit corporation itself that decides whether it must be reported as political or not. I'd say if their ad doesn't say, "Don't elect Obama" or "Don't help Romney get elected," they'd say it's not political. In fact, the federal campaign finance law requires only those donations specially designated for election ads to be disclosed to the FEC. Most donations to 501c4s are not designated, so there is no disclosure required. With the long lead times required to develop and air political ads, it is almost impossible to specify which dollar is used to fund any particular advertisement. Most 501c4s that ran election ads in 2010 disclosed no donors to the FEC.[9] Because of these fuzzy rules (as I mentioned before) regarding how 501c4 nonprofits are required to operate, and since much of the money is not reported to the FEC, it is impossible to get an accurate determination of how much money was actually spent in the 2012 election. That is why estimates on the amount of money spent on federal elections are not accurate. Some names of 501c4 organizations that you may have heard of include AARP (formerly the American Association of Retired Persons.), Crossroad GPS (started by Karl Rove and connected to American Crossroads), Citizens United, Americans for Prosperity (started by David and Charles Koch), NAACP, Heritage Foundation, Tea Party Express, Freedom Works, Organization of America (grew from Obama's old campaign organization), American Civil Liberties Union, Sierra Club, National Rifle Association and Common Cause. Any of these sound familiar? Some are legitimate nonprofits and some are not. You can decide which is which.

The *Citizens United* decision also resulted in the IRS debacle in the spring of 2013. After the decision, the number of organizations that applied to the IRS for 501c4 status more than doubled. To help streamline the qualification process, the IRS gave extra scrutiny to groups having "tea party" or "patriot" in their names. More conservative groups than liberal groups were picked for scrutiny simply because more conservative groups were applying for 501c4 status. The extra scrutiny based on the name, however, was considered to be biased and led to an IRS uproar in the summer of 2013 and the eventual resignation of Acting IRS Director Steven Miller.

The plot thickens

In October 2013, the Supreme Court agreed to hear *McCutcheon v. FEC*. In this case Shaun McCutcheon, the plaintiff, wanted to give money directly to the Republican Party in excess of the individual limit, but was blocked by FEC regulations. (Remember, individual contributions to elections campaigns are limited.)

On April 2, 2014, the Supreme Court ruled on *McCutcheon v. FEC*. In rendering the decision, the court considered many of the same factors as in *Citizens United* (i.e. that campaign contributions are a form of freedom of speech). The court did not change the limit on how much an individual can donate to a candidate or a political party. However, the court eliminated the *total* amount (or aggregate amount) that an individual could donate to all candidates, parties and traditional PACs. Before the decision, the *total* amount an individual could donate was limited to $123,200. In effect, if an individual were to donate the maximum amount to each candidate, party and election committee in a two-year election cycle, he or she could now contribute a maximum of $3.6 million. The decision was heralded as a victory by Senate Republican leader Mitch McConnell, but Senator John McCain, Republican from Arizona and co-author of the McCain- Feingold Act, said the ruling signals that the court wants to dismantle laws that limit the influence of special interest. A side effect of the new ruling is that donations to candidates must be reported to the FEC in periodic financial filings, so we might get to know who the big players are.

Conclusion

The crux of the Supreme Court's ruling in *Citizens United* is that corporations, unions and associations are groups of people and, therefore, have the same rights as individual citizens. But corporations, unions and associations are different from my Aunt Doris' bridge club. They are, as Justice Stevens implied, legal entities that are recognized by the state and are given certain responsibilities and privileges that individuals do not have. For example, corporations have limited liability such that if the corporation is sued, the stockholders in the company are not personally responsible for the debts or penalties of the company (i.e. the people are considered to be separate from the corporation). Individuals can be put in jail, but there has never been a corporation thrown in jail. The Supreme Court could have easily ruled that corporations are not entitled to the privileges of people. Instead, their ruling left the election process in turmoil.

The situation regarding two-legged individual's limit on contributions to candidates and parties, whether it be by independent expenditures or direct contributions, is much more difficult to remedy. (Whether the expenditures occur "independently" or under the candidate's or party's direction, is only a matter of speech; in either case, similar issues will be discussed and similar claims will be made. The "independent" or "direct" label that is applied is only camouflage, a cover-up.) After all, two-legged individuals are real people (in comparison to corporations) and, in so far as people use money to make their opinions heard, limitations on the amount of money they can spend could be interpreted as an infringement on their freedom of speech. Yet, how do you manage the freedom of speech issue with the real potential that the speech of one side (i.e. the rich elite) will have the power of exploding bombs while the other side (i.e. middle America) will have the power of a whimper? The equality of men (and women) — "All men are created equal" — is at risk here. One person's speech should not dominate the arena, while another person's cannot be heard.

The simplest, most direct solution to this situation is a constitutional amendment that prohibits corporations, unions and associations from donating money to political activities in any fashion whatsoever, be it an independent expenditure or a direct contribution. Corporations, unions and associations are *not* people and should not be treated as if they were. In addition, an individual's contribution to a political candidate or party, whether it's an independent expenditure or a direct donation, should continue to be limited. A constitutional amendment could do this. It would help level the playing field so that one candidate cannot achieve a significant financial advantage over another. It would also make the rules simpler and help prevent deceitful behavior. It would also greatly reduce the cost of political campaigns, reduce the influence of money on the campaign and help assure that the *people* choose the candidate, not the just the *rich*. In addition, candidates for national office (i.e. President, Senators and Congressmen) should receive public funding (e. g. through taxes) for their campaigns. This would provide funds for a vigorous campaign to get the message out to the public, but avoid the free-for-all, "money- is-king" phenomenon that exists today. It would allow more time for discussing the issues and less time spent on fundraising.

Unfortunately, there is no sign of enthusiasm for a constitutional amendment to help keep the election process in the realm of a democratic process. Such an amendment should be supported by both conservatives and liberals; after all, both sides depend on the democratic process to achieve their goals. (Or perhaps, that is what the political parties are actually trying to avoid.) Without such an amendment, the more one side spends, the more the other side must spend to keep up. It's a snowball effect.

Since a constitutional amendment or a reversal of the Supreme Court's decisions seems unlikely, perhaps another suggestion may work to revise the election fundraising system. When my wife ran for the town justice in upstate New York, we discovered that it is illegal for a candidate for a judicial office to know who contributed to her campaign fund. This is done to prevent the appearance of undue favorable judgment to the campaign donors. My suggestion is to initiate a similar system at the federal and state level. All campaign fundraising could be done like a "blind trust". Fundraising could be performed by a committee that would collect and disperse funds for the benefit of the candidate but the candidate could not know who contributed, under risk of severe penalty. In this manner, individuals, corporations, unions and associations could contribute money, but there would be less influence peddling or appearance of quid pro quo because the candidate would not know who the donors are. At the same time, the First Amendment right of freedom of speech, as interpreted by the Supreme Court, would be preserved and corporations, unions, associations and individuals could express their freedom of speech until their heart's content.

Democracy in America is not a given; we do not automatically inherit a democratic process. Democracy is fragile and must be safeguarded. Democracy's existence can easily be subverted into a paltry representation of democracy, an oligarchy, where the people are ruled by a few, the rich and powerful ones. Every day, America is slowly inching toward this pseudo-democracy. Yet most people don't realize their peril. After reading this chapter, you may realize that America's election process, the essence of democracy, is stricken with cancer and, while not dead yet, the prognosis is not good. Remember, "We're all better off, when we're all better off."

CHAPTER 2

Gun Control In America

Columbine High School

On April 20, 1999, Columbine High School in Littleton, Colorado, Eric Harris and Dylan Klebold killed 12 students and one teacher and wounded 21 others. This was the largest mass murder on any high school campus in American history. Both boys were considered gifted. Both also had signs of anti-social behavior as revealed in their emails and blog site, and both had been arrested after the theft of tools from a parked car. The boys were sentenced to a juvenile diversion program (designated for youths to prevent them from having a criminal record but requiring attendance in courses designed to improve behavior and mandating restitution or community service) and to attend anger management classes. Subsequent to the arrest, the boys' actions became more severe, as noted in their diaries, with a variety of violent plans such as blowing up the school cafeteria during lunchtime.

Dylan Klebold
Photograph from Wikipedia, the free encyclopedia

At 11:19, the two boys entered Columbine High School armed with a Savage-Springfield 12 gauge shotgun (fired 55 times), a Hi Point 995 Carbine with thirteen 10-round magazines (fired 96 times), a 9 mm Intratec TEC-9 semi-automatic handgun (fired 55 times) and a 12 gage Stevens double-barreled sawed-off shotgun. The boys freely walked around the school firing randomly at students and teachers and tossing homemade propane bombs and Molotov cocktails into classrooms, some of which exploded and some fizzled out.

Eric Harris
Photograph from Wikipedia, the free encyclopedia

Much of the time, Harris and Klebold spent in the library taunting and teasing follow students. To one girl, Harris leaned over a table and said "peek-a-boo" and then shot her in the head with his shotgun, instantly killing her. At another point, Klebold teased a student saying, "You used to call me a fag, you're a fag now." But rather than killing him, Klebold turned and walked away sparing the student's life. By 12:08, the shooting was over. Harris and Klebold had committed suicide and the police and SWAT teams outside the buildings had the school safely surrounded with the dead children inside.

Fort Hood Army Training Facility

On November 5, 2009, 13 people were killed and 29 wounded by an officer psychiatrist practicing at Fort Hood, an Army training facility in Killeen, Texas. The perpetrator, Nidal Malik Hasan, a U. S. Army major, was shot and paralyzed from the waist down during the ensuing gunfire. An FN Five seven semi-automatic handgun equipped with laser sights was used in the shootings, and the murderer was carrying several 20 and 30 round magazines during the shooting. Over 200 rounds were fired during the attack, mostly from the killer. He had no indication of mental problems before the incident. It is alleged he was sympatric to Anwar al-Awlaki, a Yemen-based terrorist group.

On August 28, 2013, the Fort Hood gunman was found guilty of 13 counts of premeditated murder and 32 counts of attempted premeditated murder and was sentenced to death. The death sentence was unanimously reached by the jury of 13 military officers. The death sentence requires a mandatory appeal by the Army. The defendant acted as his own attorney during the trial and admitted he was responsible for the murders. Hasan is presently confined at Fort Leavenworth, Kansas waiting for the sentence to be carried out.

Tucson, Arizona

On January 8, 2011, in Tucson, U.S. Representative Gabrielle Giffords was participating in a "Congress at Your Corner" meeting in a Safeway parking lot when she was shot in the head during an attempted murder. Miraculously, Representative Gifford survived the gunshot. Unfortunately, six people were killed and 12 others were wounded. The perpetrator, Jared Lee Loughner, had a history of drug possession charges and had been suspended from college for disruptive behavior. Subsequent to the shootings, the murderer was diagnosed with paranoid schizophrenia and found incompetent to stand trial. A year and a half later, he was judged competent and pleaded guilty to 19 counts of attempted murder. He is presently serving life in prison. No specific motive for the shootings has been determined.

Aurora, Colorado

On July 20, 2012, at the Century Movie House in Aurora, Colorado, a gunman dressed in military garb, killed 12 and injured 58. The shooter, James Holmes, paid for a ticket and entered the theater dressed in civilian attire. During the screening, he left the building through an exit door to retrieve his weapons and don his military clothing. He then re-entered the theater and commenced firing. He started with a Remington 870 pump action shotgun, then opened fire with a Smith & Wesson M&P semi-automatic rifle outfitted with a 100-round magazine which jammed after about 30 rounds were fired. Subsequently, he again opened fired with a Glock 22 semi-automatic handgun. The killer was arrested by police behind the theater about seven minutes after the shooting started. After the arrest, the killer warned police that his apartment was booby-trapped with explosives. Investigation by police revealed his apartment was indeed rigged to explode with 30 handmade grenades and 10 gallons of gasoline. Holmes pleaded not guilty by reason of insanity which was accepted. He was sentenced to 12 conservative life sentences without parole. No reason for the murders has been revealed.

As an aside, many of the hospital bills for the victims were reduced or forgiven, and the community accumulated more than $5 million in donations which were distributed among the victims and their families.

Sandy Hook Elementary School

On December 14, 2012, 20 children and six adults were shot at Sandy Hook Elementary School in Newtown, Connecticut. Before driving to the school, the murderer, Adam Lanza, had stolen his mother's weapons and fatally shot her while she lay asleep in bed. After entering the school, the shooter walked randomly around shooting children and teachers. All of the children were 6 or 7 years old. One teacher, Victoria Leigh Soto (Vicky) threw herself in front of a student. Both Vicky and the student were killed. After the shooting, the murderer committed suicide by shooting himself in the head. The murder carried a XM15 Bushmaster assault rifle with a 30-round magazine, a 10 mm Glock and a 9 mm SIG Sauer semi-automatic handgun although he used the rifle for the killings. The murderer did not have a criminal record and although he was reported to be autistic, there was no official diagnosis.

Mandalay Bay Resort, Las Vegas

On October 1, 2017 Stephen Paddock opened fire from the 31st floor of the Mandalay Bay Resort in Las Vegas, Nevada. Below the window were thousands of concert goers enjoying a country music festival. Paddock used a bump stock on this rifle to alter the weapon from a semi-automatic into an automatic weapon that doesn't require pulling the trigger for each shot. In the 10 minute melee that followed, Paddock killed 58, and 851 were injured, 422 from gun shot wounds and the others from the human stampede. He fired over 1100 rounds of ammunition. Paddock was a high stakes gambler and was familiar with the Las Vegas scene. Paddock's contact with the police involved only traffic citations. Following this incident, the Justice Department banded pump stocks.

El Paso Texas and Dayton Ohio

On August 4, 2019, a shooting occurred in El Paso. The shooter was Patrick Crusius. Crusius was 21 years old and a white supremacist who wanted to stop the Hispanic Invasion of Texas. He killed 22 and injured more than two dozen. He is being held without bond and is charged with capital murder and may face hate crimes and federal gun charges which carry the death penalty.

Within hours of the El Paso shoots, Connor Betts opened fire in the crowded night club district of Dayton, Ohio. Nine people were killed and more than two dozen were injured. Betts, 24, was killed at the scene by police who arrived within one minute of the start of shooting. Betts wrote articles that showed that he had an interest in killing people. No racial or political motive was found. During the gun fire, Betts shot and killed his own sister.

* * * *

All of these murderers of innocent people, except the Columbine School shooting, have occurred in the last ten years, since 2009. When are we Americans going to get tired of reading about the slaughter of other innocent Americans, especially the children? As a civilized nation we must do something!

Look at the examples presented. Almost all have multiple weapons with magazines that carry a large number of rounds. Some are committed by people with arrest records and some are not. Some of the people have diagnosed mental problems and some do not. The only thing these people have in common is they have all been male and they all killed people with firearms. Take the firearms away from these people and the murders would not have occurred.

A look at the facts

Let's look at the facts. According to the Washington Post and GunPolicy.org, there are more guns than people in the United States according to a new study of global firearm ownership. There are 393 million guns owned by civilians in the US but the US population is only 326 million people.[10] That means that, on the average, there is guns for every 100 people in the United States. America has by far the highest number of privately owned guns in the world. The next highest nations are Falkland Islands at 62.1 guns for 100 people (slightly greater than one-half of the U.S. number per 100 people) and Yemen at 52.8 guns for 100 people. Compare our gun ownership to other industrialized countries

- United States at 120.5 per 100 citizens
- Canada at 34.7 per 100 citizens
- France at 19.6 per 100 citizens
- Germany 19.6
- United Kingdom 5.03 and
- Japan at 0.3[11]

We are most assuredly armed to the teeth. We are certainly prepared for an invasion from another country! Of course, the high number of privately owned guns does not mean that every individual in the US own guns. Many people own more than one gun. In 2018, about 43 percent of the American population own at least one fire arm.[12]

So how does the high gun ownership translate into gun violence? Look at gun homicides in America. Homicide is defined as "the deliberate taking of a human life by another individual". Homicide is differentiated from suicide which is the deliberate taking of one's own life or from manslaughter or accidental death which is not deliberate.

In the United States, there were at total of 39,773 gun related deaths in 2017, the last date that data is available. Of these, 60% were from suicide (23,854), 37% were from homicide (14,542) and 3% were by accidental, law enforcement or undetermined.[13] These almost 40,000 deaths, are more than the 3,000 that were killed in the World Trade Center, more than the 2,372 Americans killed in Afghanistan up to 2018 and more than the approximately 4500 Americans killed in Iraq to 2016 COMBINED! When the World Trade Center was attacked, Americans wanted the terrorists brought to justice. When drugs are rampant in the street, we call for law enforcement and drug education programs to reduce drug use. But when gun violence infects American society killing more people than were killed at the Trade Center, some Americans shout, not for gun restrictions, but for more guns and fewer restrictions. This is absolute unadulterated lunacy! In 2016, America ranks 20th in the world in gun homicides. The highest gun homicide rates existed in Honduras at 22.5 per 100,000 inhabitants, El Salvador at 39.2 and Venezuela at 38.7. But among industrialized countries, American ranked the highest! America's 10.6 gun homicides per 100,000 in 2016 far exceed the rate in

- Canada 2.1 per 100,000 people
- France 2.7
- Germany 0.9
- Australia 1.0 and
- Spain 0.6[14]

And yet there is no outcry for laws to stop this genocide. In fact, there are louder and louder cries from the National Rifle Association to stop any legal action that may reduce these murders. According to the National Rifle Association, high gun possession is a good thing. A heavily armed America would help prevent gun crimes. That's like saying you can prevent cancer by giving the patient more injections of cancer cells. The facts are that high gun ownership translates into high homicides and countries with lower gun ownership have lower gun homicides. That's why America, with the highest gun ownership, has the highest homicide rate of any industrialized nation in the world.

Even such a simple and obvious measure as background checks before purchasing a gun is not supported by the NRA as Wayne LaPierre, chief executive officer of the NRA, stated. The NRA will maintain this position so long as Americans support them.

America's preoccupation with guns

Why is it that Americans are so fascinated with guns? Why are Americans so bound and determined to own firearms? Perhaps our history plays a part. Maybe our history of revolution against a harsh colonial government and our frontier, independent attitude of not depending on anyone, gives rise to our strong feeling about firearms. When Americans were settling the West, we lived off the land by farming and hunting. We depended on our own ingenuity. Perhaps some people still think they're frontiersmen. America sort of grew up being around and depending on firearms for protection in the lawless West and for gathering food. On several occasions in my life I have sat at a table entirely furnished by my own hands, with vegetables from the garden and fish from a lake or meat from the forest, and it made me feel good. I still have an ambition to shoot a turkey and serve it for Thanksgiving, just like the idealized Pilgrims.

Americans also feel they need guns to provide protection for their homes. My wife and I live in a rural area in Vermont. I own a Remington 870 shotgun, and we both know how to use it. I pray that neither she nor I will ever have to use it against an intruder, but I'm going to be safe and not sorry. If someone is stupid enough to try to invade our home, they may be looking at the business end of a 12 gauge shotgun, the most deadly weapon there is at close range. I wish I felt secure enough in my home that I never had to worry about a home invasion. I believe that in some countries, like Great Britain and Japan, people feel that safe. But here in the U.S., that is not the case. With 393 million weapons loosely floating around the country, owned by who knows what type of mad hatter, one has to consider the worst possibility. Here in America, "home of the free, land of the brave," we are so afraid that we must arm ourselves.

Psychologists suggest that violent movies and video games give rise to the desire to own guns and to shoot things. The satisfaction of outsmarting the video villain and having accurate aim sufficient to terminate the outlaw, over time, morphs into real life. This might be especially true for the younger generation that has grown up with these ubiquitous video games. Could it be that after hours of unsupervised video shooting each day that children somehow become confused between an electronic gun and a real weapon?

Target practice is also fun. Trying to shoot beer cans at 50 feet is challenging and gratifying when you get good at it. My father owned a .22 rifle, and I enjoyed target practicing. I used to string up a soda can and shoot at it as it swung back and forth. I got pretty good at hitting the can. My father never let me have a BB gun though. Guns are dangerous and should be treated as a weapon. BB guns are weapons that are treated like toys, so my father thought. He was absolutely right. I took gun safety in the Boy Scouts and learned how to handle a rifle safely. Shouldn't a gun safety class be required before anyone can purchase a firearm?

There are legitimate reasons to own firearms, our heritage evolved using guns. The desire to have guns for self-defense, recreational target practicing and hunting wild game are examples. However, none of these legitimate uses involve the possession of

20- or 30-round magazines or the possession of assault weapons designed for military use. Furthermore, some people, notably convicted criminals, who by their own actions, and the mentally troubled, who because of unfortunate health issues, should not be allowed to own firearms.

The Second Amendment

The Second Amendment to the Constitution of the United States of America reads:

> *A well regulated Militia being necessary to the security of a free State, the right of the people to keep and bear Arms, shall not be infringed.*

Read the amendment again. Note the ambiguity. "A well regulated Militia." Does this imply that the right to bear arms applies only to arms held by individuals in a militia? And the right to "keep and bear Arms," does this imply any person can carry any firearm any place? These questions are not answered by the Second Amendment. Surprisingly, the origin of the Second Amendment is in the English Bill of Rights of 1689, 100 years before the U.S. Constitution. In a religious war between King James of England, a Catholic, and Protestant monarchies of other nations who were fighting over the future heir of England, James was dethroned and retreated to Catholic France. Protestants King William III and Queen Mary II assumed the throne of England thus assuring a Protestant England. Upon acceptance of the throne, William and Mary signed the Bill of Rights of 1689. The Bill of Rights established the powers of the English Parliament and ended the "absolute monarchy" of England. Since King James had attempted to disarm some of his Protestant countrymen, one of the rights claimed by the 1689 bill was to established the right for noble Protestants to bear arms for their self-protection. The American Second Amendment was based on this right. It is ironic that England, the nation that was first to codify the right to bear arms, is also a nation with only a small number of firearms owners.

So the right for citizens to bear arms has been established for centuries. The right is not just limited to serving in a militia, people have a right to bear arms for self-protection. This was affirmed in the Supreme Court decision of 2008, *District of Columbia v. Heller*. In 1975, Washington D. C. enacted The Firearm Control Regulations Act. The law required that firearms must be registered. However, when Dick Heller, applied to register his handgun for home defense, he was denied. The D.C. firearm control act also required all firearms, including rifles and shotguns, be kept "unloaded and disassembled or bound by a trigger lock." In 2003, Heller and five other residents of Washington D.C. filed suit against the local law, claiming that the banning of handguns was a violation of the Second Amendment. After several years of working its way though the courts, it reached the Supreme Court in 2008. Upon reading the record of the court's deliberation on this case, the depth of the investigation and the amount of consideration and thought that go into reaching a final Supreme Court decision are impressive. The court considered the original English Bill of Rights and also the wording of initial versions of the Second Amendment in an attempt to discover the authors' intentions. For example, the initial version of the Second Amendment written by James Madison stated:

> *The right of the people to keep and bear arms shall not be infringed; a well armed and well trained militia being the best security of a free country but no person religiously scrupulous of bearing arms shall be compelled to render military service in person.*

This first version of the Second Amendment clearly recognizes the importance of firearms in maintaining a "free country." This version also had a "conscientious objector" clause contained within it. The final version of the Second Amendment, deleted this clause.

The court also investigated the use of similar language found in other parts of the Constitution to discover the amendment's intended meaning. For example, in deciding if bearing arms applies only to militia, Justice Antonin Scalia in writing the majority opinion stated:

> *Nowhere else in the Constitution does a 'right' attributed to 'the people' (i.e. the right of the people to bear arms) refer to anything other than an individual right. What is more, in all six other provisions of the Constitution that mentions 'the people,' the term unambiguously refers to all members of the political community, not an unspecified subset (i.e. the subset being the militia)… (decision of the Supreme Court of the United States, District of Columbia v Heller, No. 07-290 decided June 26, 2008)*

The Supreme Court decided therefore that the Second Amendment protects an individual's right to possess firearms unrelated to service in a militia and to use these arms for traditional lawful purposes such as self-defense within the home. The court also concluded that the act of disassembling or use of trigger locks on the firearms renders the firearm ineffective regarding the self-protection aspect of the law and therefore declared that provision also unconstitutional.

The court emphasized, however, that the decision reaffirming the individual's right to bear arms, like other rights, does not come without limitations. The Second Amendment is not a right to keep and carry any weapon whatsoever in any manner whatsoever and for any purpose whatsoever. For example, the court has held that regulations forbidding concealment of weapons are constitution. Law prohibiting possession of firearms by convicted felons and the mentally ill, laws prohibiting the carrying of firearms in sensitive places such as schools and government buildings or laws imposing condition and qualification on the commercial sale of firearms are also constitutional. Furthermore, the court's previous decision in *United States v. Miller* (1939) holding that the sorts of weapons protected by the Second Amendment are those "in common use at the time" and the carrying of weapons that are dangerous and unusual weapons are not lawful. (Jack Miller was convicted of illegally transporting a sawed-off shotgun across state lines for the purpose of sale. The court found that since a sawed-off shotgun was not a commonly used firearm and was not part of the ordinary militia's equipment that the conviction of Miller was constitutional.)

So where do the Second Amendment rights stand? The right to carry firearms in the United States of America has been repeatedly found to be lawful. How could any conscientious democratic government find otherwise? How could a government say that you do *not* have a right to carry arms for the protection of your life or the life of your family in your own home? Tying the right to carry weapons only to serving in a militia is obviously absurd. However, the right to carry arms is not absolute. There are limits. Felons and mentally ill cannot carry. This makes sense, who wants a known criminal or an unstable person to carry a weapon? Who wants firearms to be permitted in schools or courthouses? Nobody would suggest this… until recently. Who thinks that ordinary people should own rocket-propelled grenades? You don't need this type of weapon to defend yourself or your home. Reasonable people agree that there should be reasonable limitations to owning firearms. All of these limitations on the right to own firearms seem to make sense, but NOT to the National Rifle Association which has opposed every effort to limit gun ownership.

The National Rifle Association

The National Rifle Association was founded as a nonprofit organization in 1871 in NewYork. After the Civil War, it was determined that about 100 bullets were fired for each soldier who was actually hit. The "stand up in front of your enemy" methodology of the time didn't produce very good results. The NRA was originally organized to promote marksmanship and gun safety. In more recent years, however, the NRA has grown into one of the most influential lobbying organizations in America. The NRA has also grown into the staunchest supporter of unlimited ownership of firearms. The NRA appears to oppose any reasonable effort to curb gun violence in America or any effort to place any limitation upon gun ownership. As was discussed in the paragraph above, it is reasonable to place limitations on gun ownership. Felons and the mentally ill should not be allowed to own firearms. Yet the NRA opposes background checks on individuals prior to buying firearms as Wayne LaPierre stated following the shootings in Newtown, Connecticut. This philosophy has placed the NRA in an unreasonable and irrational position and against the beliefs of most Americans.

One of the NRA's mantras is that gun violence could be reduced if more people carried guns. Can you imagine every person walking down the street with a pistol strapped to their waist and rifles and shotguns in their hands? This is an incredibly ridiculous philosophy. It would result in people perpetually shooting each other. I think there are very few law enforcement agencies in America that supports such an asinine suggestion. In fact, as discussed in the section "Look at the Facts," America already has the highest rate of gun ownership in the world, far more than any other industrialized nation. America also has the highest rate of gun related homicides of any industrialized country in the world. An interesting article in the March 25, 2013 issue of USA Today investigates the issue of citizen heroes stopping a shooting. The article concluded that in 62 mass shootings in the last 32 years, not one shooting was stopped by an armed citizen. In fact, the "hero" is more likely to get shot or killed. In the case of the Gabby Giffords incident in Arizona, an armed citizen admitted coming within a split second of shooting the wrong person, a bystander who happened to tackle the shooter.[15] The bottom line is gun ownership does not reduce gun violence, it increases it.

Another outcry from the NRA "slogan machine" is "Guns don't kill people, people kill people." Well isn't this a brilliant realization? Of course, it's people that do the killing. Who else would do it? The point is that since we cannot get rid of people, we must make every effort to get rid of those people that are doing the killing from having access to firearms. That's a no-brainer, isn't it? The NRA rather than being a force of "good" to help prevent gun violence, has become a force that encourages violence by thwarting any effort to restrict guns in any fashion. While portraying itself as a true patriotic organization, the NRA is really supported to a large extent by gun manufacturers. Rather than being at the pinnacle of defending American liberties, the NRA is really just driven by money and greed.

A further often spoken claim made by gun advocates, and perhaps the most frightening, is that Americans must arm themselves against the possibility of a tyrannical government. I first heard this philosophy from a friend about 10 years ago. At the time I thought it was preposterous. We're a democracy, a nation of laws. We would never need to resort to mass violence to resolve issues concerning democracy. That's what a nation ruled by laws is all about. Our Founding Fathers were very much aware of the importance of arms in maintaining our liberties as well as defending ourselves from invasion from abroad. Of course, they were astutely aware of the necessity of firearms; they had just finished fighting a revolution. So long as the population was well-armed, the nation would never have to fear being overthrown by a tyrannical government.As Alexander Hamilton stated in the *Federalist Papers* in 1788:

> *If circumstances should at any time oblige the government to form an army of any magnitude, that army can never be formidable to the liberties of the people while there is a large body*

of citizens... who stand ready to defend their own rights and those of their fellow-citizens.

"Who stand ready to defend their own rights" is understood that defending those rights could require the use of firearms. It would be wrong, though, to believe that our forefathers fostered use of arms against tyranny over the orderly dominance of a lawful and democratic government. The founders obviously supported democracy. In fact, democracy, in addition to bestowing upon the people the right to vote for representatives candidates, requires the adherence to and consistent enforcement of laws and not the violence offered by mobs armed with guns. A hallmark of any democratic nation is rule by law. Our nation, the first to embrace democracy, is still a democracy. After almost 250 years, America has shown "beyond a reasonable doubt" that democracy can work. Do we trust the country to work out our differences in a peaceful and democratic way, as we always have, and not rely on resorting to a gun? Or has America become such an unlawful and violent country that we must all arm ourselves to protect against our fellow citizens?

The basic question then is: Do we or do we not believe in America and democracy? Many among us who claim to be true patriots will most assuredly raise their right hand to exclaim that they do believe in democracy, that they do believe in our country. Many of these same people, however, will assert that guns are needed to maintain that democracy. And here is the crux of the question: Are guns required to maintain democracy OR are laws and the consistent enforcement of those laws required to maintain democracy? I believe most people agree that the consistent enforcement of laws is the required ingredient and that rule by the gun is the opposite of democracy, i.e. anarchy. What some perceive as the solution to tyranny will itself result in tyranny. To argue then that we need to carry arms to guard against any future tyrannical rule is arguing that you don't believe in 250 years of governing by the rules of law and are prepared to replace our rule by laws with the rule of the mob. The job of reasonable people then is to make every effort to keep our democracy alive and functioning by using the vote, not the rifle. If we fail at this task and cascade into a revolt against our own government, we will have failed at this effort. We will have lost our democracy, and we will have proven that our great American experiment in democracy does not work. Remember, we are all better off, when we're all better off.

The rights of the unarmed

    Gun rights advocates harp about the right to own firearms. As we have discussed above, the right to own firearms has been repeatedly supported by the Supreme Court. There is no real likelihood that the right to own arms for self-defense will ever be withdrawn, although many Americans are numb to this fact. But the Supreme Court has also stated that the right to own weapons does not extend to mean any weapon or every person or the right to carry weapons into any place. The right applies to those sorts of weapons "in common use at the time" and the carrying of weapons that are dangerous and unusual weapons is not lawful. In an effort to pre-empt any banning of "exotic weapons," Americans have purchased assault rifles, high-capacity magazines and large handguns like a rabid dog tearing into a rancid steak. After the Newtown massacre, so many firearms were purchased that many stores sold out. In a nation of about 315 million people, there are about 300 million weapons. And the more weapons that are purchased, the more fearful Americans become and the more weapons they think they need in order to protect themselves. It is a vicious circle!

    I admit, guns scare me. Even when I'm handling my own shotgun, it scares me. I handle it very gingerly and I'm very careful never to accidently point it at anyone, even if the chamber is open and I know it's not loaded. When I was teaching my wife how to use the gun, and I knew it was not loaded, I was nervous. When I had to load a shell into it in order to teach her how to chamber a shell, I was even more nervous. And I could tell she was uncomfortable too. I'm even more apprehensive when people I don't know are carrying weapons. Contrary to what gun advocates and the NRA preach, it certainly does *not* make me feel all safe and secure when I know I'm near people with firearms. It makes me feel insecure and nervous because I believe that there may be a "crazy" among those weapon-carriers who may open fire any minute. I believe most people are like me. Most people feel uneasy and insecure when they are around people carrying guns. Guns do not make people feel safe. Guns make people feel uneasy. In America, Americans have a right to feel safe. Our original "Declaration" proclaimed that we are entitled to "life, liberty and the pursuit of happiness." How can you feel safe when you know we live in a nation loaded with firearms? Does the right to own guns trump the right for people to feel secure in their own country? This, I think, would be a great case for the Supreme Court to consider.

Proposals

The gun control proposals presented by Congress and gun control advocates are many and varied. Let's examine a few of these proposals. Banning of assault weapons and high-capacity magazines is an often-mentioned proposal. Banning rifles, however, ignores the fact that about 70 percent of firearm homicides are caused by handguns, not long guns. Banning assault rifles, therefore, ignores the most deadly weapon used in murders. Banning handguns that could have a significant effect in reducing homicides is not possible given the fascination Americans have with guns, and it would probably be declared unconstitutional since handguns are a weapon of choice for self-protection.

Another suggestion is to require background checks to prevent felons and the mentally ill from possessing firearms. Most Americans, except most NRA members, of course, support the common sense requirement of performing background checks before the purchase of any firearm. In 2015, five independent survives showed that between 85% and 93% of those polled, were in support of requiring background checks prior to obtaining firearms. However, most people who commit gun violence do not have criminal records or have not been diagnosed as mentally unstable. Background checks could prevent many dangerous people from getting weapons, If background checks is adapted though, the rule must be universally applied to *all* purchases including gun purchase loop-holes. Current federal law requires backgrounds checks only for guns bought through licensed firearm dealers which account for 78% of gun sales in the U. S. (i.e. 22% of all gun sales did not require background checks.) Those who are not involved in the business of selling firearms are allowed to sell firearms without requiring a license or keeping records.[16] In addition, straw purchases (purchase of a firearm by one person for someone else who could not legally obtain a weapon), must be prohibited by law and punishable by imprisonment. If universal checks and straw purchases aren't adapted, the measure will obviously be ineffective.

Beefing up law enforcement at schools and other sensitive sites has also been suggested. I spent a few months around Houston, Texas a few years ago. They do have armed police officers stationed at many schools during school hours every day. I don't know how effective these officers were in preventing gun violence at schools since there was no attempt to shoot students while I was there. A potential school shooter might think twice about shooting at a school protected by a police officer, or at least think about shooting the police officer first.

The idea of arming the school officials themselves or other NRA-educated citizens, as suggested by some, to protect schools is an absolute asinine idea Teachers and principals are trained to teach students, not guard a school or shoot people. I suspect that most educators would refuse to accept an armed guard role at their school, though there will always be few "heros" that would accept the role so they can stick out their chest. I'm also sure that most police agencies would not support the idea of teachers becoming guards. It's much easier to talk about shooting an invader then to actually do it. You need lots of training and years of experience to play this role.

Increased emphasis on mental health issues and access to trained professionals could play a significant role in preventing violence from all sources including suicides. Training teachers to recognize mental problems in the students and implementing zero tolerance toward "bullying" could help reduce violence in schools and on the streets. Providing easier access to mental health professionals for everyone through the Affordable Care Act or Employee Assistance Programs (EPA) at work could also prove to be beneficial. EAP provides assistance with mental health issues and can help employees maintain a more balanced and less stressful life.

In the end

In the end, no nation can ever prevent all gun violence. We can reduce gun violence, however, if we have the strength to implement gun control measures. If possession of only those weapons that are "in common use at the time" were permitted, assault weapons and high-capacity magazines would not be allowed. Shotguns, the most effective weapon for self-defense, and rifles would be allowed. Unfortunately, handguns, the weapon used in most gun related murders, would probably still be allowed. America will never significantly reduce gun homicide until possession of handguns are reduced and this, given the Supreme Court's decisions and America's psychotic obsession with firearms, is not going to happen within my, or your, lifetime.

We are left, therefore, nibbling around the edges of gun regulations. If we implemented background checks for ALL individuals purchasing a firearm, we could help ensure that only responsible, law- abiding people obtained firearms. If we outlawed straw purchases of weapons and sales at gun shows that circumvent background checks, this would also help keep guns in the hands of only law-abiding citizens. If we outlawed assault weapons and high-capacity magazines, we would help keep guns out of the hands of potential murderers. If we allowed police officers to patrol schools and other buildings, this might help reduce gun violence. If we trained people to recognize mental illness, this might also help.

I believe that a firearm training course should be mandatory before any person is allowed to purchase a firearm. Guns are dangerous. Allowing any individual to purchase a deadly weapon without training in how to handle and use it is preposterous. People are not born knowing how to handle guns just as they are not born knowing how to drive a car. We require training before we allow people to drive a car. Why shouldn't we provide training before people are allowed to own a gun? Most people, I believe, would support such a measure. Even the NRA, which started out as a gun training organization, should support this measure, but I doubt that it would.

The reality of the situation is that Congress will never enact truly strong firearm measures until the American public raises its voice in unison and demands truly strong limits on the possession of firearms. The right to own guns for self-protection is well established within America's history and legal decisions. In spite of the deceit propagated by the NRA, no one is proposing, even in the slightest way, to removal all firearms from Americans' ownership. The fact is, however, that our children and grandchildren, face an ever-increasing risk everyday of being a victim of a shooting. Until such time as America can reduce its gun violence, we will all have to live with the very real possibility that one day a wild gunman will walk into our children's or grandchildren's classroom and end their beautiful young lives. It is only by the random roll of fate's divine dice that Newtown or Las Vegas didn't happen to my children. But it could! Why should we allow the risk to persist? We have within our power the ability to reduce this risk. We can reduce the number of firearms that are loose within our country, reduce the number of assault-type weapons and high-capacity magazines. We can demand background checks be performed on all purchases of firearms. We can demand that training on the safe way to handle firearms be mandatory before the purchase of a firearm. We can do these things and reduce the risk of our children becoming victims of gun homicide. The NRA is strong, but the American public is much stronger. We need to protect our children now.

But it seems that some Americans are marching in the wrong direction. In March 2014, both Houses of the Georgia legislature passed a bill that allows gun owners to carry loaded guns in bars, on college campuses, in churches, in airports, and in schools. Since the Newtown massacre, 21 states have enacted legislation that actually expands gun rights. This is in reaction to NRA activity and to a backlash from movements to restrict gun rights following the violence at Sandy Hook Elementary School. The Georgia law, called a "Guns Everywhere Bill", is the most far-reaching gun legislation in America. As the name implies, the law permits guns to be carried "everywhere". Since the law was enacted, in 2014, the death rate from guns has steadily increased from 1394 in 2014 to 1571 in 2016, a 12.7% increase.[17] Americans who hesitate to go to countries like El Salvador or Honduras may want to reconsider going to the state of Georgia.

CHAPTER 3

Global Warming And The Environment

by William K Fifield, MD.

Introduction: A Brief History-

There are many real and significant threats (nuclear annihilation, the rise of fascism, terrorism, economic and political collapse, religious extremism) to our way of life and to our survival as a species; to say nothing of the survival of our planet with its rich diversity of life. But of all the threats, none looms larger than the threat of runaway climate change. And if you add to that threat, the human population explosion already underway, you have the makings of a humanitarian disaster on the scale of the bubonic plague (the black death), or worse. If you believe for whatever reason, that this simply cannot happen, or, quite understandably, if you choose to believe that it will not happen, stop reading and move on to the next chapter. But if you are curious about a dose of reality and if you care about the future of your home planet and your grandchildren, read on. Otherwise, your grandchildren likely will ask you someday "How could you have let this happen to us?" Another significant problem is our perception of the threat because the majority of people don't accept the fact that we are facing an extremely grave crisis.[18] It is exceptionally difficult to deal with an issue of this magnitude and complexity in a short narrative such as this, but I will at least make an attempt to articulate the most important details of our self-inflicted enigma.

Climate Change skeptics may find the following information to be of interest. Globally, eighteen of the nineteen warmest years on record have occurred since 2001 and (as of the time of this writing-fall 2019) the past five years have been the hottest five years recorded since the top weather and climate agencies started tracking global temperatures in the 1880's. July 2019 was the hottest month ever recorded in history.[19] Based on current trends, the world will warm 5.8 degrees F above preindustrial temperatures by 2100-far more than the 3.6 degree goal in the Paris agreement.[20] According to a recent United Nations report, one million animal and plant species are on the verge of extinction.

Many Americans became at least somewhat aware of the environmental movement after the publication in 1962 of Rachel Carson's landmark book "Silent Spring" in which the effects of pesticides on the environment were brought to light. I remember in the 1960's seeing the Nashua River in Fitchburg, Massachusetts being blue one week, yellow the following week and red the next week depending on what color dye the local paper mill was using at the time. At that time I found it "interesting" but in the back of my mind I remember thinking "this can't be good".

For about forty years, scientists have been warning us of the presence of climate change but the corporate owned media has greatly downplayed its significance. The fossil fuel industry and many conservative politicians alike have denied global warming, suggesting that measured temperature changes were simply normal climatic fluctuations. Even after there was no doubt that the main cause of global warming was our own combustion of fossil fuels and the release of carbon into the atmosphere in the form of the greenhouse gas, carbon dioxide (CO_2), the "experts" in the pockets of the oil industry, continued to deny that fossil fuels were the culprit and insisted that more studies were needed. Until recently at least, the mainstream media has not been particularly helpful in this regard, because in their attempt to provide a "balanced" presentation, equal time has been given to the 97% of scientists who believe in climate change and to the 3% of global warming deniers, and this has created great confusion in the public's understanding of the issue.

More than half of the carbon humanity has exhaled into the atmosphere in its entire history has been emitted in the last three decades (85% since the end of World War II) meaning that in a single generation global warming has brought us to the brink of planetary collapse-all of this has happened in the space of a single lifetime.[21]

The United Nations Intergovernmental Panel on Climate Change (IPCC) had concluded by 1995 that fossil fuel consumption had to be curtailed in order to prevent runaway climate change caused by man made global warming. Again, the skeptics tried to weaken and eliminate existing environmental protection laws.[22] Despite this, Americans were beginning to take seriously the threat of climate change until "Climategate". This was the event in 2009 in which hacked e-mail messages from climate scientists were published on the internet. In addition, mistakes in the U.N. global warming reports damaged public belief in climate science. All of this had a profoundly negative effect on the public's perception of the reality and significance of climate change. In addition, the lengthy economic crisis had overtaken climate change as the public's major concern and to most people, unemployment became a much more immediate and frightening prospect than global warming.

The IPCC, a United Nations agency, was created in 1989 for the purpose of evaluating climate information from researchers from around the world. It develops policy recommendations to help the world deal with the threat of climate change. In the past, the IPCC issued four reports; in 1990, 1995, 2001 and

2007. Each one offered more dire predictions of the consequences of climate change. In late March of 2014, the fifth report was issued and indicated that climate change was affecting all parts of the world and that the poor people of the world were the most vulnerable. The report reaffirmed that the discrepancy between the known effects of climate change and government actions to mitigate these effects is still very significant. These effects include widespread coastal flooding, drought, famine, extreme weather events, resource wars, water shortages, economic collapse and massive extinctions. The IPCC has made it clear that climate change is NOT something that will happen in the distant future but is happening NOW.

The IPCC published SR15 (Special Report on Global Warming of 1.5 Degrees C) in October of 2018. Its key finding is that meeting a 1.5 C (2.7 F) degree target is possible but would require "deep emission reductions" and "rapid, far reaching changes in all aspects of society". Limiting global warming to 1.5 degrees C compared with 2 degrees C would reduce challenging impacts on ecosystems, human health and well being and a 2 degree C increase would exacerbate extreme weather, rising sea levels and diminishing Arctic sea ice, coral bleaching and loss of ecosystems among other impacts.[23]

Larry Kudlow, director of the National Economic Council has said that he thinks the UN study "is way too difficult" and that the authors "overestimate the likelihood of environmental disaster". President Trump has stated that he didn't know that climate change is man made and that "it'll change back again, the scientists who say its worse than ever have a very big political agenda" and "we have scientists that disagree (with man made climate change)".[24]

If we keep burning fossil fuels unabated, it is felt that greenhouse gases likely will double by the end of this century. Most models suggest that this would correspond with a global temperature increase within 3 degrees C (5.4 degrees F) plus or minus 1 degree.[25] An increase of 2 degrees C (3.6 degrees F) above pre-industrial levels is the absolute maximum increase in temperature that we can tolerate, and still maintain any hope of stabilization of our planet.

At the Copenhagen meeting in 2009, a target goal of no greater than a 1.5 C increase in temperature was proposed by many participants. This number is consistent with 350.org's (and NASA scientist James Hansen's) goal of reducing atmospheric CO2 from 400 ppm to 350 ppm.[26] The choice is up to us.

How Carbon Dioxide Causes GlobalWarming-

When sunlight hits the earth, it warms its surface. Until the onset of the industrial revolution (in the mid 1700's when the burning of coal began in earnest), much of the solar radiated heat was reflected by the earth back into space due to the brightness of the earth (albedo). Ice and snow, cloud cover and aerosols (including smoke from fires and power plants) all reflect this heat in the form of infrared light.[27] Carbon Dioxide from combustion of fossil fuels, as well as methane and water vapor, has an effect like glass in a greenhouse, acting as a blanket over our planet, significantly decreasing heat loss into space, thus warming our planet.

Since the beginning of civilization about 10,000 years ago, until the industrial revolution, atmospheric CO2 had been stable at 280 parts per million (ppm). We know this because we have analyzed ice core samples and measured the CO2 levels trapped in ancient ice. Now, CO2 from burning fossil fuels increases by about 2 ppm annually. Methane is about twenty times more potent a greenhouse gas than CO2, but in the short term, can be up to 80 to 100 times as potent a greenhouse gas. This is one of the reasons that natural gas (which is methane), although it *burns* cleaner than coal and oil (as industry spokesmen are happy to tell you), is NOT cleaner (in its life-cycle) than these other fuels. Water vapor is also a greenhouse gas.

For the last 10,000 years the average global temperature ranged between 58 and 60 degrees fahrenheit. But, since the beginning of the industrial revolution, (about 250 years ago), the burning of fossil fuels has resulted in a planetary temperature increase of greater than 1.4 degrees fahrenheit.

Carbon Dioxide, Fossil Fuels and Feedback Loops

There has long been a discussion of the dwindling of world oil supplies. Until recently, most experts thought that we had reached, or almost reached peak oil. Many believed this would force the world to develop carbon-free, alternative sources of energy such as wind, solar and tidal. But the discovery of the Bakken oil fields in North Dakota, and the Canadian tar sands, has brought us fossil fuels which are much more polluting, dangerous and expensive to refine than conventional oil. There are plans in place for tar sands oil to be sent from Canada to U.S. refineries by way of the Keystone XL Pipeline but, President Obama rejected the project. On November 8, 2018, District Judge Brian Morris of the U.S. District Court for the fourth District of Montana blocked construction of the Keystone XL Pipeline. The Trump administration is expected to appeal the decision to the U.S. Court of Appeals for the 9th circuit.[28]

Also recently developed, is the capture of shale oil and natural gas by hydrofracking (fracking); injecting water and chemicals under high pressure into the shale, thousands of feet below the surface to release the oil and gas. Fracking fluids, although proprietary (secret) are KNOWN to contain carcinogens such as benzene and toluene, and these poisons, contrary to industry statements, DO get into ground water and have greatly increased the incidence of biliary tract (the bile ducts, connect the liver to the small intestine) cancer in First American indigenous peoples in Alberta, Canada as shown in the documentary film, "Gasland". Unfortunately, there are also concerns that this process could increase the risk of earthquakes. With these new found sources of hydrocarbons, should the world give a collective sigh of relief and think that our energy problems have been solved? Think again. The pollution caused by these "new" sources of energy could be catastrophic and NASA climatologist James Hansen says "There's enough carbon there to create a totally different planet".[29]

In terms of the relationship between fossil fuels, CO_2 and global warming, it is important to understand the concepts of negative and positive feedback loops. Negative feedback increases stability and has the effect of decreasing the progression of the process in question. Positive feedback, however, disrupts stability and has a positive or reinforcing effect on the underlying process, increasing its effect.

As the release of CO_2 into the atmosphere increases, the greenhouse effect increases warming of the planet. This melts arctic sea ice, creating more dark blue ocean and less bright white ice (thus decreasing albedo) which leads to increased infrared heat absorption and less reflection of the infrared heat. This is an example of positive feedback which *increases* the effect of global warming.

In addition, global warming causes increased evaporation, raising global humidity, because warm air can hold more water vapor than cold air. Since water vapor is a greenhouse gas, another positive feedback loop develops. Global warming and evaporation increase each other's effect. A third feedback loop occurs once positive feedback has overtaken negative feedback, resulting in an increasing rate of change (acceleration) that could become impossible to stop.

Bill McKibben, is thought by many to be the country's leading environmental author and has written numerous books, including *The End of Nature, Deep Economy, Eaarth and Falter*. He said several years ago that if we continue on our present course, burning fossil fuels, that within thirteen (13) years, it is likely that runaway global warming, with all of the ramifications discussed in this chapter will be impossible to stop. If this were to occur, it would take at least 1000 years to begin to reverse itself. Some scientists think that we are already there! He has also said that the biggest reason we haven't made full use of new technologies (wind and solar) has been the political power of the fossil fuel industries which have used denial and disinformation for three decades.[30]

Carbon Dioxide and Deforestation-
Deforestation is also adding to the increase in CO2, melting of ice, increasing temperature and higher atmospheric water content. Deforestation has significant effects on rainfall. When forests are cleared using a slash and burn technique, rainfall decreases. Normally the atmospheric moisture that condenses to produce rain comes from ground water, absorbed by tree roots and evaporated through their leaves (transpiration). The evaporation from the leaf surface of a single large tree equals the evaporation from a forty acre lake.[31] When trees are cut down, ground water doesn't enter the atmosphere, rain doesn't fall and the ground eventually becomes too dry to grow crops.

If crop irrigation is used, the irrigation water often contains dissolved mineral salts. These salts leach into the soil. When this leach water evaporates the soil becomes increasingly salty (salinization) and, over time, the land turns into a desert.[32] As of about ten years ago over 1500 acres of land worldwide were becoming desert every hour![33] Deforestation is taking place and irrigation induced salinization is occurring throughout the world. Whether the forest timber is burned or left to rot, the carbon contained in the wood eventually enters the atmosphere as CO2.

Trees are the "lungs" of our planet, breathing in CO2 and "exhaling" oxygen. Trees and ocean plant life use photosynthesis to take up CO2, the major greenhouse gas. Using sunlight as an energy source, trees separate the carbon and the oxygen in CO2. The carbon produces energy rich compounds and oxygen which is released back into the atmosphere. Accelerating deforestation has already increased atmospheric CO2. Every day, 200,000 acres of rain forests are destroyed in the world;[34] at the rate of 1 1/2 acres per second.[35] It is felt that at current rates of deforestation, the rain forests will be gone in a few decades.[36]

The main reason for the destruction of the South American (Brazilian) rain forests is corporate profits and the world's hunger for beef.[37]

Remembering that deforestation decreases rainfall, the loss of the Brazilian rain forest will destroy much of the world's fresh water supply. These rain forests contain 20% of the world's fresh water[38] (70% of it is in Antarctica). Every twenty years global consumption of water by humans doubles. Since only half of one percent of our planet's water is drinkable and accessible, the human need for water is likely to outstrip the planet's replenishment supply by around 2025.[39]

The Amazon rain forest has approximately one million species never categorized by man. President Bolsonaro has eliminated many key environmental officials and slashed enforcement of environmental regulations. Since his inauguration the rate of deforestation has soared by as much as 92%. According to satellite imagery about 17% of the forest has been lost already and scientists believe that the tipping point will be reached at 20 to 25% deforestation even if climate change is controlled. In August 2019 satellite data showed more than 46,000 fires in the Amazon; an increase of 111% compared with 2018.

If the Amazon reaches a tipping point it could lead to a cascade of other tipping points such as the melting of the Greenland ice sheets and the degradation of the permafrost in the Arctic which would release huge amounts of greenhouse gases held in the ice. All of these changes combined could lead to runaway global warming that would be impossible to stop.[40]

Carbon Dioxide and the Oceans-

The oceans store fifty times as much carbon as does the atmosphere, and the two primary ways that carbon is removed from the atmosphere is through the growth of trees and healthy coral reefs. Renowned oceanographer, Sylvia Earle reminds us that the oxygen in every other breath we take comes from the ocean.[41] In addition, the sea, which covers 70% of the earth's surface, absorbs up to 50% of anthropogenic (i.e. resulting from human activity) CO2. This CO2 dissolves in sea water to form carbonic acid which dissolves sea shells and the skeletons of various forms of marine life.[42] Increased production of CO2 from the burning of fossil fuels has caused the oceans to become more acidic and this, combined with warming of the oceans has led to the loss of algae needed to nourish the coral reefs. This causes coral bleaching around the planet.

Carbon Dioxide's Double Jeopardy-

Destroy the trees and the coral and you increase carbon and increase CO2. In addition, if coral bleaching continues, it has been predicted that 70% of all coral reefs could be gone by mid century.[43] If this happens the most valuable ocean habitats will be lost and this would have profound effects on many species dependent on coral reef ecosystems and for the humans that depend on them for food, livelihood and tourism.

Many scientists estimate that we have already lost at least 90% of large predatory fish, such as sharks and swordfish.[44] As if losing our large fish species isn't bad enough, global warming will also have a very negative effect on phytoplankton which are at the bottom of the food chain. This will have a ripple effect up the entire ocean food chain. Phytoplankton are responsible for about half of the world's photosynthesis which, again, takes up CO2 and produces oxygen.

Two Global Warming Drivers; Consumption and Growth Economies-

Global warming is due in large part to our selfishness fueled by the notion that we are somehow separate from nature and that everything in nature is there for our use. The ideas that the goal of humanity is to dominate and conquer the earth, that consumption is highly valued, and that the land has infinite capacity for population growth led to the fall of many great societies, including the Sumerians, the Greeks and the Romans.[45] Our civilization now faces the same fate for the same reasons. The difference this time is that homo sapiens itself is at risk.

Columnist Chris Hedges in a September 23, 2019 article entitled *Saving the Planet Means Overthrowing the Ruling Elite* suggests that the recent climate strike will not have a significant effect on the ruling elites and the corporations they serve. The elites will allow protests to occur as long as the protesters play by their rules, but if their power is threatened, the elites will respond vigorously to shut the protests down with ever greater ruthlessness in order to maintain power and their way of life including the systems of global capitalism.[46]

The energy contained in one barrel of oil is the equivalent of ten years worth of one person's manual labor and the average American uses 25 barrels of oil per year.[47] This is the reason that we, in the United States, are so prosperous and have such a comfortable life style. Have we utilized and conserved our fossil fuels wisely? Think about this. In the Pacific Ocean there is a huge "island" of plastic debris (plastic made from oil-the Great Pacific Garbage Patch). Estimates of its size vary and range from the size of Texas to an area almost as large as Russia.[48]

Our irresponsible inability to live at a sustainable level may have sealed our fate. Our complete dependence on fossil fuels is the main obstacle to effectively dealing with runaway climate change, mass extinctions and resource wars. Instead of switching to renewable sources of energy (solar, wind, tidal) we are continuing to increase our dependence on hydrocarbon fuels which simply feeds the vicious circle of runaway climate change.

Economists and policy makers alike tell us that our economy must continue to grow (a growth economy) in order for us to maintain the status quo rather than to accept a sustainable or steady state economy. In nature, nothing grows indefinitely, and the same is true for an economy which can only continue to grow if there are adequate natural resources to sustain it. So it should come as no surprise that the course we are on is absolutely unsustainable. When resources are used up faster than they can be replenished (which is what we are doing today) the carrying capacity of the planet has been exceeded.

Another Driver: We Have Too Many People-
Greatly complicating climate change is the unprecedented increase in the human population of our planet. Overpopulation leads to numerous negative consequences for our environment. These include increasing scarcity of clean water, desertification, deforestation, habitat destruction, resource exhaustion, species extinction and increased pollution. All these contribute to, among other things, climate change with all of its ramifications.

The world's population is doubling in less than fifty years.[49] Every four days our human population increases by 1 million people, worldwide.[50] We are consuming 20% more of the world's natural resources than the planet can produce, (i.e., we have exceeded the earth's carrying capacity) and the earth's population, which was one billion in 1800 is now seven plus billion and is projected to be nine billion by 2040 or 2050.

Homo sapiens has been around for about 120,000 years and now, over half of the human beings who have ever lived on our planet are alive today. We developed agriculture because our population grew beyond what could be supported by hunting and gathering and now it has grown beyond what can be supported by current agricultural technology (using irrigation of desertified land, hydrocarbon based fertilizers, etc.)[51] In addition, the United States has lost one third of its topsoil since 1950.[52] Instead of trying to limit our numbers, we have resorted to technology to save us; thus *increasing* our population. In the past, many people have believed that almost any problem can be solved by American ingenuity. The thing that is different now however, is that our population has gotten so large, and our resources have been depleted so much that no amount of ingenuity will save us unless we are willing to undertake a totally new approach and a new way of thinking about our predicament. Continued growth of our population would be disastrous. In the past, the instinct to reproduce had survival value for our species but now is threatening its very survival.

The beliefs and doctrines promoted by different religions are often contradictory and mutually exclusive and religious dogmas are held onto even when they are counterproductive.[53] As one example, the Catholic Church and some Christian Fundamentalist churches have encouraged women to be submissive to their husbands. They quote the Biblical exhortation to be fruitful and multiply. But also, in a world with seven billion people they condemn abortion and birth control.

Our population numbers will take care of themselves, either through the imposition of strict guidelines as to the size of families (i.e., limiting couples to one child; a draconian measure, to be sure) and other measures (managed decline) or through the less desirable alternative of epidemics, decreasing fertility, droughts, famine and resource wars (collapse of our civilization).

Up to 2040 or 2050, there is agreement among most experts that the world's population will increase to around nine billion people. Beyond that time, there is quite a bit of confusion about where population trends will go. A few project that the population will continue to increase to around 10-12 billion people by 2100. Many forecasters however, suggest that our population will *decrease* as we exceed the carrying capacity of the planet.

Consequences: Extinction-
The total decline of species since the Industrial Revolution will soon be worse than the asteroid impact 65 million years ago off the Yucatan Peninsula which destroyed 83% of species, including the dinosaurs.[54] As a species, we are rapidly approaching the point beyond which the planet is changing too fast for us to adapt. There have been five previous great extinctions and we are now entering the world's sixth great extinction and we, ourselves, are at significant risk of becoming extinct.[55] We MUST simplify our lives and live at a subsistence level world wide. 99.9% of all species that have ever lived on planet Earth are now extinct.[56]

Conservationists estimate that extinctions world wide are occurring at a rate 10,000 times as great as the background rate before we humans began destroying the earth. In his book *The Future of Life*, biologist E.O. Wilson warns that if we continue on our present path, half of the species on our planet could be gone by the end of this century. Only one of the five previous mass extinctions was caused by an asteroid (the Yucatan); the others were caused by climate change. All species have limited capacity for adaptation to change. Some species of living things, such as bacteria, have very short generations (the average length of time between birth and the ability to reproduce). Other species, typically large animals, adapt to change much more slowly because their generations take many years. So when there is a very sudden change in the environment, rapidly reproducing organisms such as bacteria and insects are much more likely to survive the rapid change than we are.[57]

Consequences: Global Warming and the Weather-
There are many predictable, and likely, some unforeseen consequences of a significantly warmer world. Because warm air holds more moisture than cooler air, global warming will cause much greater extremes of weather than occur now but the weather extremes will be very different in different parts of the world. There will be winners and losers in this scenario, but the losers will outnumber the winners. Places that will be the most severely affected will, for the most part, be those places least able to adapt; i.e., places inhabited by the world's poor who are the people least likely to have contributed to global warming.

Warmer water will cause an increase in the frequency of destructive storms and hurricanes and the destructive power of hurricanes has already increased by 50% in the last 30 years. Higher humidity in the air will lead to an increase in the frequency of thunderstorms and by the end of the century the occurrence of major thunderstorms could, in some areas, increase by over 100%. Global warming will cause an increase in the probability of heat waves and droughts and droughts are especially likely to occur in Africa, leading to resource wars over water. Warm water takes up more space than cold water and with global warming there will be increasing thermal expansion of the seas, increasing sea levels and flooding, especially in coastal areas. One estimate suggests that sea levels could rise by three to four feet by the end of the century, spelling the end for places like Bangladesh, Venice, the Netherlands, Tuvalu, southern Florida and many coastal cities. Melting glacial ice will add to this effect, and if all of the world's ice cover melted it is predicted that this could increase sea level by almost 250 feet.[58] One third of major cities are on the coast and at least 600 million people live within ten meters of sea level today.

The Ocean Circulation and Melting Ice-

The term "thermohaline" refers to the temperature (thermo) and salt content (haline) of sea water. These two factors determine the density of sea water. The thermohaline circulation (or ocean conveyer belt) causes ocean currents to move independent of tidal forces and the wind. An example is the conveyer belt which currently brings warm equatorial surface water, from the Gulf Stream, north, keeping western Europe relatively temperate. Glaciers are made of fresh water and when they melt, the ocean becomes less salty (desalinization). This process will interfere with the ocean currents, such as the North Atlantic conveyer belt, described above. The latitude of much of Europe and Scandinavia is the same as that of Alaska but these areas are much warmer than Alaska now because of this conveyer belt. These areas would become much colder if the currents were to be interrupted. Interference with this conveyer belt could also lead to an increased likelihood of episodic extremely cold weather (in certain areas) which in turn, could cause disruption of transportation, and increased risk of accidents (if associated with snow) as well as hypothermia and starvation.

Melting ice has endangered several species of animals in the Arctic and, as noted above will decrease albedo, further amplifying the effect of global warming. Ice sheets are extremely heavy and when they melt, the pressure they had exerted on the ground beneath them is decreased and this can free up tectonic masses which could lead to earthquakes, and volcanic activity as well as tsunamis.

As the Himalayan and Andes glaciers melt, as many as one billion people who depend on this meltwater for their water supply, could face drought, famine and starvation. The ice sheets over Greenland contain huge amounts of methane (an extremely potent greenhouse gas) and if this ice sheet melts quickly, an extremely powerful positive feedback loop will develop. Disintegration of the Greenland and West Antarctic ice sheets become likely if temperatures rise by more than five degrees, "well within the range of climate change projections for this century".[59]

More Consequences: A Plethora of Perils-

The Ogallala Aquifer which supplies water for the southwestern United States has decreased in volume by about 50% since 1986. Much of the water being pumped out of the aquifer is more than 10,000 years old and over 40% of the grain grown in the U.S. is irrigated by this aquifer. At the current rate of depletion, this aquifer may be dry within one or two decades.[60]

Another consequence of climate change and increased temperatures, is that wildfires will increase and will release even more CO2 and soot, and this will have negative health consequences for people with asthma and emphysema. There are now trapped in Arctic ice diseases that have not been prevalent for millions of years; in some cases since before humans were around meaning that we have no immunity to them. Scientists suspect that smallpox and bubonic plague may be trapped in Siberian ice.[61]

With warming of the earth and the Northern migration of all sorts of insects, there will likely be a significant increase in the incidence of diseases such as west nile virus, malaria, dengue fever, Eastern Equine Encephalitis as well as cholera and perhaps Ebola and yes, even Plague. These diseases could absolutely overwhelm public health services, especially in poorer countries.

It is not difficult to imagine the tremendous economic consequences that all of this could cause (hurricane and flooding damage, the cost of treating disease, etc.) but the dwindling of earth's resources as well as climate change, is also likely to cause tremendous societal disruption, migration, conflict and resource wars over things that today we take for granted, like water.

The question becomes whether or not climate change is happening so fast that we will soon be unable to stop it. James Hansen, director of NASA's Goddard Institute of Space Studies, and adjunct professor in the Department of Earth and Environmental sciences at Columbia University, notes that global temperature has increased by about 1 degree F since the mid 1970's and another increase of 4 degrees by 2100 would "imply changes that constitute practically a different planet... We can't let it go on another ten years like this. We've got to do something."[62] Considered by many to be one of the world's leading climatologists, Hansen, after reviewing an enormous amount of data, said in 2008 that 350 parts per million (ppm) was the absolute maximum atmospheric concentration of CO_2 that was compatible with maintaining the planet "on which civilization developed and to which life...is adapted.[63] We are now at 415 ppm and climbing! NOAA has suggested that changes in surface temperature, rainfall and sea level are largely irreversible for more than 1000 years after CO_2 emissions are completely stopped.[64]

America's Response to Global Warming-
Most Americans are primarily concerned with making a living in order to support our consumption based life style. (Remember the television footage of the "rush" at the malls on Black Friday, the day after Thanksgiving). The majority of people are clueless as to the nature of our predicament, largely because corporate America and, until very recently, the media (owned by

corporate America) are much more concerned with short term profits than the future of our planet. It is not against the law for news organizations to lie to our citizens. In addition, our representatives in Washington seem to be more motivated by their own re-election campaigns (and the corporations that support their efforts) than in serving their constituents and protecting the interests of future generations.

Americans have been *grossly* misinformed about what lies ahead and we simply don't want to think or talk about it (this is denial). Many churches are failing to discuss and deal with the reality we are facing and one has to wonder if some people are willing to accept the possible consequences of our actions as the prophecy outlined in the end of days.[65]

Climatologist James Hansen reported that the George W. Bush administration suppressed scientific evidence of the dangers of global warming and that his administration wanted to hear only scientific results that "fit predetermined, inflexible positions". Warnings about the consequences of global warming were consistently suppressed and reports outlining the potential dangers of global warming were edited to make the problem seem less serious.[66]

Senator James Inhofe (R-OK) has called global warming "a hoax". In the 2008 election cycle, his largest campaign donors represented the oil and gas industry and he received $446,900 in donations."

Exxon-Mobil, the richest company in the history of the world, "has spent the last several years underwriting an elaborate disinformation campaign to sow doubt about climate change and with reasonable success; 44% of Americans believe global warming comes from "long-term planetary trends and not the pumps at the Exxon station".[67]

If you think that the United States government would never let the scenario described above come to pass, think again. The poor nations of the world feel that the rich countries, whose actions led to global warming, *should* pay for the damage done to their countries and should help fund their adaptation to climate change. At this time, it seems unlikely that our government is in a position to do this. In fact, our political leaders are not taking the lead, they are declining to make the difficult choices we elected them to deal with and they seem almost completely unwilling to compromise on any issue.

Our government certainly should be taking a leadership position on this issue as the United States comprises only 5% of the world's population but has contributed 25% of greenhouse gases to the atmosphere. But our government is in opposition to international population control efforts (allegedly because of the fear that funding would be diverted to paying for abortions) and our government has abandoned efforts to stabilize the environment. The Kyoto Protocol, which set caps on CO_2 emissions, was adopted in 1997 and went into effect in 2005. It established emission quotas which were agreed upon by each participating country with the goal of reducing the overall emissions by 5.2 % from their 1990 levels by the end of 2012, when it expired. Initially, two nations failed to ratify the Kyoto Protocol; Australia and the United States. Ultimately, Australia ratified the treaty in December 2007.

The Paris Agreement was signed by 195 UN members. Its long term goal is to to keep the increasing global average temperature to less than two degrees C above pre-industrial levels and to limit the increase to 1.5 degrees C in order to significantly reduce the risks of climate change.

On August 4, 2017 President Trump informed the UN that the United States planned to withdraw from the Paris agreement as soon as it is eligible to do so (November 4, 2020). If someone other than Donald Trump wins the 2020 election, he or she could get the United States back into the Paris accord within 30 days. Scientist James Hansen said that most of the agreement consisted of "promises" and not commitments and that only an across the board tax on CO_2 would decrease CO_2 emissions fast enough to avoid the worst effects of global warming. Studies in

Nature have said that as of 2017, none of the major industrialized nations were implementing the policies they had envisioned and had not met their pledged emissions reduction targets.[68]

Our government, big industry (i.e. oil) and much of the media have been minimizing or lying about the problem facing us and most put the importance of short term profits above the future health of our planet and its people. Many Americans simply don't take seriously, information from other sources, such as landmark books by authors such as Bill McKibben, Al Gore and James Hansen. Again, is this because of ignorance, apathy, denial or greed, or some combination of the above?

Senator Bernie Sanders (I-VT) has said, that for important issues like this, when people in leadership positions are failing completely to act, then the people, at a grass roots level MUST take the initiative and DO THE RIGHT THING because NO one else is going to. The longer we wait, the more difficult it will be to deal with the immensity of this problem and the more people there will be on the planet to take care of. In fact, our planet may already be beyond the point of no return. With the positive feedback loops discussed above, we may already be unable to stop runaway global warming with all of its disastrous consequences.

In the past the United States government has taken some very half-hearted actions aimed at dealing with the crisis. A market based approach to control pollution by providing economic incentives for achieving reductions in the emission of pollutants was proposed. This "Cap and Trade" agreement would have set a cap or upper limit on the amount of pollutant that could be emitted by a company. The limit or cap would be allocated or sold to firms in the form of an emission permit which represents the right to emit a specific volume of a given pollutant. Firms would be required to hold a number of permits equivalent to their emissions. Firms needing to increase the volume of their emissions would buy permits from entities that required fewer permits. The transfer of permits would constitute a trade. So the company buying permits would be paying a fee for polluting while the seller would be rewarded for having reduced their emissions. In theory, this idea would reduce pollution at the lowest cost to society.

But Cap and Trade is not the long term solution to our problem of CO2 and climate change. Global warming requires nothing less than a reorganization of society and new technology that will leave the rest of the fossil fuels in the ground. Carbon trading encourages business as usual.[69]

Not surprisingly, it was Senator Inhofe who led the battle in the Senate to block cap and trade legislation after it had passed the House. The legislation finally died in Congress in 2010. President Obama launched an initiative to increase vehicular fuel economy to 55 mpg by 2025. If you remember, Governor Romney opposed this. "Why would he?" you might ask. You may also recall that at no time during the 2016 presidential debates was the issue of climate change discussed with one exception. During the Republican candidates' debates, Senator Santorum did speak of the "hoax of global warming".

During the 2020 presidential campaign, discussion of climate change DID take place among the Democratic candidates, possibly because of activists pushing for a Green New Deal, Jay Inslee's emphasis on the issue and the IPCC SR-15 report issued in October of 2018. Democratic presidential candidates spent an entire evening debating the issue of climate change suggesting that there is now a much greater awareness of the issue of climate change although the public still to some degree lacks an appreciation that this has become an existential crisis.[70]

The Green New Deal proposed legislation that seeks to address climate change and economic inequality-the name comes from FDR's project to deal with the Great Depression. The legislation was sponsored by Representative Alexandria Ocasio-Cortez and Senator Ed Markey but the resolution failed to advance in the Senate. President Trump is opposed to the Green New Deal and has referred to climate change as a "hoax". Some have claimed that the Green New Deal fails to tackle the real cause of the climate emergency; namely the concept of unending growth consumption inherent in capitalism.[71]

President Trump's approach to the environment is difficult to understand; even given that he doesn't believe in the concept of global warming. He has proposed opening the sixteen million acre Tongas forest in Alaska to logging and favors opening the Arctic, one of the world's most pristine places, to drilling for oil. His administration has lowered emission standards resulting in a significant increase in the release of sulfur dioxide, causing more acid rain to fall in the Adirondack mountains, which have suffered the most acid rain damage in the country. He has proposed relaxation of some requirements on coal fired power plants for removing coal ash and heavy metals from wastewater before dumping it into rivers and has proposed giving utilities more time to deal with the 400 plus unlined coal ash dumps that lie very close to groundwater.

What the World Must Do to Survive Global Warming-

The notion of population control; that is, temporarily encouraging couples to limit their families to one child (or adopt) is actually pragmatic although this idea would be extremely difficult to sell and will definitely seem draconian to many. But if numbers continue to increase, our society will collapse due to resource depletion, resource wars, starvation and disease.

The United States and other developed nations must assume leadership roles and must provide for developing countries, the knowledge and means to produce goods needed to develop the alternatives to fossil fuels. World energy demand will likely increase by almost 60% by 2030. Two thirds of this demand will come from developing countries.[72] If our government is unable or unwilling to take the lead, the people MUST do this. In the meantime, we must all try to minimize our carbon footprints and must rapidly convert to sustainable, nonpolluting energy sources. This will require our government to stop subsidizing the fossil fuel industry, which will vigorously resist this effort, claiming that it will take up to another forty years to recoup its' infrastructure investments. Government must also stop subsidizing the nuclear industry and start investing substantial capital in wind, solar, geothermal and tidal technology. These alternative forms of energy could replace fossil fuels within twenty years if we made up our minds to do this.[73] For a time, there may be a need to ration energy and we will need to develop alternative forms of energy for transportation.

Government spending for our military and the military industrial complex must be reduced. It has been said that the United States spends more on our military than the total combined military expenditures of the next seven countries. There must also be an effort in our country to reduce consumption (to live within our means) and to support local agriculture and manufacturing. For a time, lowered resource consumption may be needed in order to build up our renewable resource reserves.

Weighing Our Energy Sources-
Coal has been utilized as a fuel since the beginning of the industrial revolution and there is probably enough coal left to last hundreds of years. Today, coal produces almost half of the electricity used in the United States and it remains the cheapest source of electricity. It produces 30% of the world's energy. So what's the problem? Coal is the dirtiest fossil fuel there is. The concept of clean coal is a lie. Combustion of coal dumps more CO_2 into the air per unit of energy produced than any other fuel. It also contains nitrogen and sulfur which causes acid rain and smog when coal is burned.

Oil, Tar Sands Oil and Fracked Gas. The disastrous consequences of burning these fuels have already been discussed previously.

Nuclear energy has been touted as a source of energy that does not cause climate change and one can not argue against this fact. But in the view of many people, its' future as a significant source of electricity is very limited, especially after Fukushima. Despite the fact that it is non-polluting in the traditional sense, nuclear energy has two big strikes against it. The first one is its' cost which has to take into consideration not only the cost of construction of new plants but also the cost of decommissioning power plants that have reached the end of their useful lives. But the overwhelming argument against the future development of nuclear power is that there is currently no practical solution to the problem of safe long-term storage of radioactive waste which is currently stored on site at most nuclear power plants, and remains radioactive for tens of thousands of years. We are building up stockpiles of extremely dangerous material that future generations will have to deal with for thousands of years. No one knows what mankind will be like a couple of thousand years from now (if it even exists) and what capabilities they will have to deal with our incredible toxic mess. Considering that most languages don't survive for more than two or three thousand years, how can we warn future generations of the risks? In my view, continued development of nuclear power is simply irresponsible.

Biofuel production uses more energy than the ethanol or biodiesel that is generated. Ethanol does not produce a net energy gain, is not renewable and is not economical. It wreaks havoc on small internal combustion engines (lawn mowers, rototillers, chain saws, etc.) and its' production and use contribute to global warming. Turning plants such as corn and soybeans into fuel means less food for the world's increasing population and it is not a viable long-term option.[74] The one exception to all of this may be algae biofuel. It doesn't take up farmland to grow, and can be grown anywhere there is room for tanks and sunshine. Algae grow faster than corn and soybeans and may be able to utilize wastewater rather than use up fresh water supplies.[75]

Wind energy could produce electricity in a cost effective manner and the wind industry, if it took off, could employ as many people as the fossil fuel and nuclear energy utilities employ. The issue of the storage of electricity needs to be worked out (because the wind isn't always blowing). Solar production during the day somewhat balances wind production which is greatest during the night. If the U.S. shared wind technology with the entire world, it could help countries to develop steady state economies.[76] In Vermont, where I live, there seems to be more concern about the effect that wind farms will have on property values (potential noise pollution, interference with scenic vistas, etc.) than about the effects of climate change.

Solar power, likewise could replace carbon-based power in a couple of decades and could employ as many people as currently work in the fossil fuel industry. The initial upfront cost of solar power for households could be recouped in ten to twenty years and solar panels have a projected life of about forty years, resulting in solar power being much more cost effective than fossil fuel-based electricity.[77] If government subsidies were switched to the solar industry, instead of coal, oil and natural gas, it would be much more cost effective.

Both wind and solar can be decentralized, preventing losses during long distance transmission and fostering even greater efficiency.

Hydrogen-Public transportation will have to assume a much greater role in our society, especially the revitalization of our rail system. One of the biggest challenges ahead is how to provide energy for transportation. The most viable option on the horizon at this time seems to be hydrogen. When hydrogen and oxygen are combined, power and water are produced. Electricity (produced by wind, solar or hydro) could be used to convert water into two gases, hydrogen (which could be used as fuel) and oxygen (which would be released harmlessly into the atmosphere) by a process known as hydrolysis. Hydrogen made from fossil fuels (such as natural gas) is NOT the answer because it, like other processes utilizing fossil fuels will result in the continued pollution of our planet.[78]

Hydrogen can be burned in an internal combustion engine (as gas is burned in today's automotive engines) or it could be combined with oxygen in fuel cells to produce electricity to power electric motors for vehicles. However, there are some significant problems to be worked out before hydrogen can be put into widespread use. It is extremely difficult to store. For use in vehicles it would have to be pressurized and it is such a small molecule that it can leak out of storage containers. Leaked hydrogen, if exposed to a flame or a spark, is extremely explosive.[79] If you want to see an example of a hydrogen explosion, Google the Hindenburg Blimp Disaster.

Cold Climate Heat Pumps are a new thermal energy solution for the northern climate's disproportionate use of fuel oil and gas for heating. Geothermal heating units are also available for use in northern climates.

Space does not allow for a discussion of a potential solution for our dilemma known as geoengineering, which involves technologies that either remove CO2 from the atmosphere and store it somewhere (i.e. in the ground), and solar radiation management (SRM) which involves the artificial blocking of sunlight, in order to cool the planet (by building huge space mirrors to reflect sunlight back into space or pumping sulfur aerosol particles into the atmosphere to bounce sunlight back into space). If the second one of these ideas (SRM) sounds a bit far-fetched, it's because it is.

On April 6, 2011, the U.S. House of Representatives was presented with the following resolution:

"Congress accepts the scientific findings of the Environmental Protection Agency that climate change is occurring, is caused largely by human activities, and poses significant risks for public health and welfare." The final vote on the resolution was 184 in favor and 240 against.[80]

On the evening of March 10, 2014, Senate Democrats pulled an "all nighter" in order to warn fellow members of the Senate and the public, of the consequences of climate change and the risks associated with Congressional inaction on this issue. The Senate chamber was nearly empty, however. More than two dozen Democrats spoke on the issue, but only one Republican spoke, Senator Inhofe, who said that Democrats who showed up were not convincing anyone with their "stunt". Earlier in the day, Senator Mitch McConnell had said that the Democratic motivation was campaign money.

The consequences of climate change described above are very bleak, indeed, but not inevitable. There will be a tremendous need to try to repair all of the damage we have already done to our planet. It has been estimated that this period of adjustment will take between 100 and 250 years but the longer we wait, the longer it will take and the more difficult it will be. The list of initiatives outlined below will help mitigate the problem, but the only thing that will *really* make a difference is the political will to force the fossil fuel companies to leave the remaining coal, oil and gas in the ground. It seems that homo sapiens is wired in such a way that we are unable to recognize a serious threat until literally seconds before it hits us between the eyes. Stopping global warming is not about saving our planet; the earth will survive no matter what. Stopping global warming is about saving humanity. Given the course of history, what is the likelihood that the world will collectively act in time to save most of us from going over the precipice? The consensus seems to be that we will not. But there is still a chance that we can and we should act now as if our lives depend on it.

No matter what happens we must guard against despair and face this crisis together. We must follow the lead that our youth activists like Greta Thunberg are demonstrating. It is their future that is at stake.

What You Can Do? - 36 Steps to Help

1. stay informed
2. join support groups working for the sustainability of our planet
3. join climate friendly organizations such as 350.org the Sierra Club

4. vote for candidates who have made dealing with climate change a priority
5. petition political leaders to advocate the following:
   - stop the burning of coal and other fossil fuels
   - stop burning forests
   - stop fracking
   - stop polluting the oceans
6. develop renewable energy sources (wind, solar, geothermal, hydro)
7. abandon biofuels except for algae
8. phase out nuclear power
9. stop subsidizing the fossil fuel and nuclear industry
10. start subsidizing clean, renewable energy
11. turn off lights & appliances when not in use
12. use energy efficient light bulbs & appliances
13. consider purchasing a hybrid or electric car
14. carpool
15. use public transportation whenever possible
16. recycle
17. conserve and recall that the most important things in life are not things
18. downsize your home
19. use a clothesline
20. consider limiting the size of your family
21. plant trees and a garden
22. install solar panels on your home and live off the grid
23. installing a small windmill on your home
24. recognize the importance of sustainable use of our resources
25. get an energy audit
26. reinsulate your home
27. become an advocate for positive change
28. walk
29. ride a bike
30. eat less beef

31. minimize food waste
32. avoid using bottled water
33. help rekindle a sense of community in your town
34. be an advocate for restoring our endangered ecosystems and our forests
35. spread the word about climate change
36. think globally; act locally AND globally

-LIVE SIMPLY SO THAT OTHERS MAY SIMPLY LIVE

Acknowledgement- The author would like to thank retired teacher and fellow environmental advocate, Barrie Bailey, of Salisbury, Vermont for her help in the writing, editing and organization of this chapter. Without her assistance, the clarity of this manuscript would have been much diminished.

Chapter 4

Health Care In America

At the end of June 2012, after months of anticipation, the Supreme Court ruled that the "individual mandate" of the Patient Protection and Affordable Care Act, requiring that all Americans either obtain health insurance or pay a fine, was constitutional. Even though the Supreme Court had rendered its opinion, Republicans vowed that they would continue the fight to repeal the law. As Mitt Romney said while on the campaign trail on June 28, "What the court did not do on its last day in session, I will do on my first day if elected president of the United States. I will act to repeal Obamacare". Most fair-minded people would agree, I believe, that health care insurance companies should not be allowed to refuse coverage for people with pre-existing illnesses. That insurance companies should not be allowed to cancel policies if a person's health care gets too expensive or limit the annual costs of a patient's care to certain amounts and then no longer cover them. After all, the purpose of health insurance is to pay for health care. Most people, I believe, would favor a cap on the maximum out- of-pocket payments families and individuals are required to pay on health care premiums. The Affordable Care Act (ACA) provides all of these protections on health care coverage. Yet, despite the good things that the ACA does, many people are opposed to the Act because of the tax or penalty placed on individuals and companies that do not want to obtain health insurance.

This chapter discusses health care in America. It looks at the history of health care and how millions of Americans are affected by not having health care insurance. It discusses the reasons why America has the highest health care costs in the world and how these costs may be reduced by the Affordable Care Act. But in spite of these high costs, Americans do not rate as the healthiest people in the world. This chapter also looks at why many Americans are living unhealthy lives because we do not have a health care system for everyone. Then the chapter summaries what the Act requires, when these requirements take place and how the system will be paid for. At the end, the chapter discusses some of the recent Supreme Court decisions on the Affordable Care Act.

Introduction

A few years ago I was temporarily without work and my wife was between jobs. We needed health insurance. I called up local health care insurance companies to investigate the cost of private individual health insurance. To my astonishment, a policy for an individual family was over $1,500 per month, about four times what I was paying when employed. This is equivalent to $18,000 per year, or about $22,000 before taxes. Even if I were earning a salary, say about $50,000 per year, this amount is almost half of every penny I earned. How would I be able to pay the mortgage and feed my family? I knew insurance was expensive, but this was ridiculous! The only solution was to roll the dice and go without health care insurance. Fortunately, my wife and I remained healthy during this time and we didn't have any accidents. Had we had the misfortune of having a severe accident during that time, we could have wound up as paupers with our savings and retirement depleted. Hard working Americans should not have to undergo financial devastation because they cannot afford health insurance.

Our country's Declaration of Independence declares, "We hold these truths to be self-evident, that all men are created equal, that they are endowed by their Creator with certain unalienable rights, that among these are life, liberty and the pursuit of happiness." In other words, our Founding Fathers considered it an unalienable right to have a happy, healthy life in so far as our country and the creator can provide. It is one of America's founding principles. Yet to suggest that we do something that will allow everyone to have health care and some people scream bloody murder.

"I don't want to pay for everyone else's health care."

"If we make health care cheap, people will abuse it and go to the doctor for every little reason."

"If you make health care cheap, I'll have to sit in the waiting room with all sorts of people; drug addicts, drunkards, people with scabs and people who haven't had a bath in two weeks," as if health care should only be available to the privileged people.

As the leader of the democratic world, America is obligated to provide a healthy life for all of its citizens, and part of that obligation is providing health care for all. When the Patient Protection and Affordable Care Act was passed in March 2010, I thought we were finally on the right path. I thought America was committed to providing one of the basic functions of a modern democratic country.

A very brief history

Providing a national health care system is nothing new. Germany instituted a national health care system in 1883 under Otto van Bismarck, the Iron Chancellor. The health system Germany developed provides coverage for German citizens. Health care is provided by private medical services and premiums are paid by a joint effort of employers and a payroll withholding from workers' paychecks. Hmmm, sounds like the modern American plan, only 130 years earlier.

Even in America, national health care is not new. In 1912, President Teddy Roosevelt suggested that the U.S. develop a national health care system in his re-election campaign; it didn't work. During the wage and price control era of Franklin D. Roosevelt, businesses began providing health care as an incentive to hire new workers. This is how the business-oriented health care system got established in America. In 1965, President Lyndon Johnson, with the backing of a Democratic-controlled Congress, instituted Medicare for those over 65 and Medicaid for the poor. Even President Richard Nixon tried to introduce a national plan for health care where businesses would pay for the workers' health care, but it was cut short by Watergate. In 1986, President Reagan signed into law the Consolidated Omnibus Budget Reconciliation Act (COBRA), which requires employers to let former workers stay on the company work plan for 18 months. In 1993, President Bill Clinton and First Lady Hillary Clinton tried to initiate a national health plan but the plan was defeated by strong Republican and health care insurance company opposition. Through all these efforts, some backed by Republicans and some by Democrats, a national health care system has been very slowly progressing forward. Finally, on March 23, 2010, President Obama signed into law a national health care plan called the Patient Protection and Affordable Care Act. And then the fighting really began.

The cost of health care in America

In 2017, the average cost per individual for health care in the U.S. was $10,739. This totals to $3.5 trillion and amounts to 17.9 percent of the entire Gross Domestic Product (GDP).[81] The United States has the highest health care costs in the world. Americans are paying top dollar but on the whole, we're not getting our money's worth based on life expectancy and infant mortality figures.

Why is America's health care insurance so expensive? One big reason is that not everyone participates in health insurance.

This is one reason why the Affordable Care Act requires, except for a few exceptions, that everyone obtain some form of health insurance or pays a penalty. This requirement is called the individual mandate. Estimates show that before 2010 and the initiation of Obamacare in this country over 49.9 million people were without health care, about 16.3 percent of America's population.[82] Adding millions of Americans, most of whom are healthy, will add more money to the insurance pot which will help pay for those who need care. In return, when these new payers get sick or need care, funds will be available for them. Having everyone pay their own way and adding millions of Americans to insurance plans will help drive down the cost of health insurance.

Another reason costs are so high is that taxpayers and those that have health insurance are paying for those who are not insured. When the uninsured get sick or hurt, some just go without medical treatment and endure the suffering while others may receive treatment. Health care for these uninsured individuals though, is not provided free of charge. It is paid for by taxpayers through government grants, increased taxes on Medicare and Medicaid, or through hikes in the premiums paid by those who do have health insurance. While those without health insurance are crying because they don't want Obamacare, those with insurance should be demanding that everyone have insurance so those with insurance don't have to pay for those that are un-insured. When an uninsured person seeks medical attention, the hospital is partially reimbursed by the state and federal governments through grants taxes, Medicaid and Medicare. This amounts to billions of dollars which the taxpayer pays for through taxes. This money increases the cost of health care. In addition, insurance companies of course, are raising insurance premiums to cover the costs associated with those not insured. The total effect of this, according to Newsweek magazine is that Americans with health insurance are paying over $1,000 per year to cover those without insurance.[83] By requiring that almost everyone have health insurance, this $1,000 per year cost to cover those not insured will be eliminated or greatly reduced.

Other major factors for high health care costs are based in administrative, marketing and profit. Every health insurance company has a certain fee it pays the provider, (e.g. doctor, hospital, medical facility) for a medical procedure. Say you had an X-ray. That equates to a certain fee given to the provider by the insurance company. A fee is also set for a tonsillectomy, an appendectomy, for general anesthesia, and a different fee for local anesthesia. The insurance company may have hundreds of different fees it pays the provider, and the fees may differ for different providers. So the company must keep track of what procedure each provider administered. Likewise, the provider must keep track of what procedure was performed on the patient and what insurance plan the patient belonged to in order to assure proper billing. Providers are forced to hire the equivalent of a small accounting firm to keep track of varying charges which they attempt to recoup from the insurance companies. You can see that this process is cumbersome and inefficient, and even though computers aid in simplifying the process, it still takes time and money to administer. In 2018 (the most resent numbers available), the United States will spend about $10,000 per capita for health care, the highest amount of any developed nation, with Luxembourg second at $8000 per capita and Switzerland and Norway tied for fourth, at $7000. The administrative costs for this care is expected to reach nearly $500 billion, in 2019.[84] These numbers are echoed by the National Academy of Medicine and the Center for American Progresss.

Administrative costs, however, are not the only item that increases costs of our insurance. All those advertisements for Viagra, Lipitor, Caduet, even aspirin cost billions of dollars. These costs are shifted to the consumer. So we're paying more, and what we get in return are advertisements.

Then there is always profit. While some states require health care insurance companies to be nonprofit, other states allow companies to make a profit. The net effect is that administrative costs and profit can easily amount to 20 to 30 percent of our insurance premiums but provide no medical benefit.

Also, people without health care insurance do not usually receive regular preventive care. As a result, uninsured people may not receive help until there is a health problem. By this time, the illness may be in advanced development and care will be much more costly than if the illness were found and treated earlier. So late diagnosis and treatment result in higher health care costs. This problem will be discussed further in the following section.

The American Medical Association also works to increase the cost of health care. The AMA is an association of doctors whose stated mission is to promote better health care in America. It also promotes the economic well being of its doctor constituents. For example, in 1930 it prohibited its member doctors from joining health maintenance organizations, or HMOs, and in the 1950s and '60s, it opposed the creation of Medicare. The AMA effectively limits the number of doctors admitted to medical schools. In doing so, it limits the supply of doctors and therefore increases doctors' pay. U.S. doctor' salaries are on average twice as high as comparable doctors in Europe. The AMA also raises the cost of care by lobbying Congress to require doctors to perform procedures that could be carried out at lower costs and just as effectively with lower-priced medical staff, such as physician's assistants. Oh, by the way, in limiting the availability and accessibility of doctors, the AMA acts contary to its mission and actually decreases the quality of medical care in America.

The highest costs do not always result in the best care

While the U.S. has the highest health care costs in the world, until the Affordable Care Act, we were the *only* wealthy industrialized nation that did not provided health care for all citizens.[85] How can we claim to be the world's leader when we can't provide health care for all our citizens?

Our ranking among the nations of the world on quality of health care is abysmal. In spite of being the world's wealthiest nation, we are not the healthiest. According to the CIA World Factbook, out of 224 nations, the United States ranks 43th in the world in life expectancy in 2017. The British and Germans have an average life expectancy of 80.8 years. The French and Canadians also have a life expectancy of 80.8 years and the Japanese to 85.3 years. Monaco has the highest with 89.47. But in America, the average life expectancy is only 80.0 years.[86]

You would expect that in modern America we would also have a very low infant mortality rate. But in fact, from the World Alas, 2018, Japan has the lowest infant mortality rate of 2.0 deaths per thousand births; France has 3.2; Germany 3.4; United Kingdom 4.3; and Canada 4.7. Among all the nations of the Organization for Economic Cooperation and Development, **OECD**, the infant mortality rate is per 1000. The United States has an infant mortality of 5.8 per 1,000 births.[87] We ranked 54th out of 223 nations in the study. And our world ranking on infant mortality has been getting worse. The U.S. was 12th in 1960.

Most Americans believe that we have the premier medical care in the world. Some say "Our medical system may not cover everyone, but it is the BEST medical system in the world." True, America has the most advanced medical technology on earth. In 2006, the United States accounted for 75 percent of the world's R&D spending on biotechnology and 75 percent of the world's biotechnology revenues.[88] Yet despite having the medical technology, we still rank 43th and 54th on life expectancy and infant mortality. All this technology doesn't help those 49.9 million souls who are without insurance, and apparently it's not doing much to increase the number of years we live or to save our babies. If you consider spending huge sums of money, having the world's best technology and receiving huge profits to be the world's best, then yes, we are the best. If you consider a country's medical power to be the health and longevity of its citizens, and the assurance that all citizens have access to medical services, then the United States is a second-class country.

Why we need a health care system for all Americans
Americans are dying from lack of an affordable national health care program.

Most Americans without health care insurance don't seek regular health care. Some of these folks are healthy and live normal healthy lives. However, many of the 49.9 million uninsured Americans live in poor health and do not receive needed medical care. The Emergency Medical Treatment and Active Labor Act of 1986 required that all hospitals provide emergency room care for an emergency patient regardless of the patient's ability to pay. However, for those with subtle diseases such as hypertension (high blood pressure), asthma, heart problems, and diabetes, a disease can exist for years without giving any outward signs. Caught in the early stages, these diseases can be treated with lifestyle changes and drug intervention. Left undiagnosed and untreated, these diseases can be life threatening. Likewise a disease like cancer, if diagnosed early, in most cases can be treated and the patient can often experience a full recovery. If undiagnosed, cancer kills! The scenario of waiting to obtain health care and then getting care only when the disease is in its advanced stages results not only in increased costs of treatment but also an unhealthy and sick lifestyle for the patient and reduced possibility of recovery when treatment is finally delivered. The ultimate end of this process in many cases is a death that could have been prevented or delayed had medical treatment been provided. The fact is, thousands of Americans live in poor health and experience premature deaths each year because of chronic diseases that could be successfully treated with proper medical care. In 2009, The Harvard Gazette found that about 45,000 deaths each year resulted from lack of health coverage.[89] Other studies have reached similar conclusions; lack of health care can be a death sentence.

During the national debate over the Affordable Care Act, Republicans and conservatives claimed that instituting a national care system would result in "death squads" or "death panels" that would decide what care each individual could receive. This was a blatant and reprehensible lie and an attempt to scare the American public about a government health care system. The fact of the matter is that the health care system enacted by the Affordable Care Act would act much as it did before: people would be covered through an employer- sponsored plan, by Medicare or Medicaid, or through "health insurance exchanges" established as part of the ACA especially to provide uninsured individuals with insurance. Before the Affordable Care Act was enacted insurance companies routinely rejected individuals with pre-existing illnesses; you couldn't get insurance even if you wanted it. (The Affordable Care Act prohibits insurance companies from excluding individuals from coverage due to pre-existing diseases and prohibits increasing the cost of care because of an existing disease.) Uninsured individuals with chronic diseases probably won't be treated until the disease becomes severe and when treatment is less effective. The facts are exactly the opposite of the Republican claim of "death panels." Uninsured individuals with life-threatening illnesses were literally sentenced to death or bankruptcy or both. NOT having health insurance is the grim reaper's best friend. The Affordable Care Act represents salvation from a death sentence, not the "death panels" that conservatives so sanctimoniously proclaimed.

Not only is America's health reduced by not having a national health care system, but the health of babies under the age of one, is also affected. The Enviromental Pretection Agent, EPA, report on the infant mortality shows that in 2015, a total of 23,458 infants under the age of 1 (including all races and both sexes) died in the U.S. Over one-third of these deaths occurred to preterm infants.[90] Preterm deliveries can be significantly reduced by proper health and prenatal care. Instituting a national affordable health care system would provide the opportunity for all expectant mothers to get proper prenatal care and would reduce our dreadful history of infant mortality.

In spite of these horrible statistics, "Right to Life" groups and some religious organizations, object to funding prenatal care from "Planned Parenthood" and other family planning agencies that many expectant mothers, especially those in the lower income catagories, count on for care of their child. By not adequately funding prenatal care groups, "Right to Lifers" are ignoring the fact that about 24,000 infants are dying each year, many because prenatal care is not available or not affordable. How ironic, a group called "Right to Life" is actually contributing to the death of infants.

Americans are effectively indentured servants because of health care costs.

Like it or not, many Americans are servants to their jobs because of health care costs. Health care costs are expensive, and one of the ways to maintain coverage is through your employer. Many people are working largely to maintain their health care coverage, are forced to sacrifice their ambitions and goals because they know that individual insurance is prohibitively expensive and unaffordable. Some people are forced to take poorer paying jobs so they can maintain their health insurance. This is not what America is all about. America should be the land of opportunity, not the land of intimidation and servitude.

Medical Expenses are a leading cause of bankruptcy in America.

I was listening to National Public Radio a while ago and heard the story of Donna and her husband. Donna and her husband were both college-educated, employed, and living a typical middle-class lifestyle. Donna's husband developed a heart condition. Then Donna developed uterine cancer about the same time. Donna and her husband had medical insurance, but the insurance had a limit on the amount the insurance company would pay each year. (The Affordable Care Act eliminated any annual limit on health care expenses starting in 2014.) The medical bills were astronomical. Donna and her husband could not pay the bills and were forced into bankruptcy. They lost their home and life savings. Donna had to quit her job and they moved in with her daughter and lived in the basement until they could find a small apartment.

According to the American Journal of Medicine, medical expenses contributed to over 60 percent of bankruptcies in America in 2009.[91] When you get seriously ill, you may experience a double whammy: you lose your job while simultaneously your expenses go up. Most medical bankruptcies occur to well-educated homeowners, middle-class Americans, and most had health insurance before the illness occurred. About 50 percent of health insurance companies cancel the policy upon the occurrence of prolonged illnesses. The bastards! (Starting in 2014, cancellation of a health insurance policy is prohibited under the Affordable Care Act.) In the richest country in the world, no one should be forced into bankruptcy because of health problems. You may hate the Affordable Care Act, but if you have an experience similar to that of Donna and her husband, you may wind up thanking your good fortune that Obamacare was enacted. You never know! As I have said, "We're all better off when we're all better off."

Not having health care affects our Liberty and Democracy

I think you will agree that if you contract cancer or some other serious disease and do not have a health insurance plan, you won't give a damn about your right to vote. On the other hand, if you do have a medical plan and know that your medical well-being will mostly be taken care of, you are much more likely to be aware of and more concerned about other facets of life, including your freedom.

Certain fundamental necessities must be fulfilled before a democracy can work. Foremost among these are food and shelter. Those without food and shelter are reduced to the full-time effort of maintaining their very existence. There is no such thing as liberty in this environment. This is the "caveman" existence.

People must have security in their lives. If they live in fear for their lives each day or are subject to torture for dissident behavior, their existence is only slightly improved from a survival war zone. Through the 21st century people in Darfur, Sudan and Somalia have lived in this condition. Those residing in El Salvador, Honduras and Guatemata are experiencing a survival mode of existence today.

Democracy requires that the living standard of the average citizen be above a certain sustainable level. Put simply, as a country progresses and as some of this prosperity eventually trickles down to the citizens, the lives of these citizens begin moving from starvation mode to the endurance mode. But people want a better life; they invariably demand to move from endurance to prosperity, from servitude to liberty. This basic evolution of democracy has been attested to in many sociological studies. In his book, "The Future of Freedom," Fareed Zakaria reveals that democratic countries with per capita income of under $1,500 per year stay in existence for an average of eight years.[92] Those with average incomes between $1,500 and $3,000 last an average of 18 years. However, those countries with an average per capita income over $6,000 per year almost never fail. This is demonstrated proof of the relationship between economic conditions and a democracy.

Democracy and liberty require the citizenry to reach a level of education; without education people cannot make intelligent choices and a democracy cannot flourish. As Thomas Jefferson stated to James Madison, "Above all things I hope the education of the common people will be attended to; convinced that on their good sense we may rely with the most security for the preservation of a due degree of liberty."

These fundamental necessities of food and shelter, security, a minimal standard of living, and education are absolutely essential for a democratic nation to maintain itself. Unfortunately, until the Affordable Care Act, for a significant portion of Americans their security was not fulfilled. While some people chose not to have health insurance, many wanted insurance but did not have it. Maybe they couldn't afford it or maybe they were prevented from obtaining it because of a pre-existing illness. Whatever the reason, these people had lost their fundamental right of security, especially if they had a life-threatening disease. To the extent that lack of food and selter, security and a minimum standard of living and education exists, America had not fulfilled its fundamental obligations. These citizens had their liberties surgically excised until Obamacare. Instead of removing people's freedom, the Affordable Care Act actually increases the liberty and democracy of every American in terms of their freedom to choose, their financial independence (from bankruptcy), and freedom to choose where we work.

What is in the Patient Protection and Affordable Care Act?

The Patient Protection and Affordable Care Act was approved by Congress (with every Republican in both houses voting against it) and was signed into law on March 23, 2010 by President Barack Obama. It was the most recent effort by the United States to bring into existence a health care system for all Americans. The chief accomplishment, which is its most controversial provision, was to require that essentially all individuals obtain minimal essential health insurance, i.e. the individual mandate. The individual mandate was necessary because starting in 2014 insurance companies can no longer refuse coverage for patients with pre-existing diseases. The mandate prevented people from waiting until they have an illness before getting health insurance. The individual mandate required that those individuals not covered by an employer-sponsored health plan or by a government-sponsored plan like Medicare, Medicaid, or the Veterans Administration must obtain insurance coverage or pay penalty tax. To facilitate obtaining insurance for those presently uninsured, the legislation establishes what were called health insurance exchanges. These were privately owned insurance companies that were established in each state or region and offered a variety of insurance plans for the public's selection. These insurance plans must satisfy all federal government requirements and will operate under state regulations.

Some of the major provisions of the act are:
Effective in 2010
- Adults with pre-existing illnesses became eligible to join a temporary high-risk insurance pool. (In 2014 the high-risk pool was eliminated and coverage could no longer be denied due to pre-existing conditions.)
- The National Prevention, Health Promotion and Public Health Council was established to develop a prevention and health promotion strategy.
- A 10 percent tax on indoor tanning took effect.
- Insurers were prohibited from imposing a lifetime dollar limit on the amount the insurer would pay for the patient's care.
- An insurer's ability to enforce annual spending caps (e.g. your insurance only covers up to $100,000 of medical costs) was restricted but was not entirely prohibited until 2014.
- Dependent children were permitted to remain on their parents' insurance plan until age 26.
- Small businesses became eligible for a 35 percent tax credit to provide employees' health insurance. This affected up to four million small businesses.
- Insurers were prohibited from excluding coverage for people under 19 years of age with pre-existing medical conditions.
- Insurers were prohibited from charging co-payments, co-insurance or deductibles for preventive care and medical screening on new insurance plans.

- Individuals affected by the Medicare Part D (prescription drug coverage) coverage gap (called the "donut hole") received a $250 rebate. The coverage gap will be eliminated by 2020.
- Insurers were prohibited from dropping policyholders when they get sick.
- Insurers were required to implement an appeals process for coverage.
- Medicare patients with chronic illnesses must be monitored on a three-month basis for coverage of medication.
- Companies that provide an early retirement program for employees ages 55 through 64, were eligible to participate in a temporary reinsurance program.

Effective in 2011
- Insurers must spend 80% (for individuals or small group insurers) or 85% (for large group insurers) of premium dollars on health costs and claims, leaving the remaining 20% to 15% for administrative costs and profit.
- The Centers for Medicare and Medicaid Services begans tracking re-admission rates and initiated incentives to reduce readmissions.

Effective in 2012
- Employers must report the value of the health care benefits provided to the employee on the employee's W-2 form.
- All new health insurance plans must cover preventive services such as mammograms and colonoscopies without charging a deductible, co-pay, or co-insurance. Women's preventive services such as wellness visits, human papillomavirus DNA testing, domestic violence screening, and contraception are covered without

cost-sharing. (Providing contraception was the cause of the Catholic uproar that began in late 2011.)
- The Centers for Medicare and Medicaid Services (CMMS) began the Readmission Reduction Program which requires the CMMS to reduce payments to some hospitals with excess readmissions. This is an effort to reimburse health care providers based on quality of care.

Effective in 2013
- Medicare payroll tax was raised from 1.45 percent to 2.35 percent for individuals earning more than $200,000 and married couples earning more than $250,000 per year.
- The limit placed on healthcare flexible spending account was capped at $2,500.
- The threshold for itemized medical expenses on tax returns increased from 7.5% to 10.0% of adjusted gross income for taxpayer under 65.
- Starting in October enrollment in health insurance exchanges began. Coverage began January 1, 2014.

Effective 2014
- Insurers are prohibited from excluding individuals with pre-existing illnesses.
- Insurers can no longer charge higher premium rates for patients with pre-existing illnesses.
- Insurers are prohibited from establishing an annual limit on the amount the insurer will pay for patient care.
- Essentially everyone must obtain health insurance either through an employer-sponsored plan, a government- sponsored plan such as Medicare, Medicaid, or the Veterans Administration or through state-sponsored health insurance exchanges (this requirement is the so-called "individual mandate" provision of

the Act). Health insurance exchanges were opened to businesses and individuals. Individuals not obtaining health care were charged an annual tax penalty of $95 or up to 1 percent of their income, whichever is greater. This amount increased to $695 for individuals ($2085 for a family of four) or 2.5 percent of their income in 2016. Exemptions to the individual mandate are permitted for religious reasons. The IRS was able to withhold future tax refunds from those refusing to pay the penalty.

- Individuals with income up to 133 percent of the federal poverty level were eligible for Medicaid. The law also allowed for a 5 percent "income disregard" which maked the effective income eligibility limit 138 percent of the poverty limit. (The 2014 federal poverty level in the lower 48 states and D. C. for an individual was $11,670 and for a family of four was $23,850. The levels are higher in Hawaii and Alaska.) States were allowed to choose if their wanted to participate in this new program but some states have chosen not to participate.

- A maximum out-of-pocket premium cap was established for most Americans. Families and individuals making up to 400 percent of the federal poverty level ($95,400 for a family of four in 2014) were subsidized through income tax credits based on a proportional scale.The tax credit was based on maximum annual premiums families would pay out of pocket. The lower the income, the lower the annual premium the family would pay and the higher the allowable tax credit. For example, a family of four making 150 percent of the poverty level, i.e. $23,850 X 1.5= $35,775 per year (about $17.88 per hour), would pay no more than 4.0% X 35,775 = $1431 per year (about $120 per month) for a "silver" healthcare insurance plan.

(See table of Maximum Out-of-Pocket Premium Payments Under PPACA i.e. Patient Protection Affordable Care Act, below.)

Maximum Out-of-Pocket Premium Payments Under PPACA							
Income % of Federal Poverty Level, FPL	Max Premium Payment as a % of Income	Maximum Annual Premium by Family Size					
		1	2	3	4	5	6
FPL in 2014		$11,670	$15,730	$19,790	$23,850	$27,910	$31,970
100%	2.0%	$233	$315	$396	$477	$558	$639
133.00%	2.0%	$310	$418	$526	$634	$742	$850
133.01%	3.0%	$466	$628	$790	$952	$1,114	$1,276
150%	4.0%	$700	$944	$1,187	$1,431	$1,675	$1,918
200%	6.3%	$1,470	$1,982	$2,494	$3,005	$3,517	$4,028
250%	8.05%	$2,349	$3,166	$3,983	$4,800	$5,617	$6,434
300%	9.5%	$3,326	$4,483	$5,640	$6,797	$7,954	$9,111
400%	9.5%	$4,435	$5,977	$7,520	$9,063	$10,606	$12,149

Derived from 2014 Federal Poverty Levels and Private Health Insurance Provisions in the PPACA

– Employers having more than 50 full-time employees that do not offer health insurance for their workers (either through a private plan or the health insurance exchange) will be penalized $2,000 per employee. (Note that about 90 percent of companies having 25 to 49 employees already offer health insurance plans.) In July 2013, this penalty was delayed until January 2015.
– Small business employers that purchased coverage through new state exchanges can receive a tax credit for their contribution toward the employee's health insurance premium.

Effective in 2015
- Physicians' payments were based on quality of care, not numbers of patients seen.

Effective in 2016 There were no new requirements

Effective in 2017
- States can apply to the Secretary of Health and Human Services for a waiver from the Affordable Care Act. The state program can eliminate the individual mandate, creation of state health exchanges and penalties for employers. However, the state program must be at least as comprehensive and as affordable as the ACA, must cover as many of the state residents and cannot increase the federal deficit. The state program must continue to meet the consumer protection portion of the ACA such as coverage for individuals with pre-existing conditions. For example, Vermont has announced a plan to establish a single-payer plan, i.e. a Medicare-type plan, for the state. However, Vermont finally rejected this plan because it was judged to be too expensive.

Effective in 2018
- A 40 percent tax was placed on "Cadillac" plans. Health care costs exceeding $27,500 for families and $10,400 for individuals are subject to the tax.

How we will pay for the new health care act, a summary

The biggest factor in paying for the Affordable Care Act is the individual mandate requiring that everyone participate in the new health care system. The individual mandate is necessary because

- It increases the size of the insurance "pot" used to pay for the people's health care

- It significantly reduces the amount that taxpayers and those with health insurance must pay to cover those who do not have insurance i.e. about $1,000 per year
- It helps to identify illnesses earlier when health care can be initiated more cost effectively and
- Since it requires almost everyone to have insurance and prevents insurance companies from denying coverage to those with pre-existing illnesses, it eliminates the possibility that people will wait until they are sick before getting insurance.

In addition, the Affordable Care Act calls for implementing the following taxes to help pay for the program. Most of these taxes are small increases on medical companies, high income individuals who have Cadillac insurance plans, large flexible spending accounts and medical tax deductions or result from management efficiencies required to be implemented by the insurance companies.

Effective in 2010
- 10 percent tax on indoor tanning salons goes into effect.

Effective in 2013
- Medicare payroll tax was raised from 1.45 percent to 2.35 percent for individuals earning more than $200,000 and married couples earning more than $250,000 per year.

Effective in 2014
- Reduce spending on Medicare Advantage programs, reducing Medicare/Medicaid drug reimbursements and other Medicare/Medicaid spending.
- Limit flexible spending accounts (accounts set up for medical expenses which are not suggest to taxes) to $2,500. Previously the account amount was unlimited.

- New excise taxes on pharmaceutical companies based on the market share of the company. Expected to raise $2.5 billion annually.
- Medical device companies pay 2.3 percent excise tax.
- Health insurance companies pay excise tax based on market share. Expected to rise $14.3 billion annually.
- The floor for medical deductions on Schedule A of the federal tax return will be raised from 7.5 percent of income to 10 percent of income, i.e. only medical expenses above 10 percent of income is deductible.
- Employers having more than 50 employees that do not offer health insurance for their workers will be penalized $2,000 per employee, while those employers that opt to provide health care for employees will be eligible for tax incentives.
- Health Insurance Exchanges will be established in each state so that those not in an employer offered plan, or on Medicare or Medicaid will have a selection of what plan to participate in. The competition offered by the free market place will help drive down the insurance premiums.
- A series of steps will be taken to standardize and simplify the administrative procedures followed by the insurance plans. Simpler procedures should save money.

Effective in 2018
- A 40 percent tax will be placed on Cadillac plans. Health care plans exceeding $27,500 for families and $10,400 for individuals per year are subject to the tax.

The net effect of adding more members to the insurance plans, reducing taxes and other hidden costs to cover the uninsured, providing incentives to employers, instituting health insurance exchanges, and simplifying administrative procedures will reduce the cost of health insurance. In fact, the Congressional

Budget Office estimates that the net effect of these and other measures is to reduce the deficit by $132 billion over the first decade.[93] (The Congressional Budget Office is a nonpartisan agency that does financial analysis and is used extensively by both political parties.) Nonetheless, Republicans criticize the estimate, saying it neglects one cost item or another. One estimate, for example, indicated that the Affordable Care Act would increase the deficit by $562 billion. So in the future there may have to be some modifications to financing of the Act and some of the provisions of the Act. The saga of the Affordable Care Act is not over. But one thing is for sure: America needs a health care system for all of its citizens.

Why do some people oppose the ACA so strongly

Since the Affordable Care Act, ACA, was passed in 2010, Republicans in congress have lead 70 attempts, yes 70 attempts, to repeal, modify or otherwise curb the Affordable Care Act.[94] Why would people object to a health care system if it:

- provides health care for almost everyone (as of 2018, 11.8 million people have signed up for health care insurance through state and federal exchanges, about 5.5 million of these were previously not insured. In addition about 5.0 million have gained coverage through the new expanded Medicaid plan.)
- increases the overall health of the country
- reduces the cost of health care and made health care affordable for all
- reduces the deficit
- assures everyone pays their fair share
- eliminates the most reprehensible practices of insurance companies like denying coverage for patients with pre- existing illnesses and establishing maximum payments that the insurance company will provide and

– establishes maximum out-of-pocket premiums that Americans will have to pay?

All of these goals are goals that a modern democratic country would consider desirable (paying for your own medical costs for example). Yet some Americans, including some members of congress, are doing whatever they can to destroy the Affordable Care Act.

Some people oppose Obamacare because they believe it is an inefficient system that will lead to socialized medicine. Many Americans believe socialized medicine is a bad system despite the fact that many European countries use a government operated medical system that satisfies most of it citizens. The government in the U. S. is not as inefficient as many people believe. Take the US Postal System for example. The post office delievers millions of letters and parcels every day and none of them get lost. You can mail a letter to Los Angeles from New York City and the next day you can find out the exact time it was delievered. Or take Medicare which provides medical coverage older Americans. Medicare covers million of individuals each day. Yet medical treatment is delievered easily each day to most patients and medical payments are made by Medicare on time and at a reasonable price. But still, many Republicans consider medicare a form of social welfare, they want people to get work, to find a job. This is despite the fat that over 70% of the people receiving financial assistance have jobs already but still are below the poverty level. They cannot support their family on their wages and when someone suggests increasing the minimum wage, the suggestion is met with outrage. Many other people on Medicaid are unemployed because of a illness, disability or care-giving responsibility. This is not social welfare, it is Americans helping other Americans.

Finally, and perhaps most importantly to wealthy Americans, eliminating ACA will reduce taxes on the rich. To fund the ACA, taxes on the rich were increased. For example, the Medicare payroll tax for those earning more than $200,000 per year increased from 1.45% to 2.35% (a $1800 per year increase if you earned exactly $200,000). The Affordable Care Act subsidizes low income families to help them buy insurance. Eliminating the ACA would reduce the higher payroll tax, increasing the income to the rich and reduce subsidies for the poor, a reverse Robin Hood.

The Supreme Court Cases, The Individual Mandate

Much of the hatred for the ACA revolves around the individual mandate that requires all people to get health insurance or pay a fine of $695 per adult or 2.5% of income, which every is higher, starting in 2016. Millions of individuals protested the individual mandate saying that it was a violation of their individual rights for government to force them to acquire health insurance. After litigation within several U.S. District Courts, 20 states filed a class action suit with the Supreme Court to adjudicate the mandate. The arguments before the Supreme Court were heard in March 2012, and the decision was rendered on June 28, 2012 when the court, on a 5-to-4 decision, declared the individual mandate to be constitutional. To most people's surprise, Chief Justice John Roberts, a conservative, voted with the majority.

The government's justification was that under the Commerce Clause of the Constitution, the federal government is authorized to regulate interstate commerce, and health insurance falls under this provision. The opposing lawyers for the 20 states argued that the Commerce Clause applies to transactions that people are presently already doing and does not apply to transactions which the people are presently not doing, i.e. they are presently not buying health insurance. From a legal viewpoint, it is somewhat strange for the government to require citizens to participate in an activity. The state government requires me to buy a fishing license if I want to fish, but in the case of the Individual Mandate, the government is requiring me to become a fisherman. That's great with me because I love to fish, but some people would rather play golf. In the end, it was not only the Commerce Clause that makes the individual mandate constitutional but also the fact that the penalty for not participating was considered by Chief Justice Roberts to be a tax and the federal government has a constitutional right to levy taxes. The Individual Mandate was therefore held to be constitutional.

As was discussed before, since everyone will be covered by the Affordable Care Act, everyone must help pay for it. In exchange for having guaranteed health care when you get sick, you must pay your fair share of the cost of running this guaranteed system. That seems to be fair, paying your fair share. Yet millions of Americans objected and many of those objecting are not the poor but are those who are willing to forgo health insurance on the chance that they won't need hospital care. If they do need care, "we the tax payers" will pay for it. In fact, about 20 percent of the uninsured are able to afford insurance.[95]

But the story does not end here. As part of the Republican's Tax Cuts and Job Act of 2017, five years after the Independent Business decision, the penalty for not purchasing health insurance was set by congress to be $0.00. The individual mandate requiring purchase on health insurance still exists but the fine for not paying disappeared; the mandate no longer has teeth. The result is 11.4 million people signed up for Obamacare in 2018 for 2019 insurance, down from 11.8. million (a 400,000 reduction) for 2018 insurance.[96] This decrease reportedly results from sharply cut federal out-reach efforts, the open enrollment period was cut in half and the removal of the penalty for not obtaining health insurance. With the Individual Mandate now toothless, participation in health insurance is likely to decrease and so will health insurance companies' revenues. Insurance companies will be forced to increase rates to maintain solvency. In the coming year you can expect health insurance rates to increase significantly which in turn will reduce partipation. We'd be headed right back from where we started.

Another Idea, Pay at Your Funeral Plan-

I have a plan that will allow people to pay for health insurance only if they use it. Enact a plan similar to the Affordable Care Act but without the individual mandate. If people choose not to participate, so be it. However, if and when they become ill and require medical treatment, they would be responsible to pay up all their back premiums, including the inflation associated with delayed payment, from the time they stopped participating in this "New Affordable Care Act" until the time when they were admitted for care. Once in care, they would continue paying their premiums. If they died before paying up the premiums, the amount in arrears would be paid as part of their estate. In this way, people would not be allowed to receive medical care while someone else pays for it. But if they don't avail themself of the New ACA, they would still be required to pay for it. I call this plan "The pay at your funeral plan". Some would exclaim that people would still be paying for the individual mandate, only on a delayed basis. Well, au contraire, because some people will die without requiring medical care; they might be killed in a car accident or suffer a fatal heart attack for example. These people would be gambling magnate. They gambled that they would not need to maintain health insurance and they won! Of course, they would never know until they die or until they need insurance. If they never need it, then they haven't spent money on something they didn't need. If they do need care as they get older, they can pay the entire amount then or as part of their estate after they die. Either way, they pay for what they need and they wouldn't be permitted to be "free loaders" like those on welfare.

But it's not over yet

The saga to the Affordable Care Act is not over yet. In 2018, a Texas lead delegation of 20 states sued to get the entire Affordable Care Act declared unconstitutional. Judge Reed O'Connor, federal judge in the state of Texas, and a notoriously conservative judge, did hear the case and ruled the entire

Affordable Care Act to be unconstitutional. The decision was appealed to the 5th Circuit Court of Appeals in New Orleans. If Judge O'Connor's ruling is affirmed by the 5th circuit, the Supreme Court will hear the case in 2020. People can remain in the plan until the case is decided. If the Affordable Care Act is declared unconstitutional and is not replaced with another plan, about 30 million people will lose health insurance coverage. We will essentially regress back to 2010, before the Affordable Care Act was ever passed by congress.

The Hobby Lobby Decision

On June 30, 2014, the Supreme Court ruled on the case Burwell v Hobby Lobby (previously known as Sebelius v Hobby Lobby, Sylvia Burwell's name as Secretary of Health and Human Services was automatically substituted for Kathleen Sebelius after Sebelius' resignation in April 2014). Hobby Lobby is a retail art and craft store headquartered in Oklahoma City, Oklahoma. Hobby Lobby is a "closely held" (i.e. company stock is not traded on the stock market and is generally owned by a small group of stockholders) and a "for profit" corporation owned by the Green family, a devout family of Evangelical Christians. Hobby Lobby filed suit against the U. S. Government claiming that Affordable Care Act's requirement to provide contraceptive health care to women violated their religious convictions. The Supreme Court ruled in a 5-4 decision that based on religious objections, a closely held, for-profit corporation can be exempt from the law. Throughout our history America has tried to be painstakingly impartial in protecting religious freedom. However, the religious rights of the employees must also be considered. The ACA already makes exceptions for religious organizations; however Hobby Lobby is not a religious institution. This is the first time in history that the Supreme Court recognized a for-profit corporation's claim based on religious beliefs. The Court further emphasized that this ruling applies only to closely held companies; this is the continuation of a long line of assaults on the Affordable Care

Act. If conservatives can't over turn the Act by repeal, then they will disassemble it by a thousand slices.

Expanded Medicaid

As part of the Affordable Care Act, people making less than 133 percent of the federal poverty level and under 65 (those older than 65 are eligible for Medicare) were to become eligible for Medicaid assistance. This new coverage would allow people not previously covered by medical insurance to be eligible for the minimum essential benefits required by the Affordable Care Act. Under the plan, the federal government was to fund 100 percent of the state's costs of the program for the first three years and then would phase down to paying 90 percent of the costs by 2020. Under the Act, all states were mandated to implement this new system. Had things remained unchanged at this point, almost everyone in America would get health care coverage, people below 133 percent of the poverty level would be covered by Medicaid, and people above that level would receive lower premiums and lower out-of-pocket costs. However, thing did not remain constant. The Supreme Court ruled that the federal government could not force each state to offer the new Medicaid program; the states could opt to continue with the existing program administrated by each state.

The table below explains how the final system works out. Across the top is the number of people in a household. If you are the only person in the household and you make between $11,670 (100 percent of the poverty level for 2014) and $45,960 (400 percent of the poverty level), you are eligible for lower premiums under the Affordable Care Act. If you're in the lower portion of that range, between $11,670 and $28,725, you're eligible for lower premiums under ACA *and* lower out-of-pocket payments. If there are two people in the household, then the table shows what benefits you are eligible for at each income level and so on. Now if you make below $16,105 (133 percent of the poverty level in 2014) *and* your state chose to participate in the expanded

Medicaid program, you are also eligible for Medicaid. Since Medicaid costs less than the insurance exchanges, the Medicaid is a better alternative for you.

Now here's the problem. If your state did *not* choose to participate in the expanded coverage and your income is *more* than $11,670 in 2014 then you can get medical insurance coverage through the health care exchanges, but you'll have to pay premiums. However, if you make *less* than $11,670, your income is not between the two income limits, you may be without hope. You are not eligible for the health care exchanges because you don't make enough money, and you are not eligible for the federal expanded Medicaid because even though you make less than $16,105, your state is not participating in the new program. You must rely on the state programs that existed before the Obamacare. Many of these programs are very spartan. To be eligible for Medicaid in Georgia, for example, you must have children or be over 65 and handicapped. Younger adults with no children are not eligible.

You are eligible for Medicaid if you have an infant and make less than 200 percent of the federal poverty level, have a child under 5 and make 133 percent of the poverty level or have children between 6 and 19 and make less than 100 percent of the poverty level. In addition, you must have assets (bank account, stocks, bonds or real estate) worth less than $2,000 for an individual or $4,000 for a couple.[97] In other words you must have children or be over 65 and be handicapped and be really, really poor to get Medicaid in Georgia.

	Number of People in the Household					
	1	2	3	4	5	6
You may qualify for lower premiums on the marketplace insurance planif your income is between:	$11,670 to $45,960	$15,730 to $62,040	$19,790 to $78,120	$23,850 to $94,200	$27,910 to $110,280	$31,970 to $126,360
You may qualify for lower premiums AND lower-out-of-pocket costs for the marketplace insurance plan if your income is between:	$11,670 to $28,725	$15,730 to $38,775	$19,790 to $48,825	$23,850 to $58,875	$27,910 to $68,925	$31,970 to $78,975
If your state is expanding Medicaid in 2014: You may qualify for Medicaid coverage if your yearly income is below:	$16,105	$21,707	$27,310	$32,913	$38,516	$44,119
If your state is NOT expanding Medicaid in 2014: You may not qualify for any marketplace savings programs if your yearly income is below:	$11,670	$15,730	$19,790	$23,850	$27,910	$31,970

from www.Healthcare.gov, "What Income Levels Qualify for Lower Costs"

As of November, 2019, 37 states, including the District of Columbia, have accepted the Expanded Medicaid plan while 14 states have not. The fourteen states not accepting the Expaned Medicaid Plan are Alabama, Florida, Georgia, Kansas, Mississippi, Missouri, North Carolina, Oklahoma, South Carolina, South Dakota, Tennessee, Texas, Wisconsin, and Wyoming. The very poorest Americans are left without health care insurance. Texas has over 1.0 million people affected by this Medicaid gap, followed by Florida with 760,000 and Georgia with 400,000.

The states that opted out of the expanded Medicaid did so because they oppose Obamacare and "Big Government." But there are dire consequences of this decision. A study from Harvard Medical School and the City University of New York estimated that about 7.8 million additional people would have access to health care had all the states opted into the expanded Medicaid coverage plan. In addition, the report estimated that between 7,115 and 17,104 more people will die annually than would have if their states accepted the Medicaid expansion.[98] Apparently, the 14 states hate the federal government more than they care for their own citizens. They have effectively doomed some of their own citizens to death.

In addition, the Emergency Medical Trauma and Labor Act signed into law by President Ronald Reagan in 1986 makes it illegal to refuse emergency care to an individual. This means that a portion of the uninsured is going to receive some emergency medical care at the highest possible cost with the least likely favorable outcome. Some of these emergency costs will be passed along to other patients in the form of higher medical costs. These costs would be significantly reduced with proper health care offered by the expended Medicaid program. Refusing the Medicaid expansion, therefore results in higher medical costs for all residences in these 14 states.

Finally, the expanded Medicaid will provide billions of dollars to the states to provide the additional medical coverage. This means more doctors and nurses, more technicians and more administrative staff will be needed—in short, more jobs. Those 14 states are missing this opportunity. Some states hate the federal government and will do anything to reduce its power. Okay, get over it! If a good opportunity comes along, don't let your hatred overcome your common sense. Take advantage of it. As my mother used to say, "Don't cut off your nose to spite your face." After all, we're all better off when we're all better off.

Another idea of medical insurance

I was talking to a friend of mine recently about our health care system, and I explained how poorly our system ranks among the developed countries. He brought up a good point, "You can't judge a country's health care quality by life expectancy or infant mortality alone. There are lifestyle issues that affect life expectancy." He's right. Americans are fat, and I don't mean in a good way, as in "fat" with money and property. I mean fat as in obese. It is our lifestyle issues that are helping to lower our life expectancy, not just our health insurance. One source of our poor health is our poor eating habits and our lack of exercise. Any changes to America's health care system should encourage a healthier style of living. One way to do this is by determining what's bad for you and then getting restaurants and food producers to cut out the bad stuff. You can see this happening already. McDonald's, for example, now cooks its French fries in oils containing no trans fat to encourage healthy eating, particularly for school children. Another friend of mine, a medical doctor, suggested that any national health care system should consider lifestyle in determining the premiums paid by the plan members. Smokers, heavy drinkers, and obese people, for example, would pay higher premiums for their coverage than slim, fit individuals. This is a great idea. In fact, I know of at least one company medical program that asked about each participant's health habits and performed a complete physical for each employee. If you're a smoker, you pay significantly more in premiums than a non-smoker. If you're obese, you pay more. One of the employees I talked to said that he was forced to quit smoking because his health insurance was too high to continue with this killer habit. What a great idea and spectacular outcome. By quitting smoking this worker significantly improved his health and increased his life expectancy. In addition he lowered his health care premiums. If each person participated in such a health plan, the health costs on our entire country would decrease.

The cure for Medicare

Americans are living longer and healthier lives now than ever before. Even though we don't have the best health care system in the world, there is no doubt that we are all living longer. When Medicare was founded in 1965, the average life expectancy was 68. Now the life expectancy is 80. Yet the eligibility age for Medicare has remained at 65, it has never changed. It only makes sense that, over time, the age a person becomes eligible for Medicare should increase. Say, for example, that over the next five to ten years the eligible age for Medicare should be increased from 65 to 67 or 70. This would reduce the number of recipients receiving Medicare and increase the number of people paying into it and the duration of time they pay.

Medicare is a great system and has worked well for almost 50 years. It is relatively cheap, with overhead of only 3-7 percent compared with 20-30 percent for private insurance. The vast majority of Americans like Medicare, and we should do what we can to keep it. The last thing we should do is gut the system.

The Ryan Plan

However, that is exactly what the Republican Party planned to do. In 2011, Paul Ryan, chairman of the House Budget Committee and 2012 vice presidential candidate, suggested that beginning in 2022 we do away with the present Medicare system and replace it with federal vouchers to the states, allowing the states to administer the system. Until 2022, the traditional Medicare system would remain unchanged. Under Ryan's voucher system, individuals would be provided vouchers that they would use to purchase health insurance from private companies. The health insurance companies would love this system with millions of retired people coming to them with vouchers in hand. The value of the vouchers would be tied to the gross domestic product, GDP, and would increase at a rate of the GDP + ½ percent. However, the cost of health insurance increases much faster than GDP + ½ percent, so people would wind up paying thousands of dollars more out of pocket. This was a really bad idea! So Ryan modified the plan. Ryan's second plan would leave the traditional Medicare in place and give people a choice: the Ryan voucher plan or traditional Medicare. If cost of health care exceeded the payment vouchers, then the difference would come out of pocket. The new plan attempts to maintain the increasing costs of health care to the GDP + ½ percent, but if this can't be maintained, the new plan specifies that Congress must take some action, but that action is not specified. Think about this plan! Healthy people would take the voucher system and the unhealthier people would choose traditional Medicare. This would obviously cause Medicare costs to increase faster than in the past and put Medicare at a disadvantage. In either case, Medicare plan or voucher plan, since every state would administer the system differently, the proposal would increase the administrative mess that the medical system is already buried in. It would, most likely, increase the administrative costs of the system, thereby causing the premium rates to increase faster and higher. Paul Ryan resigned from the House of Representatives in January 2019.

CHAPTER 5

Business In America

The Triangle Shirtwaist Factory fire

On March 25, 1911, United Press reporter William G. Sheperd just happened to be ambling through Washington Square in New York City.

"I was walking through Washington Square when a puff of smoke issuing from the factory building caught my eye. I reached the building before the alarm was turned in. I saw every feature of the tragedy visible from outside the building. I learned a new sound—a more horrible sound than description can picture. It was the thud of a speeding, living body on a stone sidewalk.

Thud-dead, thud-dead, thud-dead, thud-dead. Sixty-two thud-deads. The first ten thud-deads shocked me. I looked up—saw that there were scores of girls at the windows. The flames from the floor below were beating in their faces. Somehow I knew that they, too, must come down, and something within me—something that I didn't know was there—steeled me...

As I reached the scene of the fire, a cloud of smoke hung over the building I looked up to the seventh floor. There was a living picture in each window—four screaming heads of girls waving their arms...

One girl climbed onto the window sash. Those behind her tried to hold her back. Then she dropped into space. I didn't notice whether those above watched her drop because I had turned away. Then came that first thud. I looked up, another girl was climbing onto the window sill; others were crowding behind her. She dropped. I watched her fall, and again the dreadful sound...

The firemen began to raise a ladder. Others took out a life net and, while they were rushing to the sidewalk with it, two more girls shot down. The firemen held it under them; the bodies broke it; the grotesque simile of a dog jumping through a hoop struck me. Before they could move the net another girl's body flashed through it. The thuds were just as loud, it seemed, as if there had been no net there. It seemed to me that the thuds were so loud that they might have been heard all over the city...

As I looked up I saw a love affair in the midst of all the horror. A young man helped a girl to the window sill. Then he held her out, deliberately away from the building and let her drop. He seemed cool and calculating. He held out a second girl the same way and let her drop They were as unresisting as if he were helping them onto a streetcar instead of into eternity. Undoubtedly he saw that a terrible death awaited them in the flames, and his was only a terrible chivalry...

Then came the love amid the flames. He brought another girl to the window. Those of us who were looking saw her put her arms about him and kiss him. Then he held her out into space and dropped her. But quick as a flash he was on the window sill himself. His coat fluttered upward—the air filled his trouser legs. I could see that he wore tan shoes and hose. His hat remained on his head He leaped with an energy as if to arrive first in that mysterious land of eternity, but her thud-dead came first...

The firemen raised the longest ladder. It reached only to the sixth floor. I saw the last girl jump at it and miss it. And then the faces disappeared from the window. By now the crowd was enormous, though all this had occurred in less than seven minutes, the start of the fire and the thuds and deaths..."[99]

This is an eyewitness account of the deadliest industrial disaster in New York City history. The disaster occurred at the Triangle Shirtwaist Factory located on the eighth, ninth and tenth floors of the Asch Building at 23-29 Washington Place just east of Washington Square. The factory produced "shirtwaist" blouses, a popular lady's blouse of the time, tight at the waist and blossoming out at the shoulders. The factory was owned by Max Blanck and Isaac Harris, who had immigrated to the United States from Russia. Blanck and Harris had ordered the exit doors and fire escapes be locked, as was the custom then, to prevent unauthorized break-ins and pilfering. The factory employed about 500 workers, most of them young immigrant women. The workers worked six days a week, nine hours on weekdays and seven on Saturdays. At 4:40 p.m. on Saturday, March 27, a fire started, probably in a waste bin from a cigarette or unextinguished match, although there is some disagreement as to the exact cause. Smoking was prohibited in the factory, but workers did occasionally sneak a smoke. As the eyewitness account indicates, the fire brigade responded rapidly and the fire was swiftly extinguished. However, the ladders could not reach to the eighth floor.

Image of Triangle Shirtwaist factory fire on March 25, 1911
http://www.ilr.cornell.edu/trianglefire/primary/testimonials/ootss_williamshepherd.html

During the fire, 146 workers died and 71 were injured. Blanck and Harris were in the building at the time of the fire and managed to escape by climbing to the roof along with other survivors.

In December, 1911, Blanck and Harris were indicted for first- and second-degree manslaughter. The lawyers for Blanck and Harris stressed that the prosecution was not able to prove that Blanck and Harris knew the doors were locked. Also because the fire was apparently caused by cigarette smoking, the employees were culpable in the fire. The two factory owners were acquitted.

In a subsequent civil suit brought against the owners by the families of the deceased in 1913, the court awarded the families $75 per victim (roughly $3800 in 2012 dollars). However, as a result of the property loss from the fire, the insurance company paid Blanck and Harris $60,000 more than their losses, an average of $400 per victim.

As another more positive consequence of the fire, the American Society of Safety Engineers was formed in October 1911.

Asbestos

Asbestos is wonderful product. It is nearly indestructible. It is abrasive-resistant, resists chemical corrosion, serves as a great thermal insulator and with asbestos gloves you can pick up a red-hot poker and hold it in the palm of your hand. It maintains these properties for thousands of years; it doesn't break down with time or sunlight. It has wonderful chemical and physical properties. As such asbestos was used in thousands of products: asbestos roofing shingles, asbestos floor tile, as fireproofing over beams, house insulation, pipe insulation, fireproof draperies, over or inside furnaces in residential and commercial buildings, in automobile brakes and clutches, insulation over hot-air or hot-water heating systems. It was even used for decorative ceiling installations. It is truly an amazing product. Only one problem: it is a serious carcinogen.

Although the wonders of asbestos were known for hundreds of years before it became popular in the United States, it wasn't until the end of the 1800s and beginning of the 1900s, during the Industrial Revolution that asbestos began to be widely used commercially. However, around the same time, people began dying of asbestos disease. In 1924, an English physician, W. E. Cooke, performed an autopsy on a 33-year-old woman who had worked as an asbestos textile worker for 13 years, and he discovered that her lungs were full of asbestos. Dr. Cooke and others started a study of asbestos industrial workers and discovered that 25 percent of the workers developed pulmonary fibrosis. The term "asbestosis" was coined to describe the lung disease.

By 1932 the hazards of asbestos exposure were plainly evident in a letter from the U. S. Bureau of Mines to Eagle-Picher, manufacturer of asbestos products. It stated "It is now known that asbestos dust is one of the most dangerous dusts to which man can be exposed."

With World War II came a gigantic leap in the use of asbestos and the number asbestos-related diseases. In 1947, the Asbestos Textile Institute, ATI, commissioned a study of the risks of use of asbestos materials. The study showed that there was a risk of disease resulting from asbestos exposure and called for the adoption of safety standards such as lowering exposure time, wearing respirator equipment and attempting to find alternate products. The asbestos industry, however, took no preventive measures, calculating that knowledge of asbestos disease would cause irreparable damage to the industry. Even when it became evident that people with no known contact with asbestos were contracting mesothelioma, the industry took no preventive action. Mesothelioma is cancer of the membrane lining of the lungs. The lining extends around both lungs and cannot be removed. It is rare but always fatal. Incidental contact with asbestos, such as wives washing the their husband's clothing, can result in mesothelioma.

Indeed, the asbestos industry used the fact that mesothelioma takes up to 40 years to show any signs of malady to its advantage. It used workers in asbestos-laden areas knowing that they could develop a terminal illness but would not have any illness or knowledge of such illness until it was too late.

So exposure to asbestos workers continued. The first successful litigation against asbestos manufacturers occurred in

1969 when a worker, Clarence Borel, filed a liability suit against several asbestos manufacturers. Borel was awarded $80,000 by the court. With this success, the floodgates were open for liability suits against asbestos manufacturers. As asbestos litigation started in the 1970s and 1980s, evidence shows that the companies knew full well about the problems of asbestos and had done absolutely nothing to protect their workers.

For example, a 1958 National Gypsum memo states:
We know that you will never lose sight of the fact that perhaps the greatest hazard in your plant is with men handling asbestos. Because just as certain as death and taxes is the fact that if you inhale asbestos dust you get asbestosis.[100]

This is just one of the many incriminating communications that came to light during the years following the Borel lawsuit. Over the ensuing 40 years, 730,000 asbestos claims have been filed against 8,400 defendants including 200,000 suits presently pending. Roughly 10,000 new claims are filed each year.[101] As a result of the superfluity of litigation and costly settlements, more than half of the 25 largest asbestos manufacturing companies in the United States have filed for bankruptcy. Among them are National Gypsum, Eagle-Picher, Amatex, Carey-Canada, Celotex and Johns-Manville.

This is not to say that the industry took *no* action at all during this time. In fact, it went to extraordinary lengths to conceal evidence and to misrepresent and distort the facts. Information related to as bestos exposure and disease was hidden from the public as well as the workers. In some cases, the company required that its workers have physical examinations and then prevented them from obtaining the results. Scientific studies were also manipulated to veil the link between asbestos and cancer. Advertisements misrepresented the content of products, saying that products were asbestos-free when, in fact, they still contained asbestos. The industry went to any and every means to shed itself of any responsibility for the asbestos poisoning of thousands of individuals.

The biggest culprit in this fiasco of distortion, deceit and conspiracy was the Johns-Manville Corporation, the biggest insulation company in the world at that time. But this was not nearly the full extent of the conspiracy. Some of the other companies involved with asbestos cover-up included: W.R. Grace, Exxon, Union Carbide (now a subsidiary of Dow Chemical), DuPont, Bendix (presently owned by Honeywell), The Travelers Insurance, Metropolitan Life Insurance,

Dresser Industries (merged with Halliburton and is now owned by General Electric), National Gypsum, Owens-Corning, General Electric, General Motors and Ford; a veritable who's who in American industry. In 1982, Johns-Manville filed for bankruptcy as a result of 6,500 lawsuits filed against it. The other companies discussed above soon followed. Pro-business leaders might complain about all the jobs that were lost as a result of these bankruptcies. Dying of an asbestos-related disease received from exposure in the workplace certainly places a new meaning on the phrase, "He worked himself to death." Workers should not become ill and face death by working. Good riddance to those types of jobs!

The estimated number of deaths due to this deceit and deception and total disregard for human life is between 8,000 to 13,000 lives per year from 1977 to 1995, about 200,000 lives in all.[102] And it's not over yet. Even today, between 5,000 and 10,000 people die each year from asbestos-related disease. These acts of deception and purposefully misconstrued information are nothing less than criminal negligence and total disregard for the value of human life, all in the name of making money. Yet not a single company executive was ever prosecuted for a crime.

Death from an asbestos-related disease strikes near my heart. My good fishing partner, Joe, died of mesothelioma. He was exposed to asbestos in his youth while he was a sailor aboard a United States destroyer. He serviced as an enlisted man in the engineer room and during maintenance periods he removed the asbestos from turbines without any protective equipment. This was the only exposure he had in his life. Later in life, Joe became a physicist and went on to become a medical doctor working on cardiovascular equipment. As a doctor, Joe was aware of mesothelioma and he had a premonition about the possibility of asbestos disease. In his sixties, while walking up a hill from a secret fishing location, Joe complained of shortness of breath. I thought he had a cold. A month later, he was diagnosed with mesothelioma. He died about eight months later. A good man was he, an excellent trout fisherman and great friend.

Even today, though, after any doubt about the consequences of asbestos exposure has been eradicated, the industry still wants to produce asbestos products. In 1998, the Environmental Protection Agency banned any products containing asbestos. Two years later, however, it was overturned by business-backed litigation. Even after the evidence is clearly on the table, the additive desire to make money thrives.

Tobacco

Asbestos is not the only example of industry causing massive numbers of deaths. The tobacco industry reaches even greater heights in terms of illnesses and deaths to the American worker and the public. No industry has contributed to as many illnesses and deaths as the American tobacco industry, all for greed and profit.

The history of tobacco goes back to the first American settlers. Virginia tobacco was exported to Europe throughout much of America's history since the 1600s. In fact, tobacco was considered to have medical uses throughout most of this time. In the 1930s, though, research began to show that smoking caused an increase in cancer. In 1952, Reader's Digest published an article called "Cancer by the Carton," which presented clear evidence of the dangers associated with smoking.

I believe it was this article that caused my mother to stop smoking. She smoked a pack of cigarettes a day, starting while she was working in a beauty shop in the 1940s. She was the first person I ever knew who actually stopped smoking on her own; I was probably about 8 years old at the time. She used to say that smoking and inhaling all that tobacco into your lungs, just couldn't be good for you, so she quit. You just can't beat good-ole homespun common sense. Mother passed away of a stroke in August 2011, two months before her 91st birthday. Had she continued smoking, she may not have made it to 60.

In response to the new public awareness of the potential illnesses from smoking, the industry created "scientific facts" and expanded advertising. The large tobacco companies hired public relations firms to obfuscate the issues and place the tobacco companies in more a favorable light. In 1954 the major companies created the "Tobacco Industry Research Council" (TIRC) to research the "true" health effects of smoking. The tobacco companies with the TIRC developed "healthier, low tar" cigarette and marketed cigarettes with filters. Kent cigarettes were introduced with "Micronite" filters, the filters were composed of asbestos. The TIRC did very little research but did help with marketing. Marketing of tobacco products was ubiquitous. Do you remember the Marlboro Man, big cowboy hat and horse galloping across the prairie. "I Love Lucy" sponsored by Philip Morris, "Your Hit Parade" with cartons of Lucky Strikes dancing across the stage? When women started entering the work place, Phillip Morris introduced Virginia Thins, playing on the psychology of women's desire for independence. And how about "Winston tastes good like a cigarette should?" During the 1950s, the tobacco industry drastically increased its advertising budget; going from $76 million in 1953 to $122 million in 1957.[103] Your recollection of these advertisements is a testament to the effectiveness of the tobacco industry's marketing campaign.

In 1964, the U.S. Surgeon General released a study unequivocally concluding a definite relationship between smoking and the development of lung cancer. The study showed that smokers were nine to ten times more likely to develop cancer than non-smokers. As a result, in 1965, the Federal Cigarette Labeling and Advertising Act was passed requiring labeling on cigarette packages and in 1971, advertising on television and radio was banned.

Also about this time, the dangers of secondhand smoke were becoming evident. Even if you didn't smoke, being around people who did smoke and breathing that smoke presented a health hazard. At the time, I remember scoffing at the suggestion that breathing secondhand smoke could cause cancer. The smoke is too diluted, I thought, to cause any adverse health effects, and I was very skeptical. Well I was wrong! According to the Centers for Disease Control, non-smokers who are exposed to secondhand smoke at home or the workplace are 25 to 30 percent more likely to develop heart disease and 20 to 30 percent more likely to develop lung cancer than those not exposed. Each year, 46,000 people die of heart disease and 3,400 die of lung cancer resulting from exposure to second hand smoke.[104] In the 1980s and 1990s, many states began to pass legislation that prohibited smoking in public places. However, it is left to the states to provide protection for their citizens from secondhand smoke, and the protection varies tremendously. For example, in my home state of New York, smoking is banned in:

- government facilities
- private workplaces
- schools, restaurants
- bars
- retail stores and
- recreational/cultural facilities.

In Virginia where I was raised, smoking is restricted but not prohibited. For example, restaurants have smoking and non-smoking areas. In other states the smoking restrictions were minimal. You can see why the restrictions are so lax. In Georgia, for example, the total funding for state tobacco protection is $2.9 billion while the state tobacco related revenues is $393 billion. You can find the smoking restrictions in your state at www.lungs.org, sponsored by the American Lung Association.

Despite growing restrictions on cigarette smoking in America, the tobacco industry is undaunted, and efforts to sell more cigarettes progress unabated. The Tobacco Industry Research Council changed its name to Council for Tobacco Research and The Tobacco Institute was formed as a separate public relations and lobbying organization that grew into one of the most influential organizations in history. In 1994, the group called Californians for Statewide Smoking Restrictions gathered signatures on a petition for a statewide referendum on California's restrictive smoking law. While the name implies support for the restriction of smoking, in fact, a signature on the petition was actually opposing any restrictions on the smoking law.[105] Fortunately, this ruse was discovered and the referendum failed.

Also in 1994, the chief executive officers of the seven largest American tobacco companies all stated before the Congressional Subcommittee on Health and the Environment that they believed that nicotine is not addictive.[106] These CEOs included: Bill Campbell of Philip Morris (Virginia Slim), James Johnston of R.J. Reynolds (Winston), Joseph Taddeo of U.S. Tobacco (today the largest producer of smokeless tobacco products in the United States), Andrew Tisch of Lorillard Tobacco (Newport), Edward Horrigan Jr. of Liggett Group (Chesterfield), Thomas Sandefur of Brown and Williamson Tobacco Company (Kool), and Donald Johnston of American Tobacco (Lucky Strike). It is truly amazing what a person can not know or can be persuaded to un-learn when money is involved.

During this period, legal actions were taken against the tobacco companies by people trying to recover financial compensation for some of the pain and suffering they had endured as a result of smoking, especially since the tobacco companies had covered up the risks associated with smoking. Until 1996, tobacco companies never lost a lawsuit at either the initial trial or upon appeal. Many of these suits were won due to "contributory negligence," which prevented guilty verdicts because the affected smoker had some responsibility for developing his own illness; he knew about the problems of smoking but did it anyway. As stated in an R. J. Reynolds Tobacco Company internal memo, "The way we won these cases, to paraphrase General Patton, is not by spending all of Reynolds' money, but by making the other son of a bitch spend all of his."[107]

Finally in 1998, 46 states and the District of Columbia came together and filed suit against the nation's largest tobacco companies. The decision, called the "Tobacco Master Settlement Agreement", is the largest civil settlement in US history. The settlement requires the tobacco company to end their most aggressive marketing practices and to fund smoking cessation programs and provide for annual payments to states to care for those having smoking related illnesses. The payments were set at $206 billion over the first 25 years and continuing indefinitely into the future. Unfortunately, the vast majority of the states did not use the funds for their intended purpose. For example, North Carolina used 75% of the settlement funds to support tobacco production. Forty states and the District of Columbia (i.e. 80% of the states) got failing grades for spending less than 50% of what the Center for Disease Control recommends should be spent on Tobacco prevention programs. In total, states spend close to $470 million on tobacco prevention and cessation programs in 2015-2016 fiscal year. However, this represents less than 2% of the $26 billion that states receive from tobacco settlement payments and tobacco taxes each and every year.[108]

The resulting health and financial burden carried by the American public due to smoking is truly staggering. According to the Center for Disease Control and Prevention, about 480,000 Americans die each year due to smoking-related diseases. Accumulated over time, this amounts to more deaths than the sum of all Americans killed in all wars we have ever fought.

But that's not all! Smoking costs money, more than $300 billion each year, $170 billion in health care expenditures plus $156 billion in lost productivity, due to premature deaths and exposure to second hand smoke for example. That about $830 for every man, woman and child in America.[109] According to testimony from the past five Surgeons General, restricting smoking is the single most important factor in disease prevention in America. There's one way to reduce health care costs: regulate smoking as a carcinogen and ban smoking in America.

Tobacco companies are responsible for more deaths and suffering than any other industry in history. They have wantonly provided people with poison with total disregard for the consequences. Even when the true nature of cigarette smoking was brought to light, the tobacco industry continued with increased fervor to sell its insidious product and it concentrated on youth. It is like handing a loaded gun to a child and then encouraging him to play Russian roulette. Even if you believe that smokers choose to smoke and it's their own fault, you can't disregard the innocent bystander who just happened to breathe the smokers' second-hand smoke. And yet the industry strives to spread its death to other places. While smoking in America has declined more than 50 percent since 1965, an estimated 46.6 million Americans, percent of the adult population, still smoke.[110] Tobacco industries are now focusing efforts on Asia and Eastern Europe and other new markets, and they are still profitable.

Environmental pollution

William T. Love was a dreamer. He envisioned building a beautiful utopian society on the banks of the Niagara River at Niagara Falls. In the early 1900s, Love started building his utopia. As part of the development, Love built a canal to supply water to the village. Unfortunately, Love ran out of funds and never finished the project. During ensuing years, the city of Niagara Falls and the U.S. army used the conveniently open trench to dump refuse and military waste remaining from World War II.

In 1942, Hooker Chemical Company began using the site to dump 55-gallon metal drums full of hazardous chemical waste. An estimated 21,000 tons of hazardous waste were dumped into the canal. In 1953, Hooker sold the land to Niagara Falls Board of Education of all people. Although Hooker explained to the school board that the property was contaminated, the board persisted; the area was growing rapidly and the area was needed to build schools. Hooker sold the canal for $1 along with a disclaimer informing the board that the land was contaminated.

Soon after, two schools were built, the 93rd Street Elementary School and the 99th Street Elementary School, and a community of houses sprung up around the schools, all setting a time bomb. In 1954, during construction of the 99th Street Elementary School, several drums of waste were exposed and the school board took the prudent steps of moving the school location about 80 feet away from the exposed drums. In the meantime, the earth above the stored dumps began to cave in, allowing the waste to float to the surface, making nice puddle-jumping areas for the kids. To make matters worse, during the housing construction, the clay walls of the canal were breached, allowing the hazardous chemicals to escape.

Heavy snowfall and an exceptionally wet spring in 1962 were enough to light the fuse. People began reporting oil and colored liquid in their yards and basements. Despite this strange occurrence, nothing happened. No samples were taken; no investigation was conducted even though some people knew hazardous waste was in the area. In 1976, 14 years later, investigative reporting by the Niagara Falls Gazette showed toxic chemicals in basements. A year later, a door-to- door survey of the community showed large numbers of children with birth defects. The bomb had just exploded! Subsequent investigation by the New York State Department of Health and the U.S. Environmental Protection Agency revealed an extraordinarily high incidence of miscarriages, epilepsy, asthma, nervous disorders, cancer, and birth defects such as cleft palates and deafness. One child was born with an extra row of teeth. New York Health Commissioner Robert Whalen stated: "Chemical wastes lying exposed on the surface in numerous places and pervasive, pernicious, and obnoxious chemical vapors and fumes affecting both the ambient air and the homes of certain residents near such living sites."[111]

Throughout this ordeal, both Hooker Chemical (then owned by Occidental Petroleum) and local officials continuously disavowed responsibility for the illnesses. (No surprise there.) They argued that the area's endemic health problems were unrelated to the toxic chemicals buried in the canal since the residents couldn't prove the chemicals had come from Hooker's disposal site, so they could not prove liability.

On August 7, 1978, President Jimmy Carter declared the Love Canal a national disaster, the first time that federal funds had been used for something other than a natural disaster. In doing this, President Carter allowed the federal government to use federal funds to purchase contaminated properties and decontaminate the site. Eventually, over 800 homes were demolished and the residents were reimbursed.

Largely as a result of the Love Canal catastrophe, Congress passed the Comprehensive Environmental Response, Compensation, and Liability Act, (CERCLA), also known as the Superfund Act, on December 11, 1980, during President Carter's term. The Superfund Act allows the federal government to respond to direct releases or threatened releases of hazardous substances that endanger public health and safety. The Superfund Act also allows for the creation of the National Priority List (NPL) that searches out and determines where these hazardous sites are located. As of February 27, 2014, there were 1,319 sites listed on the NPL; 375 sites have been decontaminated and delisted but 53 sites have been proposed to be added.[112] The Act provides for those who are responsible for the hazard to clean it up. However, where the responsible party cannot be determined, is not cooperative, or is no longer in business, the Act allows the government itself to clean up the hazardous site. After all, these hazardous sites should not be left sitting until someone is found to clean them up. To pay for the government cleanup, the Act established a trust fund, the Superfund, funded by fees paid by the petroleum and chemical industries that, for the most part, caused the mess in the first place. The Act then allowed the government to institute legal action against those that are felt to be responsible in order to recover the costs of the cleanup, thus helping to finance the Superfund. The last year the fees were collected, though, was in 1995. In 1996, the Superfund balance was $6 billion. By 2003, the fund balance was exhausted. Since that time, funding for cleanup where the responsible party cannot be determined has not been appropriated by Congress.

So where are these 1,319 hazardous site located around the United States? Almost every large town has at least one site listed on the NPL; a site may be near your home. For example, in the areas I'm most familiar with, NPL sites include:

- Old Salem Tannery and Dixie Caverns Landfill, in Salem, Va.;
- Nelson Electric Company on Holly Spring Road in Richmond, Va.;
- General Electric Company Moreau site in Saratoga County, N.Y.;
- Malta Test Site, in Malta, N.Y.

For a complete listing of the National Priority List or to find out if a Superfund site exists near you, go to EPA.gov/superfund.

It turns out that one of these Superfund sites was located less than quarter mile from my parent's home in Salem, Virginia. In November 1976, people near my parents complained about discolored drinking water. In that part of Virginia, people use ground wells for water. It turned out that the water was contaminated with chromium, nickel and cyanide. Matthews Electroplating, a small company that refinished automobile bumpers, had been dumping electroplating chemicals on the ground probably since it started business in 1972. The site was listed as a Superfund site and placed on the National Priority List on September 8, 1983. The EPA extended water lines from the Salem Municipal water system to my parents home in 1986 and the site was deleted from the NPL on January 19, 1989. Of the 31 Superfund sites listed in Virginia as of March 2010, there have been only four sites that have completed remediation and been removed from the list. My parent's home was included in one of them. My parents dodged a bullet; it could have been much worse. Never say it can't happen to you.

Another important environmental regulation is the Resource Conservation and Recovery Act (RCRA). Signed into law on December 13, 1976 by President Gerald Ford, RCRA (it seems that government officials love to use acronyms) was enacted to control handling and disposal of municipal and industrial waste to protect human health and the environment, to conserve energy, to reduce and recycle waste and to establish government authority of waste for "from cradle to grave." Most of the RCRA requirements are implemented by the states, not the federal government. My purpose here though is not to examine the national regulations for hazardous waste disposal and remediation. Rather, it is to point out that municipalities and industries pollute the environment, and a centralized governing authority is required to provide guidance on how to manage and control that pollution.

Air pollution

On December 8, 2008, Blake Morrison and Brad Heath of USA Today, published an article discussing air quality at the nation's schools titled "Toxic air and America's schools, Health risks stack up for school kids near industry." The newspaper's investigative reporters used a computer model developed by the Environmental Protection Agency that simulates the spread of toxic air contaminants from industrial sites throughout the country. The model used the most recent data reported (2005) from over 20,000 industrial sites. Then, based on the computer simulation, the newspaper ranked the 127,800 public, private and parochial schools in the nation for their potential to have poor air quality. The results showed that for 16,500 schools, the air quality outside the school was potentially at least twice as toxic as within the surrounding community. Further, for about 3,000 schools, the air was potentially at least ten times more toxic than in the surroundings.

So okay, all of this is based on a computer model, and computer models can be wrong, but we do have some real air quality measurements. In 2005, the Meredith Hitchens Elementary School near Cincinnati, Ohio, was closed down because air samples showed high levels of chemicals coming from a nearby plastics plant. Air samples indicated that the risk of contracting cancer was 50 times more than what the Ohio Environmental Protection Agency considered acceptable. However, based on the USA Today analysis, there are 435 schools that have worse air quality than Meredith Hitchens! These schools are scattered throughout the nation from the East Coast to the West, in 170 cities and 34 states.

- At Abraham Lincoln Elementary School in East Chicago, Ill., the model indicates high levels of manganese. Manganese is associated with mental and emotional problems after long exposure. The school is located within blocks of three factories that released a total of more than six tons of manganese each year.
- In Follansbee, W.Va., the middle school is located next to plants that turn out tens of thousands of pounds of toxic gas and metals each year.
- In Huntington, W.Va., Highlawn Elementary School had elevated levels of nickel, which is a carcinogen.
- At Oro Grand Elementary School in the Mojave Desert in California, students breathe high levels of chromium, manganese, and lead.

- At San Jacinto Elementary School and the Deer Park Elementary, Middle and High Schools in Texas, data showed higher levels of butadiene and other carcinogens emanating from the petroleum refineries near the schools.[113]

Several years ago, I worked near San Jacinto (where Sam Houston defeated General Santa Anna during the Texas Revolution of 1836) and Deer Park, Texas. I remember looking out across Texas City where the petroleum plants are located to where a gray haze loomed over the area. This was not every day, mind you, but it did occur on many occasions during the six months I was there. It was obvious that the air in that area was not healthy; anybody looking at the cloud would know that.

All of these areas could represent a health hazard to children. Schools are where most children spend a lot of time, and children are more susceptible to foreign substances than adult bodies because they are smaller and still growing. Exposure today may not manifest itself for years out into the future.

Following analysis using the computer simulation, USA Today joined with scientists from John Hopkins University and the University of Maryland to take actual air samples at schools. They selected 95 schools in 30 states. About two-thirds of the schools, i.e. 63 schools, were selected from among the worst schools found from the computer simulation. The other one-third, 32 schools, were selected from schools having the cleanest air. The results showed that 64 schools had high levels of air contamination, some higher than what their state considers acceptable. These schools are located along the Louisiana coast, as well as in affluent areas like McLean, Va., and Lakewood, Colo. At seven of the worst schools, the analysis showed concentrations of the heavy metals manganese and chromium, known to cause mental disorders, as well as benzene and naphthalene, known carcinogens, at levels well above the EPA thresholds for long-term exposure.

The Environmental Protection Agency has air quality standards for 187 air pollutants as part of the Clean Air Act. However, the EPA had never used its database of air emissions and the computer simulation to establish where air pollution may be occurring for schools. Following the USA Today article, the EPA announced that it would commence a study of outdoor air quality at 63 schools in 22 states. The study would take about three years to complete and in order to get an accurate evaluation of the air quality, it would require sampling for duration of 60 days at each site.

In June 2011, the EPA announced the results of the air quality sampling. In most of the schools, air quality was below the established levels for air pollutants. However, all areas were not judged to have satisfactory air quality. For example, in East Elementary School in East Liverpool, Ohio, in Warren Elementary School in Marietta, Ohio, and Neale Elementary School in Vienna, W.Va., air sampling showed high levels of manganese above the allowable exposure limits. Also in Follansbee Middle School and Jefferson Primary School in Follansbee, W.Va., high levels of benzene, arsenic, and benzopyrene were discovered. The EPA announced that they are commencing further sampling at these areas. Additionally, the EPA is commencing the second round of school sampling late in 2011. The full set of results of school sampling to date can be found at on the EPA website, EPA. gov/schoolair/schools.html.

Installing scrubbers (devices that remove harmful contaminates from the exhaust of a smoke stack) on the factory stacks can reduce all of these industrial pollutants. In fact, where scrubbers have been installed, the air quality has improved. The EPA data shows that between 1980 and 2010, total emissions of the six largest air pollutants have been reduced by 67 percent. This is despite the fact that the gross domestic product, energy consumption, population, and total vehicle miles traveled have all increased.[114] This, of course, is a good thing.

However, in some areas, the air pollution actually increased due to added industry, for example. Although there are regulations governing the amount of pollution companies can discharge and the concentration of pollutants in the air, companies are not following these regulations because the Environmental Protection Agency is not enforcing them. This goes to prove the old adage, "You get what you inspect." It is left up to good citizens like "USA Today" to help ensure the regulations are followed. This is not a good thing.

Deepwater Horizon

At about 9:45 p.m. on April 20, 2010, the Deepwater Horizon oil drilling platform exploded killing 11 people. The platform was located about 45 miles from the Louisiana coast and about 250 miles southeast of Houston, Texas. Subsequent efforts to extinguish the fire were unsuccessful, and the entire rig sank to the bottom of the Gulf of Mexico on April 22.

These ocean going oil rigs are gigantic. The Deepwater Horizon was 396 feet long by 256 feet wide, only slightly smaller than two football fields placed side by side. This rig could not propel itself, so it was carried to its drilling from US Coast Guard

Deepwater Horizon offshore drilling unit on fire 2010.jpg

official files entire rig sank to the bottom of the Gulf of Mexico on April 22 location by a heavy-lift ship, which picked up the Deepwater Horizon piggyback and carried it to its location. A similar technique was used to carry the USS Cole home after it was damaged by a suicide bombing attack in Yemen. Deepwater Horizon was classified as a semi-submersible, meaning that it was built on pontoons which could take in water to submerge the vessel partway into the ocean to help stabilize itself but still maintain its superstructure (its work areas, living space, etc.) well above the ocean to avoid waves and tides. The rig was held in a stationary location by planting anchors in the sea floor that were adjusted by automatic winches using GPS locations.

These platforms are true engineering marvels. They contain their own electric generators necessary to operate the platform and all of its equipment: including motors for hoists, pumps, and drilling gear, a derrick and all the pipes, cables, and supplies required for the drilling operation as well as the living quarters required by the crew members who operate the platform 24/7. The platforms must also store fuel for generators and reservoirs for storage of drill lubricates. The logistics to support these platforms are also impressive, as additional pipes, drill bits, cables, and other equipment as well as food for the crew must be supplied from shore.

Deepwater Horizon was built in South Korea by Hyundai Heavy Industries and at the time of the explosion was owned by Transocean, a Swiss firm, and leased to British Petroleum. Halliburton, the Texas oil company, designed and managed the operation. The leasing fees for BP were $500,000 per day in addition to the operational fees for the crew of another $500,000 per day. That is $1 million per day total. Deepwater Horizon was just completing an exploratory well in 4,132 feet of water and was about 30,918 feet below the ocean bottom. In other words, the well was 6.6 statute miles below the surface of the ocean. At the time of the explosion, the rig was preparing to leave the drill site to go to another location. A "production" vessel was scheduled to replace the Deepwater Horizon at the site to begin collecting petroleum for refinement.

To understand what happened on the Deepwater Horizon to cause the explosion, we must first understand just a little bit about how oil wells are drilled. The location of where to drill is determined by geologists using acoustic technology, causing loud noises to be transmitted into the earth, and looking at the acoustic echoes from the rock formations below. Once a likely location is determined, a drill rig is established on the site, e.g. the Deepwater Horizon. A pipe is sent down and buried in the ocean floor. The pipe serves to connect the rig to the floor. From this point, drilling an oil well is basically the same whether on land or on sea.

- Using a pipe with a drill bit attached, called a drill pipe, the well hole is started. The drill pipe and bit is sent through the connecting pipe to the ocean bottom. The drill bit looks like a beefy tripod with hardened steel gears attached to the bottom of each leg of the tripod. The drill pipe is rotated by motors on the rig, causing the bit to "eat" into the rock.
- During the drilling, a hose is connected to the top of the drill pipe. A swivel is placed between the hose and the pipe to prevent the hose from winding up like a ball of twine. "Mud" (a mixture of water, clay, and chemicals) is pumped through the hose, down through the center of the drill pipe, out through the bit, and up between the wall of the hole and the outside of the drill pipe. The purpose of the mud is to carry the loose rock up from the bottom and to lubricate and cool the drill bit. As the drill gets deeper, the mud also acts as a weight on the well, sort of like a bottle stopper, to help stop any eruptions that might occur from the well. At the top of the drill pipe, the mud is captured, sent through a sieve, and reused.
- As the process gets deeper into the well, new sections of pipe are added to the drill pipe.
- At a certain depth, the drill pipe is pulled out and a steel casing pipe is inserted into the open bore hole all the way to the bottom. A cement mixture is then pumped into the casing pipe all the way to the bottom and pressure is applied to the top of the cement to force

the cement up between the outside of the casing pipe and the wall of the hole. The cement pushes up outside the casing until it reaches the top of the casing pipe. When the cement hardens, it forms a ridged structure to protect the integrity of the wall of the casing pipe.
- After the cement casing is hardened, drilling starts again using a slightly smaller drill bit to go inside the casing pipe and the process is repeated: drill, install casing pipe, pump in concrete, and commence drilling again.
- At a certain point in time, before the depth where the oil and gas is expected, a blowout preventer is installed over the casing and placed on the ocean floor. The blowout preventer is attached to high-pressure hydraulic hoses that operate two steel jaws called "shear rams" that can cut through the casing wall and seal off the oil well. This is the ultimate safety device.

Deepwater Horizon oil spill - May 24, 2010
locator.jpg from US Coast Guard official files

When the correct depth for the oil is reached, explosive charges are placed into the bottom of the borehole and blow perforations in the casing. This allows the oil to leak into the piping. In some cases, water is put into the bottom of the pipe to pressurize it. This fractures the rock layers where the oil is found and allows the oil to drain out faster. Hence the reason it's called "Fracking." (For a more thorough view of oil drilling and what can go wrong, go to www.wvsoro.org/ resources/how_a_well_is_drilled/index.html.)

After the Deepwater Horizon explosion, a herd of commissions was established to determine the cause. The federal agencies that control offshore oil drilling is the Bureau of Ocean Energy

Management, Regulation, and Enforcement, BOE, (also known by its previous name, Minerals Management Service) and the U.S. Coast Guard, since the drilling was in coastal regions.

President Obama also established a special commission to investigate the oil spill. The National Commission on the BP Deepwater Horizon Oil Spill and Offshore Drilling was a bipartisan committee headed by Senator Bob Graham and William K. Reilly, former Environmental Protection Agency Administrator.

On June 1, 2010, Attorney General Eric Holder announced that the Justice Department was opening up an investigation into possible criminal and civil violations involved with the explosions.

In addition, the House Committee on Energy and Commerce conducted hearings on the oil spill and took testimony from BP, Halliburton, and Transocean. One could say that the occurrence was well-investigated. And, of course, each company also performed its own independent investigation and, needless to say, was eager to blame every other company for the spill.

The resulting aggregate list of most of the possible causes discovered by the various studies and commissions include:

- The hydraulic hoses that connect to the shear rams in the blowout preventer were leaking, potentially preventing the shear rams from fully closing.
- At least one of the control panels that activate the shear rams in the blowout preventer contained a dead battery which would prevent the shear rams from initiating.
- One of the control panels was disconnected from a shear ram and placed on a test ram.
- BP ordered Transocean operational personnel to replace drilling mud with sea water too early in the "mothballing procedure." Seawater is not heavy enough to cap the well in the event of eruption.
- One of the blowout preventers was connected to a test pipe instead of the pipe intended to convey oil to the surface.

- The concrete placed to strengthen the well casing was not properly tested and was not strong enough. One study concluded that this weak concrete allowed natural gas and oil to flow outside the well casing and into the raiser pipe connecting the ocean floor and rig and onto the rig.

The final report from the White House oil spill commission was released on January 5, 2011. The report found that BP, Halliburton, and Transocean made decisions based on saving costs and not on safety. The report stated, "Whether purposeful or not, many of the decisions BP, Halliburton, and Transocean made that increased the risk of the blowout clearly saved those companies significant time and money."[115] A similar conclusion was made by other investigations. Subsequent to the report, BP released a statement saying it was already revising its safety procedures. Transocean released a report blaming BP. Halliburton released a report asserting that it was only following orders from BP and that it was the government's fault for not making BP use a cement log. Sort of sounds like the three stooges; multi-billion dollar stooges.

On November 16, 2012, British Petroleum agreed to pay $4.5 billion in fines (spread over five years) resulting from the Deepwater Horizon oil spill. BP agreed to plead guilty to criminal negligence and 11 counts of felony manslaughter related to the deaths of the employees caused by the disaster. In addition, BP agreed to pay the Securities and Exchange Commission $525 million (spread over three years) for misrepresenting the volume of oil that was released into the gulf. This settlement does not bar the potential for additional fines resulting from violations of the Clean Water Act. These violations could result in as much as $21 billion in fines. Furthermore, these fines do not include the estimated $7.8 billion resulting from litigation brought by over 100,000 individuals and businesses for damages resulting from the spill. BP's net income in 2011 was $16.03 billion.

Massey Mining in West Virginia

On the morning of April 5, 2010, Gary Wayne Quarles got up and went to the Massey Upper Big Branch coal mine to work, just as he had done for years. At 3:27 that afternoon, the mine sirens screamed out their alarms indicating that there had been an accident in the mine. Gary never came home! He and 28 other workers in the mine perished in an explosion and the worst mining disaster in 40 years.

The miners knew that the work conditions were bad. Quarles had remarked to a friend before the accident, "Man, they got us up there mining, and we ain't got no air. I'm just scared to death to go to work because I'm just scared to death something bad is going to happen."[116] Unfortunately, Gary Quarles' premonition came true.

The Upper Big Branch coal mine, located in Raleigh County in Montcoal, W.Va., about 30 miles south of Charleston, was operated by Massey Energy, one of the largest coal mining companies in the United States. Following the explosion, a federal investigation was initiated by the Mine Safety and Health Administration, MSHA, (the equivalent to the Occupation Health and Safety Administration, OSHA, for mines), under the Department of Labor. Additionally, the governor of West Virginia, Joe Manchin III, appointed a special independent team to investigate the accident lead by J. Davitt McAteer, a former federal mine safety chief. The resulting reports revealed a company that was fanatically concerned with making a profit to the detriment of any other consideration, including workers' safety. The story as it unraveled during the investigations involved lies, deceit, conspiracy, bribery and threats.

The independent investigation team issued its final report on May 19, 2011, a little over a year after the accident. The report found Massey failed to meet even basic safety standards. The report concluded, "The story of Upper Big Branch is a cautionary tale of hubris. A company that was a towering presence in the Appalachian coal fields operated its mines in a profoundly reckless manner, and 29 coal miners paid with their lives for the corporate risk-taking." The ventilation system was not adequate and allowed explosive gases and combustible coal dust to accumulate in the mine, "behaving like gunpowder carrying the blast forward in multiple directions" and killing miners far from the original explosion. The report also disclosed that safety equipment was not functioning, the track duster designed to dilute coal dust was frequently clogged, and miners who should have been reducing coal dust were frequently called away to other tasks.[117]

The report also revealed that Massey threatened workers with termination if they stopped work in areas that lacked oxygen. When Dean Jones shut down his section due to lack of air, Chris Blanchard, a company boss, "called the dispatcher and told him to tell Dean if he didn't get the section running in so many minutes he'd be fired." Dean, afraid for his job, complied.[118]

The independent report was also very critical of the Mine Safety and Health Administration. The report revealed that the Upper Big Branch mine had been issued 515 citations by MSHA in 2009 yet failed to require corrective action or levy fines. Additionally, three major methane-related events had been experienced previously at the Upper Big Branch mine: in 1997, 2003 and 2004. Yet MSHA had not required Massey to implement corrective action. Instead, Massey chose to treat each methane release as an anomaly. The report also showed that in 2007, another mine owned by Massey, Aracoma Alma No. 1, experienced a fire that killed two miners and MSHA had failed to enforce safety requirement there as well.

The independent report also claimed that Massey used its influence and money in an attempt to control West Virginia's political system. The report indicated that politicians were afraid the company would use its financial resources to influence elections.

The final Mine Safety and Health Administration report was issued on December 6, 2011. The report had been delayed almost three months due to methane buildup in the mine. The report concluded that the disaster was an entirely preventable event caused by the buildup of coal dust. The day the report came out, MSHA issued 369 citations to Alpha Natural Resources, the company that had acquired Massey Energy in 2011. The report stated that the investigation concluded that physical conditions that led to the coal dust explosion resulted from Massey's disregard for basic safety standards. The report stated that Massey practiced intimidation of workers, maintained two sets of books (one with actual hazards recorded by internal production and one that the company showed to MSHA inspectors), and enforced a culture of production over safety.

Subsequent to issuance of the report and citations, the U.S. Attorney announced a settlement with Alpha National Resources for Alpha to pay a civil fine of $10.8 million plus $209 million to the Department of Justice. The $209 million constituted $46.5 million for restitution, $34.8 million in fines for safety violations, $48 million for health and safety research and development, and $80 million for safety improvements. The restitution payments consisted of $1.5 million to the families of the 29 miners who died plus two survivors of the explosion.

The only person convicted of criminal liability was Gary May, a former superintendent, in March 2012. May confessed to providing advance warnings of inspections and concealing violations, including poor air flow in the mines, piles of loose combustible coal and scarcities of rock dust used to cover the coal dust. May was sentenced to up to five years in jail and a $200,000 fine.

The Opioid Crisis-

In the late 1990s, American pharmaceutical manufacturers began aggressively selling miracle drugs that could eliminate severe pain for individuals who had experienced traumatic injuries or treatment of a life threatening disease. One of the makers of these drugs was Perdue Pharmaceutic owned and operated by the Sackler family, originally located in Greenwich Village in New York City and then in Stamford, Connecticut. Over time, the family built the company into a thriving drug manufacturer whose most profitable drug was OxyContin. Salesmen for the drug called oxycodone, a generic name for OxyContin, would travel throughout the country attesting to the miraculous natural of the drugs. Eventually Perdue Pharma partnered with Abbot Laboratories to market OxyContin. Abbot lab was a much larger pharmaceutical firm and could sell OxyContin to a much larger population. To seal the partnership, Perdue agreed to indemnify Abbott Labs from any malfeasants that Abbot may experience. To sell OxyContin to doctors, Abbott Labs and Perdue salesmen would show up at the doctor's office with a box of donuts or meet them for a takeout lunch or at the book store to pay for their purchase. Over time the companies became partners in selling OxyContin. The two companies played up the benefits of OxyContin while claiming benefits which were not substantiated. If asked about the addictive nature of the drug, salesmen were coached to say that OxyContin has less euphoric effect and less abuse potential than short-acting opioids. Salesmen also told physicians that OxyContin is misused by "street users" but not by "true pain patients."[119] None of these sales claims were verified. As incentive, the company sponsored sales contests among its salesmen, featured a $20,000 bonus and luxurious vacations to its highest salesmen.[120] These techniques proved very effective for selling OxyContin. From the year 1996 to 2002 (6 years), total sales of the drug reached nearly $5 billion and from 2003 to 2006 (only 3 more years) total sales of OxyContin reached another $6 billion.[121]

It wasn't just Perdue Pharma and Abbott Labs that was selling the narcotic pain killers. Drug companies like Johnson & Johnson, McKesson, Cardinal Health, AmerSource Bergen and Teva Pharmaceuticals were all involved in selling OxyContin.

The pitch delivered by the sales force were strong on the use of the drug but weak on its side effects. Over a seven year period from 2006 to 2012, over 76 billion pills (that's 76,000,000,000 pills) were distributed to the American public. That is a nationwide average of about 36 pills per person each year. The distribution of pills throughout the country is not equal though. The states of Oklahoma, Kentucky, and Ohio were especially hard hit. In some places in West Virginia, for example, the number of OxyContin pills averaged over 200 pills for every man, women and child living in a particular county[122] and since children aren't normally prescribed painkillers, the number of pills available for adult consumption is even higher. The problem with these huge numbers of pills is that the pills are not M & M candies. They were habit forming; they were opioids, which the OxyContin salesmen didn't stress. The Opioid epidemic has now spread throughout the entire nation involving over 2000 lawsuits from state and local governments that claim Purdue has miss lead the public about the dangers of OxyContin while using deceptive practices and downplaying the risk. According to the Center for Disease Control and Prevention, more than 218,000 people have died from overdoses since the epidemic stated in the late 1990s.[123]

Unlike tobacco, OxyContin provides a useful medical purpose, i.e. elimination of pain to an inflicted patient. OxyContin is also regulated by the Food and Drug Administration. The use of OxyContin is controversial however. In a legal case in North Dakota, Judge James Hill expressed the controversy most cleanly. Judge Hill ruled in 2019 that "Perdue cannot control how doctors prescribe its products and it certainly cannot control how individual patients use and respond to its products" the judge wrote, "regardless of any warning or instruction Purdue may give."[124] The issue here is complex, balancing the good provided by opioid pain killers against their additive nature. However, under strict liability laws, the manufacturer of a product for use by the public must divulge information regarding adverse effect resulting from use of the product. After all, who should know of the adverse effects of a drug better than the manufacturer? Also doctors are ethically bound to provide reinforcement of possible adverse effects of medication. This should not be at the control or discretion of the drug distributor. But Purdue did not properly control the use of OxyContin. In fact, they propagated falsehoods about OxyContin and actively encouraged its use. These actions by Purdue Pharma make the drug company more culpable and more responsible for contributing to these thousands of deaths. The legal actions against Purdue Pharma and other drug manufacturers continue to unfold in our courts.

There are many more

I have presented in this chapter some of the most outrageous acts committed by American businesses since the early 20th century and continuing until today. But there are many others. For example:

- IBM helped Nazi Germany manage the mass murder of millions of Jews. IBM developed a system to gather vital statistics on Jewish citizens: information like location, occupation, and inmate number, that the Nazis used to select those to be executed.
- Bechtel, the construction company, gained control of the water supply in parts of Bolivia through privatization. Then Bechtel charged exorbitant prices for the Bolivian citizens to use the water.
- Monsanto and other agricultural product manufacturers have developed seeds that will not reproduce. This causes farmers, many already struggling, to purchase new seeds each year instead of using seeds from harvested plants, which increases the farmers' costs to grow crops.
- According to the September 2013 AARP bulletin, makers of popular brand name drugs are paying smaller drug companies to delay bringing cheaper alternative generic drugs to market. When a pharmaceutical company patents a drug, it has a monopoly to produce that drug. When the monopoly expires, other companies can start production of generic drugs. What some

companies are doing is paying the other drug companies to delay marketing of the alternative drug. This extends the brand-name drug monopoly and increases the profits from the drugs. The losers in this are the consumers who must pay higher prices for a longer time. AARP states that consumers are paying $3.5 billion per year in higher drug prices. Some ill patients must forego treatment because of these higher prices.

So what do you think?
We have:

1. a fire in the garment industry that killed 146 over 100 years ago;
2. asbestos companies in the construction industry that willfully exposed their employees to asbestos for years, resulting in the deaths of thousands;
3. the tobacco industry that knowingly sold (and continues to sell) poisons to people and that indulged in massive cover-ups to purposefully deceive the public;
4. thousands of industries of various types that dumped toxic waste throughout the country and left it to others to cleanup;
5. hundreds of energy companies that continue to spew air pollutants into the atmosphere, poisoning our air, especially for our children and,
6. oil-drilling and mining companies in the energy industry that place much more importance on making a profit, even if it involves breaking the law, than in protecting the lives of their employees or the environment.
7. nation wide spread of an opioid that results in thousands of citizens becoming drug dependent.

These are only a few examples of business malfeasance. There are many more. Of course, not all businesses are corrupt and do harm but there are enough to require close scrutiny. Based on these examples, you can see that there must be governmental agencies to overview and protect the environment and the citizens from businesses destructive and harmful practices. This is not government overreach, it is good governance. In spite of what some people preach, reducing regulations and taxes on businesses will not necessarily increase employment. The purpose of business is not employment of workers Workers are only a by-product of business, a resource, for business. The overriding purpose of business, as the examples above testify, is to make a profit. It is profit, not employment, which is business' "Holy Grail." In fact, in the pursuit of profit, a business must reduce expenses as much as possible. That means the work force will only be expanded if absolutely necessary. If the company can replace workers with efficient machinery, it will do just that. If the company can hire illegal immigrants who work for less, it will do that, and if it can more economically send work overseas, it will do that too. In this regard, business' purpose is to reduce employees, not hire them.

Of course, businesses do employ people and many businesses are honest, forthright companies, but some, especially big businesses, are not. When there's a bad apple in the basket, you must examine them all.

Companies know when they are breaking the laws or violating human dignity, even if it's not unlawful. Massey knew it was violating MSHA safety requirements when it did not install proper mine ventilation and when it put miners in unsafe conditions. Polluting companies knew that dumping toxic waste could be harmful, even before the Environmental Protection Agency was created and certainly after it was created. Some say that regulations hinder business. Yes, regulations do prevent companies from doing whatever they damn well please, from killing people to polluting the environment. But regulations can help ensure that we are all much better off and that our lives and property are not devastated. And if the regulations are enforced, all companies will be working on a level playing field; one company competing against another on the basis of innovation and efficiency, not destruction. This is how "Capitalism" is supposed to work.

A righteous conscientious company would refuse to participate in activities that are obviously detrimental to humanity. However, when rules and regulations are not persistently and consistently enforced, the righteous company is placed in a competitive disadvantage. Other companies can produce their product cheaper because they don't obey the rules. The righteous company may be forced to likewise break rules in order to be competitive. This is why state and federal regulations must be uniformly and consistently enforced. Contrary to relaxing regulations, we should enforce them to assure a safe, environmentally friendly and level playing field. Contrary to those citing the harmful effects of regulations, increased enforcement should not harm businesses because they are supposed to be complying with the rules already. Proper regulation enforcement would ensure that businesses compete based on efficiency and management acumen, as they are supposed to, and not by cheating and violating human principles. Honest companies would make honest profit. Remember this: We're all better off when we're all better off.

CHAPTER 6

The Financial Crisis

The fox is at the hen house and the door is wide open.

During the Great Depression in the 1930s, the Roosevelt administration established certain agencies to protect the American public from the possibility of fraudulent practices by the financial industry. This was a reasonable and just action to take since protecting the people and regulating business to assure fairness is what a democratic government is supposed to do. I'll briefly discuss a few of these agencies that played a significant role in the recovery from the Great Depression:

- The Security and Exchange Commission (SEC) was created in 1934 to regulate stocks and securities market trading to prevent fraud, insider trading and dissemination of false information and other devious actions.
- The Commodity ExchangeAct of 1936 created the Commodity Exchange Authority. In 1974, this Act was amended to create the Commodities Futures Trading Commission (CFTC). The CFTC was created to protect the users and public from fraud, manipulation

and abusive practices related to the sale of commodities and to foster open, competitive and financially sound commodity markets.
- The Glass-Steagall Act of 1933 created the Federal Deposit Insurance Corporation (FDIC) to provide deposit insurance, which guaranteed safety of deposits in member banks. Originally the FDIC insured deposits up to $2,500 but currently the insurance applies to deposits up to $250,000. The FDIC also examines financial institutions for safety and sound business practices and manages failed banks. Perhaps more importantly, however, the Act also separated "Wall Street" type investment banks from commercial depository banks and insurance companies.

For 70 years, these laws served well to protect us Americans from unscrupulous financial dealers. Yes, there were financial upheavals during this period—like the savings and loan crisis in the late 1980s and early 1990s—but by-and-large the period was a time of financial stability and continuous growth.

Then came the late 1990s. The financial philosophy changed as a result of several simultaneous and related events. A major factor was the growth in popularity of so-called "Supply Side Economics." This economic theory was extolled during the Reagan administration and suggested that a strong and vibrant business community was required to create jobs and to stimulate and grow a strong economy. Government regulations and high taxes only hindered growth of free enterprise businesses, effectively clogging up the machinery. Let businesses run free and business will prosper, and in doing so, will increase employment and bring prosperity to the country.

Another component to Supply Side Economics was a reduction in taxes. Taxes only take money away from businesses. Let companies keep their tax dollars where the money will be reinvested to create jobs and a stronger, richer economy. In fact,

Reagan did decrease taxes. In 1982, taxes on the top income bracket were reduced from 70 percent to 50 percent and by 1988 the top bracket was reduced to 28 percent.

Reagan implemented Supply Side Economics with the appointment of Allen Greenspan, who served as chairman of the Federal Reserve from 1987 to 2006. Greenspan was a strong supporter of reducing business regulations. (In testimony before Congress years later, Greenspan recanted his regulation free philosophy. Greenspan expressed "shocked disbelief" that financial companies failed to execute proper control over their own trading standards.)

Alongside Greenspan, Robert Rubin—Treasury Secretary under President Clinton and a past member of the Board of Goldman Sachs—begin to disregard overview responsibility of the treasury department. In fact, Rubin encouraged deregulation of financial institutions. In 1998, Brooksley Born, the head of the Commodity Futures Trading Commission (the commission originating under FDR), became aware that some banks were trading financial derivatives without proper public disclosure and federal regulation. Derivatives are financial securities that derive their value from the value of something else. Such derivatives, as we will see, prove to be a chief culprit behind the financial crisis of 2008. In June 1998, Rubin recommended that Congress strip the CFTC of its regulating authority for these derivatives. A year and a half later in 2000, the Commodity Futures Modernization Act was slipped into a spending bill at the last minute and was passed Congress. The Act eliminated the CFTC's authority to regulate derivatives.

With little regulation of the financial institutions and elimination of the CFTC's responsibility to regulate the financial derivatives market, the financial community was ready to plunder the economy. However, they weren't finished just yet. Congress, not just the regulators, had to get into the Act. In 1999, President Clinton signed into law the Gramm-Leach-Bliley Act sponsored by Senator Phil Gramm, Republican from Texas, and

Representatives Jim Leach, Republican from Iowa, and Thomas Bliley, Republican from Virginia. Gramm-Leach-Bliley sponsored a law that would repeal a portion of the Glass-Steagall Act of 1933 that separated the investment banks, commercial banks and insurance companies. The banking industry had been trying since the 1980s to eliminate the distinction between commercial/savings banks and investment banks. The banks argued that many people have both savings bank accounts and financial investments and that merging the two banks would make it more convenient for the bank's customers. Of course, banks ignored the inherent conflict of interest that uniting commercial and investment banks would have. Commercial banks offer saving accounts for deposits in a comparatively risk-free environment, since savings are insured by the FDIC. Investment banks use people's money to invest in securities, an inherently risky business. Merging the two banks allowed commercial banks to act like investment banks and use funds in saving accounts as capital to invest in securities. It was the reason for the Glass-Steagall Act in the first place: to separate the two purposes in order to eliminate this conflict.

When President Clinton signed the Gramm-Leach-Bliley Act into law on November 12, 1999, the banking institutions finally accomplished several of their most important goals. First, it allowed commercial banks to enter the investment market and insurance business. For example, Citicorp was allowed to merge with Traveler Insurance, forming a huge financial company. Second, the revised law allowed commercial banks to use their depositor's money—basically their savings—to invest in the risky securities market. Next, since the FDIC insures deposits in commercial banks, if the bank invested in the stock market and lost all the savings, the Federal government and the American taxpayer would insure the losses. The bank's incentive to invest with prudent care was reduced. And finally, it allowed the creation of gargantuan financial institutions, bigger than the world had ever experienced. This was one of the factors leading to the "Too Big to Fail" phenomenon. What a wonderful, glorious arrangement the banking system had created; wonderful at least for the banks but maybe not for the taxpayers. The fox was at the hen house and the door was wide open.

How the financial industry works, a little primer

In 2005, my wife and I were on vacation in Wyoming with my brother and his wife and the subject of home mortgages came up. My brother would invest a portion of his savings in rental property. He rented the property, covering the mortgage, repairs and other expenses, and then sold it after a few years of appreciation or held on to it to save the incomefor his retirement nest egg. He seemed comfortable doing this so I asked him how he got the money for the down payment.

"What down payment?" he asked me.

"You mean you can buy a house with no down payment?" I asked him.

"That's right."

When I bought my home around 1985, I had to have 10 to 15 percent down payment on the house, as well as show continuing employment and good credit rating. No longer! It was almost like you walked in, asked for a mortgage and got it. I was thinking what "rocket scientist" would lend money like that? The bank has no collateral on the house; if the house lost value, the bank would have a property worth less than the mortgage. The mortgage lenders turned out to be Chase Bank, Wells Fargo, Bank of America and especially Country Wide, as well as all of the other big mortgage banks.

Think back to the years, say between 2002 and 2006 for example. People were buying houses like crazy. A friend of mine bought a house, painted the interior and did a few other interior projects and sold it for a $70,000 profit one year later. Who wouldn't want to make that kind of profit? He was extremely lucky. Had he bought the property a year later, he would have been sitting on a house that was worth far less than his mortgage.

The de-regulation efforts in the 1990s, along with the philosophy of reducing government involvement in business, allowed the financial industry to participate in some very questionable practices. Subprime mortgages are mortgage loans given to individuals who are considered a higher financial risk than prime mortgages because they have a poor credit rating, below 620 or so. Banks are usually reluctant to provide loans to such individuals because they represent a higher risk. In the 1990s though, things began to change. To understand this change, one must understand a little about the home mortgaging business.

In the old days, when a person wanted to buy a home, he would go to his hometown bank and ask for a mortgage. Actor Jimmy Stewart wonderfully portrayed the hometown banker in the movie *It's a Wonderful Life*. If the bank thought he (but not "she" since banks didn't give loans to women back then) was an honest person of integrity, the bank would loan him the money. The homeowner would make payments on the loan throughout the years until the loan was paid off. Bank investors provided the money for the bank to loan. The investors would invest in the bank and reap the benefits of that investment through the principle and interest payments that the homeowner (the borrower) would make.

Those days died a long time ago. Today, when a commercial bank or mortgage company makes a loan, most times they don't keep the mortgage. They sell that mortgage or package the mortgages into large bundles and sell the entire bundle to someone who is willing to invest in mortgages. Selling of mortgages to investors is referred to as "securitizing the mortgage," i.e. making a security out of it. The bundles of mortgages are called Mortgage Backed Securities, MBS. Throughout the years, security companies have taken mortgages and other things of value, such as car loans and credit card payments and placed them into sellable securities. These are called Collateralized Debt Obligations, CDOs, or asset-backed securities. They are all forms of derivatives, the same derivatives that were discussed previously.

Selling the mortgages has several advantages. For example, say I got a thirty-year fixed mortgage for $100,000 at 6 percent interest from the bank. Over the life of the loan, the bank would collect a total of $115,838 dollars in interest plus the original $100,000, for a total of $215,838. However, the banks would have to wait a considerable time—thirty years in this case—in order to collect the money. If the bank sold the mortgage to an investor, say for $150,000, the bank would then get the money up front. After taking out a reasonable profit, the bank would then have more money available to make further mortgage loans. It is a beneficial arrangement for both the banks and the borrower. It gives the banks finances to make more mortgage loans and allows mortgages to be more available for people desiring to buy a home. The bank, or some other company, would continue to collect the mortgage payments from the homeowner and would forward the payments to the investor. This allows the investor to make a reasonable profit from his investment because he collects interest at about the original rate of 6 percent. In addition, selling the mortgage allows the original bank to escape the risk that the homebuyer will default, and not pay. The risk is transferred to the investor. The process of selling mortgages on the secondary market does have at least one problem though, it gives banks the incentive to make loans as fast and hard as they can and not pay too much attention to whether the borrower can repay the debt.

The secondary mortgage market, i.e. selling the securitized mortgages to interested investors, worked so well that in 1934 under the Roosevelt presidency, Congress created the Federal National Mortgage Association—known by the nickname Fannie Mae. The purpose of Fannie Mae was to provide low cost mortgage funds by providing reliable secondary markets. Fannie Mae deals only in the residential mortgages in the secondary market, its entire purpose is to provide affordable loans for home ownership. In 1970, Congress created a sister organization to Fannie Mae called the Federal Home Loan Mortgage Corporation, or Freddie Mac. This was done in order to provide competition between the agencies and to spread the risk associated with mortgage finance, i.e. to avoid putting all your eggs in one basket. Fannie and Freddie bought big bundles of mortgages, Mortgage Backed Securities (MBS), from banks in order to assure that there is a secondary market so that banks will have sufficient funds to loan to homebuyers. Fannie Mae and Freddie Mac worked so well at providing a stable secondary market for mortgages that they were the biggest players in the secondary mortgage market, purchasing about 40 percent of the mortgages in the late 2000s.[125]

Of course, Fannie and Freddie themselves must have funds to buy the MBS from the banks. So, in addition to raising funds by selling equity, i.e. stocks, in the companies, Fannie and Freddie also sell thousands of MBS to investors.

As you can see, the whole process is a big daisy chain. The homebuyer borrows money from the bank to buy a home. The bank then sells the mortgage on the secondary market, primarily to Fannie Mae and Freddie Mac but also to other investors, to obtain additional funds to loan to potential homebuyers. Fannie Mae and Freddie Mac in turn bundle their mortgages together and sell them as MBS to other investors to help finance Fannie's and Freddie's own leaning.

So who are these investors? Anyone who thinks that investing in mortgages is a sound and profitable investment. The investors include pension funds, municipalities, school systems, state investment funds, mutual funds, investment banks, foreign investment companies and, of course, individuals. Mortgage based securities are sold throughout the entire world.

This process is risky but worked perfectly fine for years so long as the risk was managed. So long as the mortgages were lent to people capable of repaying the loans and there were sufficient reserve funds in the system so that if a few homeowners defaulted, the system was solvent enough to be able to withstand some adverse financial events.

In fact, banks and the financial institutions were supposed to be regulated. Banks are regulated by the FDIC—which, as we have seen, is charged with ensuring banks follow safe business practices—and the Office of Thrift Supervision (an agency under the Department of Treasury). Fannie Mae and Freddie Mac have their own special agency to regulate them, the Office of Federal Housing Enterprise Oversight, that has the responsibility to assure that Fannie and Freddie are operated within certain guidelines. However, with the declining involvement from the government regulator agencies—fueled by Secretary Greenspan's philosophy that businesses are efficient and logical institutions—these government organizations fell asleep at the throttle of a raging locomotive.

So why did the train wreck?

During the late 1990s and up to 2006, the real estate market was booming. Mortgage rates were low and the demand for housing was taking off like the Japanese Shinkansen high-speed rail line. Thirty-year fixed mortgages between 1992 and 2000 generally varied between 7.0 percent and 8.0 percent. Between 2002 and 2006 though, a thirty-year fixed mortgage was between 5.5 percent and 6.5 percent, a 1.5 percent decrease. This meant that on a $100,000 mortgage, the owner would pay $700 per month in 1998 but only $600 per month in 2005. However, Adjustable Rate Mortgages, ARM, decreased initial monthly payments even further. The initial payment on a thirty-year 4.5 percent ARM for a $100,000 mortgage is about $510 per month. The interest rate on Adjustable Rate Mortgages, however, increases after one or two years and is generally at a higher rate than the conventional thirty-year mortgage. These ARM mortgages were particularly attractive to people with low-incomes. Mortgage lenders and mortgage banks like Countrywide Financial, Ameriquest, Washington Mutual, Wachovia, JPMorgan Chase, Wells Fargo, Citigroup, Bank of America and others began an intense push to place ARM type mortgages. In addition, there were extra incentives for mortgage loan officers to place ARM type mortgages, and many of these ARM loans were made to subprime borrowers people with a poor credit rating. In fact, between 2004 and 2006, 18 to 20 percent of the loans for the entire mortgage market were made to subprime borrowers.[126] The fact that many of these borrowers couldn't repay their mortgages didn't bother the lender banks one bit. They just kept lending. Anyone could qualify for a loan. The banks even had an acronym for those with no qualifications for a mortgage loan, NINA-no income, no asset—which became know as Ninja loans. For about 40 percent of these loans, no down payment was required, just as my brother told me years earlier.

Part of the motivation to place loans to low-income borrowers came from Fannie Mae and Freddie Mac. Home ownership has long been an American dream. Both Republican and Democratic administrations have encouraged home ownership, especially for people in the lower income levels that traditionally have been neglected by banking establishments. In 1996, the Department of Housing and Urban Development (HUD) set goals for Fannie and Freddie to purchase at least 42 percent of their mortgages from borrowers with incomes less that the median wage in their region. In 2000, this percentage was raised to 50 percent and in 2005 to 52 percent. Although all low-income borrowers are not subprime borrowers—many low-income individuals live within their means and have good credit ratings—encouraging mortgages be placed with low-income borrowers did tend to increase the number of subprime loans.

With interest rates low, and mortgage banks loaning money to anyone standing vertical and still breathing, the demand for houses soared. When the demand goes up, so does the price. Many people saw the opportunity to "flip" houses: buy them, and fix them up a little, or maybe don't even fix them up, wait a little while and then sell the house to the next person in line. This speculation in housing exacerbated the situation, driving the housing market up even further. The demand for houses increased the price, which in turn increased the demand for houses, which again increased the price. A vicious circle.

Of course, there were supposed to be people watching the banking industry to ensure that not too many bad loans were placed. That's part of the job the Federal Deposit Insurance Corporation, the Office of Thrift Supervision and the Federal Reserve are supposed to be doing, and "suppose" is the operative word here. These regulating agencies did nothing: they never checked the loans being made; they never checked the number of subprime mortgages that were being placed; they never investigated the level of risk that the financial companies were engaged in and they never investigated the capital ratios that the banks were carrying. In 2004, at the encouragement of Henry Paulson—CEO of Goldman Sachs and later Secretary of the Treasury—the Security and Exchange Commission changed the way the SEC calculated the Net Capital Ratio. The Net Capital Ratio is the ratio between debt and capital (think of capital as the money the bank uses to operate its business). For example, if the Capital Ratio were twelve, the bank would have twelve times the value of loans as they had money on hand. If the capital ratio isn't too large, a bank can withstand defaults on some mortgages because the bank has sufficient capital to overcome the small drop in income. For the four largest banks (Lehman Brothers, Merrill Lynch, Morgan Stanley and Goldman Sachs) and two commercial banks (Citigroup and JPMorgan Chase), the SEC changed the method of calculating the risk associated with the bank's loans by using a computerized mathematical model. In essence, the bank said that loans were not as risky as they thought they were so they could extend the amount of money lent without increasing their capital. Of course the computer model was wrong but they didn't know that. So the SEC agreed with the banks and changed the rules in 2004. Banks that once were required to maintain a capital ratio of about 12 to 1 now increased the ratio to 30 to 1; they effectively had 30 times as much debt that they loaned customers, as they had money on hand to pay if the customer defaulted. With "geniuses" like this running the financial market, it's a wonder how this country ever got as prosperous as it is.

Many of these loans went to mortgages and many of the mortgages were subprime mortgages. By 2006, subprime mortgages represented about 20 percent of the total mortgage market, up from 10 percent in 2003. This represented about $1.3 trillion and 7.5 million in mortgages. Of course, most of these mortgages were securitized, turned into Mortgage Back Securities, and sold to investors throughout the entire world. The value of all mortgages in the United States was about $10 trillion in 2007 and MBS constituted about $7.3 trillion.[127]

So why did people invest so much money in risky securities? Several reasons, one was that mortgages had always been secure investments in the past. There were some defaults but these were a small percentage of the total number of mortgages. Another reason is that interest rates paid by MBS were higher than the rates paid on government bonds, so naturally people invested in MBS. In addition, the agency that once investigated derivatives, the Commodities Futures Trading Commission, which could have potentially stopped the raging train, no longer had the regulatory responsibility for derivative financial instruments. This was thanks in part to Robert Rubin. A further reason that people invested in MBS was that the financial rating agencies that rate the risk associated with financial securities continued to give the highest rating to these derivatives. These agencies, Standard & Poor's (S&P), Moody's Investor Service and Fitch Group failed in their jobs. They didn't really investigate the Mortgage Backed Securities but rather, they took investment banks and mortgage banks at their word and trusted them. This, of course, is partly due to the fact that these rating companies are paid by the people they are supposed to be investigating. There was an obvious conflict of interest. I've always found that it's really difficult to squeal on the people who are paying you.

The train derails

Now what do you think happens when those Adjustable Rate Mortgages loaned to subprime borrowers reset to the higher rates? That's right, the homeowners couldn't make their monthly payments. If you and I can figure that out, you know the big time wheeling- dealing finance people knew what would happen. With many mortgage payments not being made, investors holding mortgages and MBS didn't get their dividend checks. Banks had no money to lend to new homeowners so they started hoarding their own money to meet their obligation and had no money to loan to anyone.

One of the first overt signs that the financial system was headed into trouble occurred on May 24, 2008 when Bear Stearns was sold to JPMorgan Chase for $10 per share, down from its twelve month high of $133 per share. At the time of the sale, Stearns' capital ratio was about 35 to 1; they didn't have enough assets to weather the crumbing mortgage securities market. Then in September 2008, Merrill Lynch announced that it had entered into an agreement to be sold to Bank of America. Later, during government hearings, it was claimed that the Federal Government used some heavy persuasion to promote the sale of Merrill Lynch. This was immediately followed by Lehman Brothers' announcement that they could not find a buyer and had filed for bankruptcy. This was the biggest bankruptcy filing in American history. When Lehman Brothers went under, their net capital ratio was 31 to 1.

With the bankruptcy of Lehman Brothers, the proverbial train was totally derailed and careening through the city, knocking down everything in its path. People lost confidence in the stock market and the outlook of American businesses. From January 1 to October 11, 2008, owners of stock in U.S. corporations lost $8 trillion as stock value dropped from $20 trillion to $12 trillion, a 40 percent decline.[128] As a result of this drop in stock value, anyone who owned stock in America lost tremendous amounts of money. Pension funds were depleted. City, town, county and state investment portfolios plummeted, along with school districts and non-profit institutions. The entire society sank.

With reduced confidence in the value of American business, demand for American products declined as people started to pull in their spending in preparation for bad times. As a result, businesses began to layoff employees. America was entering a recession (defined as several, usually two, consecutive quarters with declining GDP). In January 2008, before the financial crisis started, unemployment in the United States was at about 5 percent. By January 2010, only two years later when the crisis was well underway, unemployment was at 10 percent and 15 million people were out of work. In fact, this number is probably low because it didn't include those people who were working part time but wanted a full time job or who wanted a job but stopped looking because they were frustrated.

As subprime borrowers failed to make their mortgage payments, the banks started foreclosing on the mortgages. This was exacerbated by layoffs and unemployment, which made even more people incapable of making their mortgage payments. In 2007, there were 1.3 million properties in foreclosure and in 2008, 2.3 million properties, and by 2009, 2.8 million properties were in foreclosure proceedings.[129] Families losing their homes was becoming a common occurrence. In some areas, whole neighborhoods sat with empty homes.

As the number of foreclosures went up, the demand for houses rapidly went down. The days of buying a house and "flipping" it had come to an abrupt halt. In 2008, the average U.S. home declined 20 percent in value over their 2006 peak. 8.8 million borrowers, over 10 percent of all homes in America, held a mortgage loan that was higher than the value of their home. By September 2010, this number had risen to 23 percent of all homeowners having negative equity in their home.[130] Remember that discussion I had with my brother in Wyoming, that if the price dropped, the mortgage would be higher than the house value? This is exactly what I said would happen and I'm not a rocket scientist.

Tight money, sinking house prices, mortgage backed securities defaulting, unemployment rising, the stock market plunging and people everywhere losing their houses. Everyone was affected. School systems, individual retirement funds, as well as corporate pension plans; all saw their assets evaporate. Municipal governments—from small towns to large cities, to county and state governments—were unable to meet their obligations. With people out of work, the tax base decreased. Governments could no longer meet their payrolls or make payments on bonds they had issued to finance new construction projects. States were in danger of defaulting on their loans and began to look for ways to cut costs and increase revenues. Some unscrupulous governors, like Governor Scott Walker of Wisconsin, used the impending crisis to cut the bargaining power of the State employee unions, as if the unions caused the financial problem. Governor Walker claimed the union's high pay and benefits were bankrupting the state, even though the unions had agreed to cuts in pay and benefits. The unions had nothing to do with the financial crisis but they, like many other Americans, would pay the price for other people's greed.

This financial crisis isn't just isolated to the United States, although the instigators of the crisis are in the United States. American banks vigorously marketed derivative investments throughout the world. Because so many countries invested in mortgage backed securities and other derivatives, when the U.S. market began to fail, other countries also followed suit. In addition, the financial greed infection infested other nations; they too began to participate in highly leveraged bank deals and risky financial practices. Countries that depend on those investments to support government programs really suffered. Further with American economic decline, America's demand for foreign products decreased and so foreign production decreased. Employers laid off workers and people were without work, so taxable income decreased and foreign governments were in trouble just as the American government was. When the U.S. banking system began to sag, countries with banks emulating America also sagged. This made the economic situation even more severe. In December of 2007, America officially entered a recession. But we were not alone. Iceland, Greece, Spain, Portugal, England, Germany, Ireland—in fact, the entire European Common Market—were all suffering because of the financial crisis. And it wasn't just limited to western Europe. By the third quarter of 2008, Japan, Sweden, Hong Kong, Singapore and Turkey were in a recession. It was truly a Global Financial Crisis.

Putting the train back on track

So what does a country do to pull itself out of a recession, to put people back to work and to get the country back to prosperity? You do things to get the economy going again and you do things to create jobs and increase demand for products and services.

When the Great Depression hit the United States in 1929, President Herbert Hoover did nothing for three years to help reduce the effects of the country's downturn. Hoover believed that governments should not interfere with the economy and the government was not responsible for creating jobs or providing economic relief. Hoover believed that business prosperity would eventually return and the nation's economic condition would naturally improve without government interference.

It took three years before Franklin Delano Roosevelt was elected President in 1932, FDR reversed Hoover's philosophy and instituted large government programs to assist the economy. Some of the programs created during the Great Depression by the Roosevelt administration, including the Federal Deposit Insurance Corporation and the Security and Exchange Commission, were discussed previously. But Roosevelt instituted other programs to help stimulate the economy. Here are a few examples:

- The Tennessee Valley Authority was created to build dams for flood control and to supply electricity to the poorer southern states, and in doing so it created jobs. TVA is still in operation today and is continually providing valuable services to southern states.
- When the Great Depression occurred, the United States was the only industrial country that did not provide some form of unemployment insurance or retirement pensions. When Roosevelt came into office, he created the Social Society Administration to protect the elderly. It also placed money in the hands of people who would spend it and help create demand for products.
- The Work Progress Administration was created in 1935 and was initially funded with $1.4 billion, 6.7 percent of the GDP. The WPA hired unemployed people to build public works projects like public buildings, bridges and roads. They built, built, and built. There is hardly a community in the country that does not have a structure built by a WPA worker. At its peak in 1938, the WPA provided income to three million people and between 1935 and 1943, the WPA employed a total of almost eight million people.

As a result of these programs, the unemployment rate dropped from about 25 percent in 1933 to 14.3 percent in 1937.[131] However, in 1937 the nation was hit again with a recession and employment again plummeted. This "double dip" recession was caused in part by the Federal Reserve Bank's decision to reduce the amount of money circulating within the country: no money, no purchases, no jobs. In the end, it was World War II that got the American economy going again. As Europe came under Nazi control and Asia under the control of Japan, demand for American made military supplies soared. When America entered the Second World War, and American service men joined the military, the Great Depression finally came to an end.

So why can't we institute such government instigated programs today? The answer is because they are government instigated. Massive government employment programs in the United States are invariably labeled "Socialism;" praising the benefits of socialism is akin to promoting syphilis. Additionally, the size of the American economy in the 1930s is miniscule compared to the enormous economy of today. The government does not have the capacity to directly employ such massive numbers of people anymore. But the idea of instituting programs that encourage people to spend and increase the demand for goods and services remains the same.

The recession officially started in December 2007 but of course, we didn't know we were in a recession. It takes several months of analysis for economists to determine that the economy is in a decline. However, with unemployment and mortgage foreclosures increasing, the Bush administration astutely perceived an upcoming economic downturn. On February 13, 2008, way before Bear Stearns was sold to JPMorgan Chase in May, or the failure of Lehman Brothers in September, the Economic Stimulus Act of 2008 was passed by Congress and signed by the President. This Act provided $152 billion of stimulus money to the economy. The core of the Stimulus Act provided a tax rebate to low and middle income taxpayers of $600 per couple ($300 for singles) or for those couples with adjusted gross incomes of less than $150,000 per couple ($75,000 for individuals).

I remember receiving that $600 check in the spring of 2008 and I did what I was supposed to do with it: my wife and I spent it on a new canoe. Providing taxpayers with tax refunds helps. It puts money into the economy and if people spend the money instead of saving it, it increases demand for goods and services, thereby increasing the economy. The results of the Stimulus Act increased spending but it was not enough to stop the recession.

In October 2008, the Bush administration instituted another economic recovery package designed to forestall a downturn. On October 3, 2008, President Bush signed the Emergency

Economic Stabilization Act into law. The Act designated up to $700 billion to purchase distressed assets, such as mortgage backed securities, from banks and other financially troubled companies. The idea was to buy the bad investments to prop up the banks or companies and to provide money for the banks to lend other companies to operate. The only problem was that it was difficult to determine the value of the assets and only about $432 billion of the $700 billion authorized was eventually doled out. The bill became known as the Troubled Assist Relief Program (TARP) but it is also known as the Financial Bailout. Some of the participants in the TARP bailout include:

> Citigroup - $45 billion
> Bank of America - $45 billion
> AIG - $40 billion
> JPMorgan Chase - $25 billion
> Wells Fargo - $25 billion
> GMAC financial - $17.3 billion
> General Motors - $13.4 billion
> Goldman Sachs - $10 billion
> Morgan Stanley - $10 billion
> Chrysler - $4 billion

Some of the largest creators of the crisis received bailout money. These funds were *not* gifts to the banks though. The U.S. government purchased securities, bonds, preferred stock or loans in the case of the automakers. These securities earned dividends and interest and when they were sold, they went to repay the bank's debt. By 2011, most of the securities had been redeemed and most of the money had been repaid to the government.

Both of these economic packages, the Economic Stimulus Act and Troubled Assist Relief Program, were developed and put into law by the Republican President Bush. The process of pumping money into the economy had not finished with President Bush though. When President Obama was elected, one of the first things he did was to institute the American Recovery and Re-investment Act. This was a true stimulus package. Its main purpose was to create jobs by pumping money into the economy but it was much more widely cast than TARP. Republicans today criticize President Obama's economic recovery plan. But you'll note that the Republican plan—to put money into the economy to get the economy moving—is exactly what President Obama did. Here are some examples of how money was invested among a myriad of projects:

- Individual tax incentives: individual workers got a $400 tax credit ($800 for couples); the child tax credit was increased to $1,000 and there was $2,500 tax credit for college tuition.
- Tax credit to companies: businesses were allowed to use current losses to offset profits made over the previous five years instead of the past two years and also extended tax credits for renewable energy production.
- Healthcare: provided funds for health information technology; helped provide COBRA insurance for the unemployed; helped build community health centers and military hospitals.
- Education: provided funds to help prevent school layoffs and modernized schools; increased Pell Grants and increased funds for Head Start programs.
- Unemployment: extended unemployment; increased funds for food stamps; gave a one-time payment of $250 to social security recipients and increased funds for vocational school training and job training.
- Transportation: invested funds in highway and bridge construction; provided funds to purchase new equipment and provided funds to upgrade air traffic control centers.
- Water, sewage, environmental: provided funds to Army Corps of Engineers for infrastructure projects;

provided funds for clean water and wastewater treatment projects.
- Government Buildings and Facilities: provided money to modernize Defense Department facilities; improved housing of service men and women; improved Job Corps training and improved facilities for the National Guard.
- Communications and security technology: provided funds to complete Internet access and to detect explosives in airports; updated computer center at social security and upgraded fire stations.
- Energy infrastructure: provided funds to cleanup radioactive waste; modernized electric grid system and upgraded power transmission systems.
- Energy efficiency and renewable energy research: money was provided for weatherizing modest-income homes, carbon capture technology and advanced car battery systems.
- Scientific Research: provided funds to the National Science Foundation and the Department of Energy and other scientific oriented government agencies like NASA and NOAA.
- Others: provided funds for state and local law enforcement agencies and child support enforcement and aid to AmeriCorps and the Small Business Administration for loans.

The bill was enacted on February 27, 2009 for a total of $787 billion. You can see that this stimulus was spread over a much wider area of the economy; it was less focused than the TARP—which was basically only for the financial sector—or the Bush stimulus plan that gave money to taxpayers. There is something for everyone in the Recovery Act and this is good. It hit a wide variety of economic sectors to provide some stimulus to each sector. In August 2011, the congressional Budget Office estimated that by 2012 the American Recovery and Reinvestment Act would increase the nation's GDP between 3.5 percent and 9.5 percent.[132] In fact, between the 3rd quarter of 2009, after the bill was enacted, and the 4th quarter of 2011, the GDP increased by 5.8 percent, they hit their mark.

There are other things that the government can do to get the economy going again. With about 14 million people out of work, it is important to provide people with unemployment insurance. The average unemployment check is about $300 per week. Those who are unemployed are likely to spend every cent of these funds and the items they spend their money on will go to other people who will also spend the funds. This money has a multiplicative effect. The U.S. Department of Labor estimates that every $1.00 provided by unemployment insurance generates $2.00 of growth in the economy and helps increase employment as well as the GDP.[133] Unemployment insurance is sort of like a tax refund, except that the funds don't go to everyone, only to those unemployed and most likely to need it and spend it.

Another method to revive the economy is to lower interest rates. Since the start of the Financial Crisis, the Federal Reserve Bank (Fed) has steadily lowered the Federal Fund Rate. This is the interest rate that banks charge each other for short-term loans and is determined and controlled by the Fed through the supply of money. In 2008, the Federal Fund Rate was set between 0 and 0.25 percent, the lowest level since the 1950s. The Federal Fund Rate influences other rates such as the Prime Interest rate which in turn, affects various other rates including: all consumer rates, credit card rates, home loans, auto loans and student loans rates. Keeping the interest rate low encourages people to borrow money to build or buy something. Interest rates on a thirty-year fixed mortgage for example in January 2012 were about 4 percent. This is the lowest rate I can ever remember. This would have been a great time to re-finance your home, lower your monthly payments and buy a new car or pay off your credit card debt. It's a great opportunity but once the economy gets going again, interest rates will go up.

Has it worked? Is the train rolling again?

Has all this effort to restore the economy worked? Has the effort and debt we have incurred to save the financial system and the economy of the United States of America been effective? If you're a Republican or a Tea Partier, you may say NO! But let's look at the factual record. Below is the percent change in the Gross Domestic Product by quarter developed by the Bureau of Economic Analysis part of the Department of Commerce as of the end of 2013. All the information is adjusted for inflation and presented in 2009 dollars. The table starts in 2006, two years before the recession, so you can see what the GDP changes were leading up to the train wreck and how the GDP has performed since the recession.

In 2006 and 2007, the average annual GDP change was 2.7 percent and 1.8 percent. However, in 2008 and 2009 when the recession was in progress, the GDP was decreasing. The GDP reached its largest rate of decline at -8.3 percent in the 4th quarter of 2008. You can also see that in 2011, 2012 and 2013 the GDP had been increasing at an annual rate of 1.8 percent, 2.8 percent and 1.9 percent respectively; about the same rate of increase that was experienced in 2006 and 2007 before the recession started. In fact, going back ten years before the recession, 1998 to 2007, the average GDP increase was 2.6 percent. The recent GDP increases of 1.8 percent, 2.8 percent and 1.9 percent compare favorably with this 2.6 percent rate.

Percent Change of GDP (in Constant 2009 Dollars)

	2006	2007	2008	2009	2010	2011	2012	2013
1st Quarter	4.9%	0.3%	-2.7%	-5.4%	1.6%	-1.3%	3.7%	1.1%
2nd Quarter	1.3%	3.1%	2.0%	-0.4%	3.9%	3.2%	1.2%	2.5%
3rd Quarter	0.3%	2.7%	-2.0%	1.3%	2.8%	1.4%	2.8%	4.1%
4th Quarter	3.2%	1.5%	-8.3%	3.9%	2.8%	4.9%	0.1%	2.6%
Annual	2.7%	1.8%	-0.3%	-2.8%	2.5%	1.8%	2.8%	1.9%

Now let's look, not at the rate of change, but at the Gross Domestic Product itself. Below is the GDP starting from 2006.

Again, this information is from the Bureau of Economic Analysis as of the beginning of 2014 and is in constant 2009 dollars (i.e. adjusted for inflation).

GDP in Billions of Dollars, Constant 2009 Dollars

	2006	2007	2008	2009	2010	2011	2012	2013
1st Quarter	14,546.4	14,728.1	14,895.4	14,372.1	14,597.7	14,894.0	15,381.6	15,583.9
2nd Quarter	14,591.6	14,841.5	14,969.2	14,356.9	14,738.0	15,011.3	15,427.7	15,679.7
3rd Quarter	14,604.4	14,941.5	14,895.1	14,402.5	14,839.3	15,062.1	15,534.0	15,839.3
4th Quarter	14,718.4	14,996.1	14,574.6	14,540.2	14,942.4	15,242.1	15,539.6	15,942.3
Annual	14,615.2	14,876.8	14,833.6	14,417.9	14,779.4	15,052.4	15,470.7	15,761.3

Before the recession, the GDP reached a high of $14,996.1 billion (or $14.996 trillion) in the 4th quarter of 2007. After that, the GDP declined for most of 2008 and half of 2009, hence we see the minus sign in front of the rate of change in the first table, reaching a low of $14,356.9 billion in the 2nd quarter of 2009. After mid 2009 though, we see that the GDP is increasing and has been increasing steadily except for 1st quarter of 2011. By the 2nd quarter of 2011, the GDP reached a new all-time high of $15,011.3 billion, higher than the highest point before the recession started.[134] So in a period of four years, the GDP had regained its previous record high; during the Great Depression of the 1930s, it took ten years to regain the all time high GDP. Add to this the fact that General Motors regained its slot as the world's largest automaker in 2011, producing about 9.0 million vehicles and increasing sales by 7.6 percent. This coming from the auto giant that was nearly bankrupt only a few years ago.

Now let's look at unemployment. According to the Bureau of Labor Statistics, national unemployment in September 2012 was 7.8 percent, down from the peak unemployment rate of 10.0 percent in October of 2009. Over 3.3 million people have found employment since the peak.[135] Although the unemployment rate has seen ups and downs since October 2009, the general trend is clearly declining unemployment (i.e. increasing employment). Note too, that historically the average unemployment rate is about

5.5 percent, you never get to percent unemployment; somebody is always without work. So, in effect, we are about halfway back to the historic average employment level. So to answer the question, have the Economy Stimulus Act, the Trouble Assets Relief Act (both enacted by President Bush) and the American Recovery and Reinvestment Act (enacted by President Obama) worked? There is no logical answer other than YES, they have worked and they have helped to increase the country's productivity and have saved the country from a new depression.

Yet, if the economy is doing better than before the recession started, then why is there still a 7.8 percent unemployment rate and millions of people out of work? There could be several reasons. For one, the construction industry is recovering slowly because people aren't building new homes. Construction employs a lot of workers so even through the economy as a whole is making money; some of the more labor-intensive work categories aren't doing so well. In other words, the business mix has changed to emphasize the less labor-intensive categories of business. Another reason could be that the work force is not trained and educated to staff the new, more technically demanding positions that present day companies require. There is no denying that more emphasis needs to be placed on educating and training workers.

Uncertainty about the future of the economy could be yet another explanation for high unemployment. Companies are uncertain about the economy and are unwilling to hire new workers. Apparently over four years of continuous growth is insufficient persuasion. The fragile European Common Market and Congress' inability to decide on a way forward does represent a road hazard to America's sustained recovery.

Another explanation for high unemployment is that businesses are just holding out. They are squeezing the labor force to get as much production as they can and are using fear of lay-offs and unemployment to "motivate" the workers. Business profits are up, and businesses have stashed away trillions of dollars that could be used to increase production and employment but they're not putting it to good use.

President Obama asked American businesses to start reinvesting in American jobs but to no avail. It seems that Supply Side Economics— the theory advocating increased business profit will stimulate economic growth and employment—just doesn't seem to work. (More on this discussion is included in the chapter on Debt and the Economy.)

How to prevent the train from ever wrecking again

The economic and financial crisis has caused the world economy to crumble. Every nation has felt the consequences of the financial misconduct perpetrated by the United States financial community. What do you do to prevent such a train wreck from ever happening again? One answer would be to disassemble the big banks that controlled a significant portion of the country's financial transactions. At the time the crisis struck, five financial banks (JPMorgan Chase, Bank of America, Citigroup, Wells Fargo and Goldman Sachs) held assists amounting to 43 percent of the financial assets in the country.[136] If Congress had broken these large banks up into small banks, the smaller banks wouldn't have had the financial where-with-all to cause a worldwide catastrophe. Also, if a small bank failed, the consequences would not be so large that it would cause a worldwide problem. The bank would fail, the Federal Deposit Insurance Corporation would protect the depositors' money and there would be no bank bailouts. It would also seem that many small banks competing in the marketplace would agree exactly with the true capitalist's viewpoint. The "many small banks concept" it seems, would have been the best answer to avoid any future crisis. When power gets concentrated in the hands of a few and only a few control the marketplace, that's not capitalism; that a monopoly or oligarchy (rule by the few).

There are some disadvantages, however, with having many small banks operating independently. One such disadvantage is that the finance system becomes cumbersome. Big corporations require big loans and big loans are difficult to arrange with only small banks. One of the biggest reasons that the banks weren't broken up is that by the time the financial regulations were on the table, the banks had already recuperated. A huge lobbying effort by the people who caused the crisis and who received benefits of the bailout were now in control again. With huge donations to their campaign war chests, politicians caved in and the big banks remained whole. Congress opted to "regulate" the banks instead of breaking them up. In December 2009, Democratic Senator Chris Dodd from Connecticut and Democratic Congressman Barnie Frank from Massachusetts introduced the Financial Reform Act. Versions of the bill passed through both Houses of Congress along party lines and after committee hearings to reconcile differences, the bill was passed. On July 21, 2010, President Obama signed into law what has become known as the Dodd-Frank Wall Street Reform and Consumer Protection Act.

This Act represents the largest change to the financial system since the Great Depression. Look back at what caused the financial crisis:

1. Elimination of overview authority of the Commodity Futures Trading Commission to regulate derivatives such as Mortgage Based Security.
2. Repeal of the Glass-Steagall Act, which separated investment banks from commercial banks, thereby allowing commercial banks to invest in risky securities markets.
3. Very lax regulations on mortgage loan approval, thus resulting in massive loans to subprime borrowers, which eventually lead to the collapse of the real estate market.
4. Bank incentives to mortgage officers to place ARM type mortgages.
5. Obligation on Fannie and Freddie to purchase loans made to low-income homebuyers.

6. Lax overview of the financial industry by the Federal Deposit Insurance Corporation, the Office of Thrift Supervision and Federal Reserve.
7. Relaxation of the Net Capital Ratios allowed by the Security and Exchange Commission changed the ratio from about 12 to 1 to about 30 to 1.
8. Rating agencies like Standard & Poor's and Moody's totally inaccurate rating of MBS was spurred on by the fact that they are paid by the people that they rate.
9. Banks were "Too Big to Fail." Failure would cause an even worse catastrophe.

The Dodd-Frank law is complicated. The legislation created three new agencies: Financial Stability Oversight Council, the Office of Financial Research and the Bureau of Consumer Financial Protection and eliminated one agency: the Office of Thrift Supervision. The stated aim of the law is:

> To promote the financial stability of the United States by improving accountability and transparency in the financial system, to end "too big to fail," to protect the American taxpayer by ending bailouts, to protect consumers from abusive financial services practices and for other purposes.

A laudable aim indeed.

So, let's see how the legislation contained in the new Dodd-Frank Act compares with what we know are the causes of the crisis. (For those looking for a new house, read this section carefully. It affects you.)

1. No overview of derivatives
   Title VII is designed to restore some overview of the derivatives market, the overview which were

eliminated in 2000 by Robert Rubin and Congress. Regulatory authority was returned to the Commodity Future Trading Commission and to the Security and Exchange Commission. The organizations were tasked with regulating derivatives and with fostering more transparency within the derivative market by establishing trading exchanges and cleaning houses (sort of like stock markets) for most derivatives. The legislation also established a code of conduct for dealers of derivatives. Furthermore, Subtitle D of Title IX requires that companies that sell derivatives must retainat least 5 percent of the credit risk. So if they're selling crap, they atleast have to live with some of it in their own house.

2. Repeal of Glass-Steagall Act that separated investment banks from commercial banks
Under Title VI, the Volcker Rule—originally introduced by Paul Volcker former chairman of the Federal Reserve—would prohibit the banks from using private money for their own gain. This title effectively would have restored the Glass-Steagall Act, which prevented commercial banks from investing in risky securities. However, as the bill went through Congress, it was significantly weakened, largely through the efforts of Senator Scott Brown of Massachusetts, and the extent and effect of the title has yet to be tested.

3. Lax regulations on mortgage loan approval
Title XIV is designed to simplify mortgage processing and prevent predatory lending practices like No Income, No Asset, NINA loans and ARMs on those who can't afford it.

Subtitle A: Requires that Resident Mortgage Originators (companies that take mortgage applications and find lenders for residents) get paid per person. This ensures that the mortgage (to avoid kickbacks from finance companies) is based on the amount of the mortgage and not based on the type of loan (e.g. paid more if it is an ARM).

Subtitle B: Establishes national underwriting standards for residential loans. These include for example verifying through documented information that at the time of the loan, the borrower could repay the loan. Income verification is mandatory and other payments are considered in the loan. (In other words, it makes the originator do some investigation to help assure the borrower can repay, unlike what existed before the loan crisis.)

Subtitle C: High Cost Mortgages High Cost Mortgages are defined as loans secured by the borrower's principle residence (such as second mortgages) or points and fees that exceed certain specified amounts. To obtain High Cost Mortgages, the borrower must have pre-loan counseling to explain the loan. Also, balloon payments, prepayment penalties and encouraging default on an existing loan are no longer legal.

Subtitle D: Office of Housing Counseling Creates a new Office of Housing Counseling with HUD to educate the general public in home ownership and home financing.

Subtitle E: Mortgage Servicing Requires an escrow account to be established by the borrower to pay taxes, insurance, flood insurance (if applicable) and other required periodic payments.

Subtitle F: Property Appraisal Requirements Requires that a property appraisal be conducted for the mortgaged property. A certified or licensed appraiser must conduct the appraisal.

Subtitle G: Mortgage Resolution and Modifications Develops a program to ensure protection of tenants and multifamily properties. The program will include creating sustainable financing of these properties that include rental income and government subsidies.

4. Bank incentives to place ARM type mortgages
Incentives to place ARM mortgages to barrows is prohibited within the language of Subtitle A of Title XIV above. Obviously lawmakers are aware that this reprehensible behavior was occurring within the mortgage community.

5. Obligation on Fannie and Freddie to purchase loans from low- income buyers
It is still the policy of the U.S. Government to provide loans to low-income families. In fact, title XII provides micro-loans ($2,500) and financial education and counseling to low and moderate-income families.

6. Lax Overview of the Financial Industry by the Federal Deposit Insurance Corporation, the Office of theThrift and the Federal Reserve
Title I and II introduced significant changes to the regulatory agencies and how regulations will function in the future. Title I creates the Financial Oversight Council and the Office of Financial Research.The responsibility of the Oversight Council is to identify threats to the financial stability of the United States and to respond to emerging risks to that stability.The

Office of Financial Research is the data-gathering wing of the Oversight Council; they are the number crunchers. Financial Research provides technical and budget analysis information to the Oversight Council. The Oversight Council is a powerful agency. It can require the Federal Reserve to assume oversight control of institutions that pose a risk to the financial stability of our country. The Council can even place non-banking financial companies or domestic subsidiaries of international banks under the Federal Reserve if they pose a threat to financial stability. Both the Oversight Council and the Office of Research must make regular reports to Congress of the country's financial stability. Title II is the Orderly Liquidation portion of the Act and deals with the "Too Big to Fail" issue of the Financial Crisis as well as lax overview issues. The Federal Deposit Insurance Corporation and the Securities Investor Protection Corporation already have the authority to place banks, insured depository and security companies into liquidation. This new law allows insurance companies and non-bank financial companies to be placed into liquidation as well. The law also requires, among other things that:

– Shareholders of the failed institution do not receive payment until all other claims are fully paid.
– The management and board of directors responsible for the failure are removed from office.

In addition, the taxpayers will not pay for the cost of liquidation. Funds expended for liquidation of financial companies will be paid for by the *assets of that company* or from a new "Orderly Liquidation Fund" established to pay for the cost of liquidation. The fund will be established by the FDIC from assessment fees placed on financial institutions having more than $50 billion in assets. Taxpayers shall bear no loss from liquidating any financial company. Losses will be the responsibility of the financial sector recovered by assessments.

Note also that Title III reduces the overlap between bank regulating agencies by eliminating the Office of Thrift Supervision and transferring its authority to other agencies.

7. Relaxation of the Net Capital Ratio
   Title XI required the Federal Reserve Bank to establish prudent standards for the companies they regulate. For example:

   – New standards regarding required capital and leverage, i.e. their net capital ratios.
   – New standards regarding public disclosure and contingent capital requirements.

8. Inaccurate rating by the rating agencies.
   Title IX deals with investor protection and the nationally recognized statistical rating organizations, such as Standard & Poor's, Moody's and Fitch. The title encourages more transparency, honesty and divulgence of interest. The SEC is authorized to require information regarding costs, risks and conflict of interest be revealed upon purchase of investments. Also the SEC is authorized to impose "fiduciary duties" on brokers and investment advisers.

   A new "whistleblower bounty program" is established by this title that leads to financial rewards for information leading to a successful SEC conviction of violation of the law.

   The title also creates an Office of Credit Ratings (OCR) to provide oversight and regulations, including some very interesting common sense requirements on the rating agencies.

- The office of credit has the authority to temporarily suspend registration of a rating company that cannot produce credit rating with integrity.
- The OCR is required to audit each rating company annually and produce a public report.
- The national rating organizations are required to disclose information on credit rating issues, including credit rating methods.
- The national rating organizations are required to establish and maintain a control structure governing methods for determining credit ratings and submit an annual report to the OCR.
- The rating companies are required to adhere to rules designed to prevent sales and marketing considerations from influencing the rating.
- Requires a report to the SEC when a rating agency employee goes to work for a security firm he or she has rated within the last twelve months.
- Requires rating agencies to include creditable information received from a source other than the organization they are rating.
- Allow investors to file suit if the rating agency knowingly or recklessly fails to conduct a reasonable investigation or to obtain analysis from other sources.
- Requires analysts to pass a qualification exam.
- Compensation of the compliance officer cannot be linked to the financial performance of the rating company.
- Duty to report credible allegations of unlawful conduct to authorities by issuers of securities.

- The SEC will conduct a study to strengthen the independence of the rating agencies and to reduce conflicts of interest.

It seems that most of these requirements are indeed common sense for most honest people. Now they are written down. Does this mean that if they're not written down, that brokers are free *not* to use common sense?

9. "Too Big to Fail"

Title I deals with preventing systematic banking failure and Title II discusses how to deal with banks that are heading for bankruptcy. In addition, part of Title XI requires companies supervised by the Federal Reserve (large banks are supervised by the Feds, some state chartered banks are supervised by the FDIC) to periodically present plans to rapidly and orderly liquidate their own companies. In essence, they must plan their own funerals.

In spite of the proven hazard of allowing banks to become too big, the five largest U.S. banks (JPMorgan Chase, Bank of America, Citigroup, Wells Fargo and Goldman Sachs) control assets amounting to 56 percent of the economy of America at the end of 2011; more than the 43 percent they held before the crisis.[137] The financial institutions are more powerful and wealthier today than in 2007. They haven't learned a thing and they are not repentant or remorseful and clearly they represent a danger to America's financial stability. Title I of the Dodd-Frank Act gives the Financial Oversight Council and the Federal Reserve the power to take action against these threats, yet no action has occurred. We will see.

Further Regulations contained in the Dodd-Frank Act

In addition to those regulations that were developed in response to the Financial Crisis, the Dodd-Frank Act provides several other protections to the American consumer. One of the most controversial is the creation of the Consumer Financial Protection Bureau under Title X. The CFPB is charged with regulating consumer financial products and services from payday loans, student loans, personal mortgages and credit cards. This part of the Act was controversial because Congress refused to confirm the Director who is appointed by the President and confirmed by a sixty-vote majority in the Senate. ElizabethWarren—a Harvard Law Professor, championed the creation of a Consumer Financial Protection Bureau—was strongly opposed by Republicans as being too aggressive for consumer protection regulation. President Obama appointed Warren as a Special Advisor to the President. In July 2011, Obama nominated Richard Cordray, an Attorney General from the State of Ohio, to be Director of the CFPB. Cordray was also opposed by Senate Republicans as being too active and was opposed by a Senate filibuster in December. On January 4, 2012, six months after Cordray's nomination with no action from the Senate, President Obama appointed Cordray as the Director during a recess appointment. The new Consumer Financial Protection Bureau will entail the following five units to help consumers with financial affairs:

- Research
- Community Affairs
- Complaint Tracking and Collection
- Office of Fair Lending and Equal Opportunity
- Office of Financial Literacy

Title IV introduces reporting regulations on hedge funds and other investments for the first time. (Hedge funds are investment funds for the super rich, usually requiring large investments. Hedge funds are managed to produce a high rate of return but also incur a high risk. Before this, hedge funds had very little reporting responsibilities.)

In addition, Title V brings insurance companies under the financial regulatory purview. Title V establishes the Federal Insurance Office within the Treasury Department. Some of the tasks to be performed by the Insurance Office are:

- Monitoring the insurance industry (except health insurance) including gaps in the regulation of insurance companies.
- Monitoring the availability of insurance to underserved communities, minorities and low-income individuals.

In response to the obscene compensation provided by some financial companies to their executives, Title IX subtitle E requires that at least every three years, executive compensation for publically held companies will be submitted to the shareholders for approval. This may be in part due to companies like Goldman-Sachs' payment of $10 billion in compensation and benefits in 2008 (the year the Financial Crisis started). The shareholders must also be informed of the relationship between executive compensation and financial performance of the company. Matching company performance with executive pay, what a novel idea! This provision does have teeth. In April, 2012, stockholders rejected the $15 million pay package of the CEO of Citibank, Vikram K. Pandit. Mr. Pandit was seen as not being able to implement strategy quickly and effectively, and that he lunged from crisis to crisis. On October 16, 2012, Mr. Pandit resigned as CEO.

Other actions resulting from the Dodd-Frank Act

In January 2012, the Consumer Financial Protection Bureau took its first action. Capital One Bank was fined $210 million for misrepresentation of the benefits of their credit cards. Consumers were sold products, such as payment protection plans, without their consent and were automatically charged. Some consumers were lead to believe that the product was free of charge. When some people tried to cancel the product, Capital One gave them "the run around." In addition, some consumers were signed up for the product even though they did not qualify for them.[138]

In July 2012, the Justice Department announced that Wells Fargo agreed to pay $175 million to settle claims that it discriminated against 34,000 African American and 36,000 Hispanic borrowers. These borrowers were steered into subprime mortgages or paid higher fees than white borrowers with similar qualifications. In the Chicago area for example, African Americans seeking a $300,000 mortgage paid an average of $2,937 more than similar qualified whites. In Miami, Hispanic borrowers paid an average of $2,538 more than whites for a $300,000 mortgage.[139]

JPMorgan Chase has been fined about $25 billion for unlawful actions that occurred during the financial crisis. In November 2013, JPM was fined $13 billion to settle claims over its underwriting practices and sale of mortgages before the financial crisis. As part of the settlement, JPMorgan Chase "acknowledged it made serious misrepresentations to the public."[140] In January 2014, they were fined $2.6 billion for not providing warning concerning Bernie Madoff's activities, as they were required to do by the Secrecy Act. Other illegal or improper activities JPMorgan Chase has plead guilty to include:

- settlement of losses on mortgage backed securities sold to institutional investors;
- settlement to credit card customers who were sold credit cards based on improper information, and
- improper carrying out of foreclosures.

Added together, JPMorgan Chase has paid $25 billions in fines.

All the regulatory titles of the Dodd-Frank Act are now covered except for Title VIII, Title XIII and XV, for those who are keeping track. Title VIII aims to mitigate systemic risk by asking the Feds to create uniform standards of risk management for large companies. Title XIII just de-obligates funds allocated from the TARP program which were not spent and Title XV deals with miscellaneous issues like developing a report on "blood diamonds" and the effectiveness of the Inspector General.

Our review of the Dodd-Frank Act, which is meant to be the future railroad for the financial industry, and a comparison with the causes of the Financial Crisis, is now complete. Dodd-Frank, it seems to me, addresses each of the fundamental causes of the crisis in a practical and reasonable manner. It restores some old laws that had served the financial industry well for many years, and enacts new regulations that can serve as a guide into the future. Dodd-Frank has brought insurance companies, hedge funds and derivatives that played a significant role in the Financial Crisis, within the financial regulatory framework and at least attempts to look into the financial future and take pre-emptive action against impending crises.

The train is back on the track and has started moving slowly forward. However, legislation is only as good as the enforcement of the legislation. Even after the devastation caused by the crisis, financial companies and some members of Congress relentlessly continue calling for a reduction in regulations. After the sorrow and grief these companies have caused, why on earth would anyone want to reduce regulations? The financial industry has proven, beyond any doubt, that they can only operate honestly and to everyone's benefit if they are heavily regulated. They are incapable of self-regulation, as Federal Chairman Alan Greenspan has belatedly discovered. Given the animosities that exist in Congress to implementation of the Dodd-Frank Act, it may never be fully implemented.

Let's face it, the fundamental cause for the Global Financial Crisis is greed. The financial power elite manipulated Congress and the legislative process to allow for reckless risk-taking and to make legal what was before illegal. Then the financial community at large lent money with thoughtless disregard for the future consequences of their actions, spreading their cancerous disease worldwide. They must have known that what they were doing would in time result in trouble, but they didn't care. All the while government regulators took a vacation; comforted by the "knowledge" that business is rational and will act rationally. Despite Gordon Gekko's claim in the 1987 movie *Wall Street* that greed is good; greed, at the expense of investors who place their trust in a company or who placed their trust in the protective nature of their government, is NOT good. It is reprehensible! Yet, to date, not one member of this disgraceful group has been legally prosecuted.

The final analysis.
Some members of the public will defend this reprehensible behavior. They believe that businesses should be allowed to make a profit. No, not just a profit, but the largest possible profit they can make, no matter the consequences. I also believe that businesses should make a profit; after all, a business that doesn't profit won't last long. I also believe in the capitalist system and competition. By competing, the best ideas flourish; the best "widgets" are produced. But there must be a limit. Suppose you're an investor in a bank. Is it acceptable to provide mortgages to people who you know cannot make the mortgage payments and thus cause the bank to go bankrupt? Or to cause a retirement fund that invested in the bank to lose its assets and cause millions of people to forego their retirement? Suppose you're buying a house. Is it acceptable to obtain a loan at a higher rate than you could have qualified for because a devious mortgage broker didn't inform you about a better loan? I believe this is NOT OK! While businesses must make a profit, they must do it fairly and honestly. All businesses have a fiduciary duty to deal with their customers honestly; otherwise it is not an honest profit. Some businesses have proven themselves

to be incapable of dealing on an honest basis. Thus we have Allen Greenspan's "shocked disbelief" in business' inability to regulate itself. Oh, surprise!

In view of the fact that at the very least the financial businesses have proven themselves incapable of acting honestly, we must implement rules in an attempt to force these businesses to do what is honest. We must regulate them. To the Republicans, regulation is the antithesis of the free marketplace and they strongly oppose any regulation of the financial industry. Well we've seen what happens when regulations are relaxed, starting with Ronald Reagan and leading up to today. I'm reminded of the quote, credited to Albert Einstein, Mark Twain or Benjamin Franklin, take your pick, "Doing the same thing over and over again and expecting different results is the height of insanity." This truism definitely applies to those who want to reduce financial regulations. Never the less, in 2018, congress removed the strictest requirements of Dodd-Frank from most banks leaving only 10 banks that are still required to follow these rules. Also congress relaxed the Volcker Rule and hence allowed, once again, banks to use depositors money to engage in the riskiest forms of financial investment i.e. like hedge funds and derivatives.

CHAPTER 7

The Tea Party, A Comedy Of Contradictions

Everyone saw the power of the Tea Party and Tea Party sympathizers during the 2010 midterm elections. In the House of Representatives, Republicans gained 63 seats of the 435 seats contested and in the Senate, Republicans gained 6 seats. The result was that President Obama and the Democrats who had control of both Houses of Congress, lost control of the House and became weaker in the Senate. This was a major blow to the Democrats; they took a "shellacking" in the words of the President. Who is the Tea Party? How did they get started and how did they get so much power so fast? Most importantly, what do they stand for?

The party gets started

Although many people try to get credit for the creation of the Tea Party, the first nation wide attention drawn to the Tea Party was from Rick Santelli. A CNBC Business News broadcaster, he fell into a tirade on February 19, 2009 during one of the business news broadcasts. Santelli was irate, touting "the government is rewarding bad behavior" and was "subsidizing the mortgage losers." Santelli then challenged Obama to have a referendum and vote on whether the "government should reward those who can buy cars and houses in default and have a chance to prosper down the road and give them to those that can carry the water rather than those who can just drink it." Santelli then called for a capitalist Chicago Tea Party.[141]

This was the perfect signal that the disgruntled conservative community was waiting for. Santelli's referendum became known as the Tea Party movement. The Boston Tea Party occurred in Boston Harbor in 1773 and was a perfect symbol to embody the patriotism of our forefathers and the anger that conservatives felt. As explained in the book, *The Tea Party and the Remaking of Republican Conservatism* by Theda Skocpol and Vanessa Williamson, the Tea Party provided vast opportunities for conservative organizations. FreedomWorks and Americans for Prosperity, for example, were now able to further their long-standing conservative agendas such as reducing taxes on businesses, reducing government regulations, revamping Medicare and privatizing Social Security. Unlike the Tea Party though, FreedomWorks and Americans for Prosperity are not new organizations. FreedomWorks has been around for years. Funded by the billionaire Koch Brothers, David and Charles, it's a petrochemical company and the second largest privately owned business in the United States. FreedomWorks is headed by Dick Armey from Texas, who also served as the Republican Majority Leader in the 1990s. Americans for Prosperity is also a Koch supported organization with ultra-conservative goals. It was the Wisconsin branch of the Americans for Prosperity that awarded Paul Ryan the "Defender of the American Dream" for his budget "RoadMap" that entailed huge tax cuts for the rich, and reduced spending on Medicaid and college aid, and switched Medicare to a voucher system.[142] It was the financial support of these organizations that helped the fledgling Tea Party spring to the American forefront.

However, it was not just financial support that helped launch the Tea Party movement. Fox Network provided a tremendous boost to the Tea Party's reputation and popularity among conservatives. Just six months after Santelli's tirade, Glenn Beck of Fox News sponsored the "9/12 Tea Party" march on Washington. Then, on August 28, 2010, Beck and Sarah Palin sponsored the "Restoring Honor" march at the Lincoln Memorial, the same date as Martin Luther King's famous "I Have a Dream" speech. News media—Fox News especially, with over 2 million viewers during prime time—and radio talk show hosts such as Glenn Beck, Sean Hannity, Rush Limbaugh, Bill O'Reilly and Laura Ingraham played a significant part in publicizing and popularizing the Tea Party. Without this heavy news coverage, the Tea Party movement may have floundered.

So the Tea Party was formed by grass root activism, funded by billionaires and publicized by powerful media networks and personalities.

Who are the Tea Partiers?

Although it's called a party, the Tea Party is not a "political party." For example, it will not place the name of a candidate into nomination in opposition to the Republican or Democratic parties. Although it is becoming very closely associated with the Republican Party, it is a loosely knit group of organizations that basically support similar political ideals. Rather than nominating a separate candidate, the Tea Party has been successful at endorsing candidates for office or endorsing candidates to oppose those the Tea Party did not favor. This tactic was successful, the following merely a few examples: In Kentucky where Rand Paul defeated John Conway, or in Wisconsin where Ron Johnson defeated the incumbent Democrat Russ Feingold and in Massachusetts where Scott Brown was elected to take over Senator Edward Kennedy's seat after Kennedy's death. In other words, the Tea Party is more closely monitoring the Republican Party, to assure they keep the faith, rather than being a separate political party.

Skocpol and Williamson have also done an excellent job of characterizing who Tea Partiers are. Based on their personal experience in attending many Tea Party meetings and interviews with the members throughout the country, members of the Tea Party can be characterized as follows:

- Generally white, married men, although there are women who play a vital role.
- Most are middle aged in the middle or upper middle-income level. Most did not experience the full effects of the recession due to being in retirement and having a larger financial cushion.
- Many are Evangelical Protestants (not mainline Protestants, Catholics or Jews) and have at least some college education. Many, but not all, are anti-evolution and anti-birth control, right-to-lifers.
- Many are small business owners, many in the construction industry. Only a few are employed in the public sector.
- The largest tea party groups are located in the South.
- They are very conservative or libertarian. One of the trademarks of the Tea Party is their non-compromising stance on political issues. For example, early in 2011, clashes over the size of budget cuts pitted the GOP house against the Democratic Senate. Two thirds of the Tea Party wanted to shut down the government rather than compromise.
- The vast majority of Tea Partiers watch Fox News as their main source of news information.

Another interesting characteristic about Tea Partiers are their willingness to accept, without hesitation or consideration, the most outlandish conservative accusations as being a given fact. It is widely believed among the Tea Party that President Obama is not a United States citizen. The fact that Obama is President and his citizenship was most assuredly verified by government agencies before the election holds no sway. Even after the President offered his birth certificate, some are still not convinced. The belief that "Obamacare" will add to the national debt is still widely held despite the Congressional Budget Office's estimate that the healthcare plan will actually decrease the debt by $132 billion over ten years. Still, there are others who hold the opinion that President Obama is a Muslim. This is in the face of Obama's membership in the Trinity United Church of Christ and the well-publicized remarks by Reverend Jeremiah Wright that it's not "God bless America but God damn America" that prompted Obama's subsequent leaving that church. The belief that the Affordable Care Act, aka Obamacare, contains "Death Panels" is still believed among many Tea Partiers. Apparently, they think that some people, particularly the elderly, must go before a panel of white Anglo-Saxon men dressed in white lab coats to seek permission to undergo life saving medical procedures. If you're too old, the gavel slams down. "You are too old, you must die." They feel that America will have panels that will effectively sentence its own citizens to death. Then, they turn around and speak of America as being the greatest nation on earth. Sentencing your citizens to death doesn't sound like a great nation to me. Where these panels materialized from are unknown. There are advisory panels like the American Medical Association that do exist, however, to provide recommended and approved medical procedures and treatments for illnesses and injuries that form the basis of treatment for all healthcare providers in the United States. These procedures, if anything, tend to overprescribe to protect the patient, not to disallow needed treatment.

The Tea Party Agenda, a comedy of contradictions
From the Dilbert cartoons, Boss is talking to Dilbert.
"I like to have opinions but not informed opinions. It takes so much work to get informed that it defeats the whole point of having an opinion in the first place."

Dilbert replies, "What exactly do you think is the 'point' of having an opinion?"
To which Boss answers, "The point is that it feels good."
(Dilbert 10/7/12)

The Tea Party website, TheTeaParty.net, states that the Tea Party supports the United States Constitution as the Founding Fathers intended. This includes:

- limited powers of the Federal Government;
- individual freedoms;
- personal responsibilities;
- free markets and
- returning political power to the states and the people.

The details of what each Tea Party group endorses varies somewhat from affiliate to affiliate and within the various regions of the country. Generally though, Tea Partiers are in favor of reduced taxes and a smaller federal government.

Individual freedoms

Famous among the Tea Party agenda is their purported love for "Individual Freedom." Their stance on "Individual Freedom" is absurd. Tea Partiers are against gay marriage, abortion and contraception. These most fundamental choices of life—an individual's choice, in which no other individual deserves a voice—are considered open topics for the Tea Party. How can anyone say with a straight face that the Tea Party stands for individual freedoms? The individual freedoms in the Tea Party lie only with those who believe the Tea Party doctrine that gay marriage, abortion and contraception are against God's will. "I'm for individual freedom unless I don't agree with you, then I'm against it." And what if you don't believe in God? In the Tea Party you do not have a right to NOT believe in God. "Ocktung! You vill believe in God!" Not just God, but the one whose son is Jesus; it doesn't count if your God is Allah or Adonai (Jewish God). In fact, it is curious that Tea Partiers even consider endorsing Mitt Romney, a Mormon. A religion founded less than 200 years ago, this religion follows the Book of Mormon as well as the Bible and whose founder, Joseph Smith, had 87 wives!

Reduce the Power of Government.
Following right on the trail of individual freedom is limiting the power of government. Of course, many Tea Partiers are in favor of a law to ban gay marriages and would repeal Roe v. Wade in a heartbeat. Is this what the Tea Party means by limiting government powers? How much more intrusive can government regulations be? Once again, Tea Partiers are in favor of limited government unless it's something that they support, and then they're in favor of a big and intrusive government.

But, look at some of the other functions of government:

- government monitors the flights of aircraft and assures aircraft safety (FAA);
- it assures that the medicine we take are safe (FDA);
- it monitors the water we drink to guarantee it's safe and drinkable (EPA);
- it helps assure that we work in a safe work environment (OSHA);
- it helps ensure that the air we breathe is clean (EPA);
- it protects our country from invasions from abroad and protects our citizens and their assets from terrorist attacks (Dept of Defense and US Military);
- it provides a source of funds for our businesses so they can operate (Dept of Treasury, Fed Reserve);
- it establishes communications with the other nations of the world because the U.S. cannot live in a vacuum (Dept of State);

- it decides if laws passed by the states and the federal government are legal (in other words, it assures that the constitution is followed) (Supreme Courts);
- it constructs interstate highways and it regulates trade between the fifty states in spite of the fact that all fifty want to do it differently (FHWA);
- but that's not all. It develops energy policies to help save the earth from pollution (EPA);
- it regulates nuclear power to assure it is safe (NRC);
- it provides healthcare for our citizens and tries to keep the nation healthy regardless of the desire to smoke, drink and eat ourselves to death (HHS);
- it provides medical help for our service men and women (VA);
- it protects our national parks and forests, spectacular regions that are under attack each day from business interests (NPS);
- it assures the food we eat, fruits and vegetables, meat and milk—whether produced at home or from aboard—are healthy (USDA, FDA) and many other important functions that a government must provide.

It does thousands of other vital jobs. Now Tea Partiers, I ask you, which one of these jobs do you want to eliminate? They are all important! This is not to say that a government for over 300 million people living in the U. S. is not gigantic and costly; and it is not to say that there is no waste and that cost saving measures cannot be instituted. We can save money by inspecting for waste and fraud and we should do this and we do. Of course, Tea Partiers are against providing funds for inspection and auditing agencies because they increase the cost of government; never mind that those inspections often save more money than they cost. Saying that we need to cut government and make it smaller, as if you can do that by waving a magic wand, is just like a whining unhappy child who can't get his or her way. <u>One thing is for</u>

sure though, most laws and regulations result from some business or some person doing something immoral, unethical or illegal.

Reducing the budget and increasing taxes.

During World War II, the entire country was behind the war effort. People were saving rubber bands and shoe soles to aid in the supply of rubber and tin cans to help with our steel supply. While the men were at war, the women worked. Tom Brokaw is right, that was the "Greatest Generation."

Today we're in a similar situation. Due to the financial crisis of 2008 and two wars, our national debt is about equal to our entire GDP, and our economy is in the worse condition it's been in since World War II. We are fragmented and need to get on a better financial footing. So yes, we need to cut federal programs and reduce spending so we can reduce the nation's expenditures. But we also need to increase taxes so we can increase the revenue coming in; a balanced approach. This is only common sense. Yet 80 percent of Tea Partiers polled by Skocpol and Williamson oppose any increase in taxes on the rich, those making more than $250,000 per year. Most Tea Partiers don't make $250,000 per year, so a tax increase would not affect them directly. But raising the tax rate on the wealthy would help us crawl out of this deficit, which would help all Americans. Instead, Tea Partiers support *only* reducing federal programs, even though many of the programs to be cut would hurt them personally. Republican proposed budget cuts would reduce the deficit by increasing interest rates on student loans—requiring students to pay more for their education—reduce the benefits of Medicare, privatize social security and would make large cuts to many programs like the U.S. Park Service that many Americans enjoy. In addition, federally funded programs like food stamps and Medicaid would be drastically cut, betraying Christianity's belief in providing charity for the poor. So, the Tea Party is in favor of spending cuts and reductions in government programs—an action that would actually harm many Tea Party members—but are against tax increases on the rich—an action which would actually benefit most Tea Party members and the entire nation.

So let's look at the richest 1 percenters. Between 1992 and 2007, the income of the bottom 90 percent of households increased 40 percent while the income of the top 1 percent of households increased 275 percent, almost seven times faster than the 90 percent.[143] In 2008, the top 1 percent actually received 21 percent of the income for the entire nation. This results in the biggest disparity in income since 1928.[144] To be included in this elite group, you must have made at least $343,927 per year in 2009 and you'd be considered poor compared with the average member making $960,000 per year.[145] When it comes to wealth (i.e. wealth is considered to be the stuff you own, not the money you receive as income) the top 1 percent owns 34.6 percent of the country's wealth and the top 20 percent owns 85.1 percent of everything in the country. The middle class owns a paltry 15 percent of the country's wealth. That was in 2007. By 2009, the top 20 percent increased their ownership to 87.7 percent of the country's wealth, not because they necessarily bought more stuff, but because everybody else lost their stuff, like their homes.

Given these statistics, it is obvious that our country does, in fact, have a lopsided distribution of wealth. Republicans and Tea Partiers decry Obama's statements about redistributing the wealth. Hell, redistribution has already occurred, except in the wrong direction! Over the last ten years, our country has seen tremendous growth. In fact, the GDP is the largest it has ever been. The growth has not "trickled down" to the middle class though. The rich have developed a way, through relaxed tax rates and reduced government regulations, to keep most of the profits themselves, not sharing it with the workers who actually produced the growth. Even more miraculous, through the efforts of people like the Koch Brothers and Fox News (which is a Roger Ailes creation), they've been successful in convincing about half the nation, the Republicans, and a few hundred thousand Tea Partiers, that this is the way it should be. By opposing tax increases on the richest among us, Tea Partiers and Republicans are actually encouraging and perpetuating this system. There are at least two things wrong with this. First, the American Dream that you and your family will prosper through diligence and hard work, is denied. Tea Partiers apparently think the dream should be "Work hard and the rich will prosper." One might call this "Reverse Socialism." Secondly, you cannot have a democracy if all the wealth is owned by only a few. A democracy requires that almost everyone participate on an equal basis. It is not equal if the news media, the means of production and the country's government representatives are heavily influenced by the wealthy.

Deregulation of business.
Almost all Tea Partiers are in favor of reducing regulations on businesses. Let's review the causes of the Financial Crisis. In the early 1980s during President Reagan's administration, a philosophy of government developed that praised the wisdom of business deregulation and "Supply Side Economics." Under Allen Greenspan— Chairman of the Federal Reserve—and Robert Rubin—former Co- Chair of the Board of Goldman Sachs—as Secretary of the Treasury, government overview agencies such as the Security and Exchange Commission and the Department of the Treasury, for all intents and purposes, were non-existent.

In addition, the financial industry pushed two bills through Congress that were crucial for causing a worldwide disaster. The first bill eliminated regulation on derivatives. Derivatives you'll remember are financial securities that derive their value from the value of another security. For this discussion, derivatives were developed by bundling large numbers of mortgages together into what's called a "Mortgage Backed Security." Mortgages have value and they were traditionally very safe, as almost everyone pays their mortgage. So the mortgages were bundled up and sold around the world as safe investments that paid higher interest than U.S. Savings Bonds. The Commodity Future Trading Commission had regulated derivatives, but in 2000—with

Secretary Rubin's encouragement—Congress stripped away the authority of the CFTC to regulate derivatives.

The second bill passed by Congress repealed the Glass-Steagall Act. Glass-Steagall separated depositor banks (i.e. the banks where people have their savings) from investment banks (i.e. banks that make risky investments in stocks, bonds and derivatives). The Act that repealed Glass-Steagall, the Gramm-Leach-Bliley Act, allowed the two banking systems to effectively merge, thereby allowing all the savings deposits to become eligible for risky investments. To compound the impending disaster, the Federal Deposit Insurance Corporation, FDIC, insured the saving deposits. If the deposits were lost because of bad investments, the federal government would have to reimburse the depositor. The bank wasn't risking any of its own money!

So, with the stage now set, investment banks such as Goldman Sachs, Wells-Fargo, Lehman Brothers, Charter One, Countrywide Financial, Ameriquest, Washington Mutual, Wachovia, JPMorgan Chase, Citigroup, Bank of America, Merrill-Lynch, Bearn-Stern, essentially every investment bank in America, started making loans to almost anyone regardless of their ability to repay the loan. Twenty percent of the loans in 2006 were made to these sub-prime borrowers, people who had poor credit ratings and should not have been eligible for a mortgage. And what happened when the sub-prime borrowers could not make their mortage payments? The mortgages couldn't be paid; the millions of people who had Mortgage Back Securities lost most of their money and the whole stack of cards came tumbling down.

So, I ask you, what is the root cause of the Financial Crisis? Tea Partiers say the people getting the mortgages knew that they couldn't pay their mortgage and shouldn't have applied for it. People with low credit ratings, many with only a high school education or even less, were being offered the American dream of owning their own home. They should have had the knowledge and self-discipline to know that they shouldn't have applied for a mortgage. Or did the college educated home loan mortgage agents with years of experience, who knew the applicants could not make the mortgage payments, cause it? They shouldn't have made the loans, even though, the mortgage agents were being offered huge bonuses to make loans? No, it's neither of these. The root cause is because THE INDUSTRY WAS NOT EFECTIVELY REGULATED! This is proven by the fact that before de-regulation, the system had worked well since the 1930s. But after de-regulation, no one was regulating derivatives. The Securities and Exchange Commission wasn't looking at derivatives, while the security rating companies like Standard & Poor's continued to give the highest rating to the derivatives—even though they were crap—and the Treasury Department wasn't looking at bank lending practices.

Now, the same scenario plays out with the DeepWater Horizon disaster and the Massey Energy Coal Mine accident in West Virginia. The regulatory agency, OSHA, wasn't watching the company that was willfully and frequently violating regulatory standards for safety. It happens over and over again. Despite this evidence, the Tea Party wants to continue doing the same thing (i.e. reduce regulations) and expects different results.

Obamacare

Tea Partiers unanimously want to repeal Obamacare. The recent Supreme Court decision upholding the requirement that almost everyone obtain healthcare coverage makes the possibility of repeal unlikely. Still, Tea Partiers continue work to bury the plan.

The Declaration of Independence claims "life, liberty and the pursuit of happiness" to be self-evident, inalienable rights. The Tea Party's claim to follow the intent of the Founding Fathers obviously doesn't apply to the Declaration of Independence. When the Founding Fathers stated Americans have the right to "life," they were suggesting a happy, healthy life; a life assisted along the way with medical care. However, without healthcare insurance, the vast majority of Americans cannot afford the high costs of medical treatments. So, to sustain healthy lives, access to medical insurance effectively becomes an inalienable right. Obamacare allows everyone to get health insurance. Health insurance companies cannot deny coverage due to pre-existing illnesses or cancel insurance due to a patient making claims. But, if insurance cannot be denied to any individual, then everyone must have insurance or some would avoid paying the premiums and wait until they're sick before getting insurance. They would become "moochers" and "free-loaders" of the system. There is nothing Tea Partiers hate more than "moochers" and "free-loaders" who don't work and who exist off of government handouts. So, logically, by opposing a national healthcare system, the Tea Party is NOT supporting the intent of our Founding Fathers but IS supporting the "moochers" and "free-loaders." Two comical contradictions over only one issue!

But, hold on to your hat, that's not all! There is still the American dream: work hard, be a good citizen, pay your taxes, love your wife and kids and you will prosper. This sounds good and every Tea Partier—in fact, almost all Americans—support this dream. Some Americans want to adopt policies that make that dream come true. Not the Tea Party! Around 1.53 million Americans, 1 in 150, filed for bankruptcy protection in 2010.[146] The largest factor involved in individual bankruptcies is medical debt. You do work hard all your life; you buy a house and raise a family. Then, when you're 60, you get cancer. Who knows why? You have insurance that pays the bills until one day you've exceeded your annual limit on medical expenditures and the insurance company cancels your policy. You spouse's income will not support the mortgage and hospital expenses, so your house goes, then your savings are exhausted, then your retirement is wiped out. Soon you're totally bankrupt with absolutely no chance of recovery. All of this will be prevented with Obamacare. Insurance companies cannot place a limit on medical treatments. Opposing Obamacare is working in opposition to the American dream. The Tea Party is opposing what they are for! Along with the two contradictions above, this makes three comical contradictions over one issue! "A three-fer."

Global warming

Despite the opinion of the vast majority of climatologists, the shrinkage of the polar ice caps and melting of glaciers in Greenland, many Tea Partiers completely reject the idea of Global Warming. They oppose any regulation that would require expenditures by companies to limit carbon dioxide emissions. This is why the United States did not approve the Kyoto agreement that would limit greenhouse gas emissions or any regulation that would regulate carbon emissions. We only have one earth! We can protect it or we can destroy it so that some people can get rich. It is all our choice. What else do I need to say?

Immigration

"Build fences, check driver's licenses and deport all illegal immigrants." The Tea Party is strongly in favor of enforcing the immigration laws to its fullest extent despite the fact that immigrants— both legal and illegal—provide a valuable service in America. They work at a wage rate below where many Americans will work. In doing this, they help make products cheaper for the consumers; they pay into social security and Medicare and, by the way, help make larger profits for the owners.

There is a simple solution to the illegal immigration problem. There exists today a national database under the U.S. Citizenship and Immigration Service (USCIS), part of the Department of Homeland Security, called E-Verify (electronic verify). The database contains names, birthdates, and social security numbers of U.S. citizens as well as green card numbers of legal immigrants. Simply require that all businesses search E-Verify before hiring new employees. (Federal Law requires all government contractors to use E-Verify. The only states that presently require it are Arizona, Mississippi and South Carolina. In 2008, only 8 percent of all U.S. businesses used E-Verify.) If a potential employee is in the database, then hire them; if not, then don't. Simple. If the USCIS (I know, here comes big government again) investigates the business and finds the business employs individuals not in the database, then place heavy fines on the business. (Arizona can suspend or revoke business licenses for non-compliance, although as of 2009, it has not yet taken this action.) Implement this procedure and the immigration issue will go away. But it must be implemented nationwide, otherwise illegal workers will just move to other states. Oh, businesses won't like this! It places additional burdens on them because they have to learn how to use the system and to check on immigrant status and it will cut down on profit. The Tea Party wouldn't like it because it requires the BIG GOV to enforce the law and provides an impediment to businesses for making money. (In spite of the Tea Party, this is another example where big government can fulfill a useful purpose.)

However, E-Verify is not perfect yet. Some unauthorized workers are categorized as legal workers (false positive), mostly due to identity theft, and some qualified workers are categorized as unauthorized (false negative). However, the system has methods in place to manually verify adverse results. This system is the best we presently have and it is much better than stopping every Hispanic driver and asking for his driver's license. It could improve with time by adding fingerprints or pictures to the data files, for example. So, the Tea Party must decide: does it want to stop illegal immigrants by using E-Verify or does it want to protect businesses and reduce big government? They cannot have it both ways. Luckily, the decision will probably *not* be theirs.[147]

Conclusion

I remember years ago saying that the Environmental Protection Agency did more to take people's freedoms away than any other government agency in history. This was because recycling was becoming popular and people in some states were required to place recyclables in separate cans. How inconvenient. When the law requiring people to wear seatbelts while driving was enacted in New York State, I remember saying, "How can the state require me to wear seatbelts? That's against my personal liberties. I don't like wearing a seatbelt, they're uncomfortable." When the smoking laws prohibiting smoking in restaurants and bars and other public places were issued, I said, "How can the government tell people where to smoke?" I was irate, even though I'm not a smoker.

Over time though, I began to realize that the Mohawk River in New York was once again harboring fish: large and small mouth bass, pike, walleye as well as thousands of sunfish. My wife even caught a 50-inch tiger musky once. You could eat fish from the river once a week. This was because the EPA banded dumping pollution into the river. I also realized that recycling really is a good idea; it conserves our resources and reduces waste. Wearing seatbelts helps save lives, especially kids who are the most precious of all and it helps bring down car insurance premiums. Now I feel naked if I drive without a seatbelt. And banning smoking in public places is also a good idea. It reduces risks of getting lung disease from secondhand smoke and it makes eating in a restaurant so much more enjoyable. I can actually breathe while I'm eating.

It seems that the Tea Partiers never reach this "aha moment", this re-thinking stage in their maturing process. They grab onto their first gut reaction to a new proposal or idea and they cling onto it forever, never questioning their conclusion and never adding any facts to support their beliefs. This is the only way I can explain why seemingly intelligent and educated people can behave so irrationally.

I hope this discussion has helped clarify your considerations of the Tea Party and has shown that what the Tea Party believes is contradicted only by something else the Tea Party believes. But as Dilbert's boss said, "It makes you feel good."

CHAPTER 8

Debt And The Economy

The World Trade Center was destroyed on September 11, 2001. By October, we were dropping bombs in Afghanistan. Afghanistan provided a haven for the fanatic Taliban Muslim sect who, in turn, provided shelter for al Qaeda and Osama Bin Laden. We were justified in going after a terrorist organization that ruthlessly attacked the United States, killing about 3,000 Americans. However, war has a price, not only in lives, but also in treasury. As of the end of 2012, about $600 billion has been appropriated by Congress for fighting in Afghanistan.[148] There was no increase in taxes to help pay for this unplanned event and we were forced to borrow to pay for the war.

In 2003, President George W. Bush, along with Vice President Dick Cheney and Secretary of Defense Donald Rumsfeld, thought it was a good idea to go to war with Iraq, while simultaneously fighting the war in Afghanistan. Based on accusations that Iraq possessed weapons of mass destruction and was in league with al Qaeda terrorists—claims that later proved to be totally false—the United States waged war on Iraq from March 2003 to December 2011 when U.S. troops pulled out.

During that time, 4,486 United States military personnel were killed, about 50 percent more people than were killed in the World Trade Center. In addition, the "Iraq Body Count Project" estimates about 120,000 Iraqi civilians have been killed and it could actually be much higher.[149] The estimate of the total costs appropriated by Congress for the Iraq war and the war in Afghanistan is about $1.3 trillion. These are only the costs appropriated by Congress. If you included the cost of long-term care for veterans, continuing aid to Afghanistan and Iraq and interest on loans, the total cost is estimated to be $3.2 to $4.0 trillion and possibly as high as $6.0 trillion.[150] Once again, these funds were not paid for by the American taxpayer. Had Americans been asked to pay for the Iraq war with a tax increase, we probably would not have gone and many American and Iraqi lives would have been saved. However, just as in Afghanistan, we borrowed the money to pay for the Iraq war. From 2001, when Bush became President, to 2008 when he left, the Total Gross Federal Debt increased from $5.77 trillion to $10.0 trillion.

In 2008, in the midst of the Afghanistan and Iraq wars, the American financial industry came crumbling down like a sandcastle in a tsunami. The tsunami—fueled by lack of oversight on the derivative securities market, particularly Mortgage Backed Securities, the narcolepsy experienced by the investment rating companies like Standard & Poor and Moody's and criminal behavior of the largest financial companies—permitted the financial firms to offer mortgages to anyone who could apply. Subprime mortgages (i.e., mortgages to people who had a poor credit rating and probably could not pay off a mortgage) increased from about 10 percent of mortgages in 2003 to above 20 percent in 2006 and constituted about $1.3 trillion of investments. When people could no longer pay their mortgages, the castle crumbled. In 2008, the stock market fell by 20 percent, losing $8 trillion in the process. By 2010, unemployment rates reached over 10 percent with 15 million people out of work.

With people out of work, the country's finances suffered. Tax revenues dropped while people were out of work and wages fell. Additionally, tax expenditures increased as the government tried to stimulate the economy by placing more money into society. In early 2008, President Bush created the Economic Stimulus Act of 2008, which pumped $152 billion into the economy, mostly through tax rebates, in an attempt to forestall a downturn. Then in late 2008, TARP worth $700 billion was initiated to help bail out troubled banks. When President Obama took office, he instituted the American Recovery and Reinvestment Act, ARRA, spending $878 billion on a wide range of programs in an attempt to increase economic growth. All of these expenditures drove up the deficits and increased our nation's debt. When Bush left office in 2008, the Federal Debt was $10.0 trillion and by 2012, the debt was $16.0 trillion and climbing.

Although these are very large numbers, they don't really present a clear picture of the magnitude and severity of the debt. If your income is $50,000 per year and you have debts of $250,000, you are in a very bad position. If your income is $500,000 though, with debts of $250,000, you're in a much better position. In other words, you must compare the debt to something else, e.g., your income, to get an idea of your condition. The gross domestic product (GDP) is the measuring stick that's used to determine the severity of our debt. Now, having some debt can be a good thing. In the entire history of the U.S., 1835 is the only year that we've had no debt. Just as businesses fund future growth through borrowing, (e.g., businesses may borrow to build new facilities and buy new equipment or to fund bringing a new product to the marketplace) the government can also introduce new programs (e.g., modern controls for the electric energy grid, mass transportation and better transportation infrastructure) by borrowing. This allows these programs to be instituted faster and in doing so, provides needed services and facilities sooner. This is why a balanced budget amendment to the constitution is a really bad idea. However, Congress must have the fortitude to limit the debt to reasonable amounts. Fighting two wars at the same time without funding does not constitute "reasonable fortitude."

From 1960 to 1980, the debt-to-GDP ratio (the ratio of total debt to the gross-domestic-product) decreased from 56 percent to 33 percent. From 1980, the ratio rose back up to 67 percent in 1995 but by 2001 returned to 56 percent.[151] So except for a few years, the debt- to-GDP ratio has held between 30 percent and 60 percent. Table 1 below shows the debt-to-GDP ratio from 2000 onward. From 2001, the start of the Afghan War, until 2013, the debt-to-GDP ratio has increased continuously every year until it reached 106 percent of GDP in 2013. Our national debt exceeds all the money that this country makes in a year!

\multicolumn{3}{c}{Table 1}
\multicolumn{3}{c}{Total Federal Debt and Percentage of GDP from 2000[152]}
End of Fiscal Year	Total Federal Debt, in $Millions	Total Federal Debt, % of GDP
2000	$5,628,700	57.3%
2001	$5,769,881	56.4%
2002	$6,198,401	58.8%
2003	$6,760,014	61.6%
2004	$7,354,657	63.0%
2005	$7,905,300	63.6%
2006	$8,451,350	64.0%
2007	$8,950,744	64.6%
2008	$9,986,082	69.7%
2009	$11,875,851	85.1%
2010	$13,528,807	94.3%
2011	$14,764,222	98.9%
2012	$16,050,921	103.2%
2013	$17,249,239	106.5%

This is not a good situation. Everyone—Democrat, Republican, Tea Partier and Libertarian, whomever—will agree that having a debt- to-GDP ratio exceeding 100 percent is bad. This has happened before, though, in our history. Toward the end of World War II, between 1946 and 1947, when the country was producing mass quantities of weapons to fight Germany and Japan and was borrowing heavily to do so, the debt-to-GDP ratio was over 110 percent (almost 122 percent in 1946). As the troops came home, however, the demand for homes and new automobiles—stimulated by cheap loans for the military— surged while new industries such as aircraft and electronics flourished. The economy was growing at a healthy clip and the GDP along with it. Meanwhile, the national debt also grew, but at a much slower pace. Between the beginning of 1946 and the end of 1960 (fifteen years), the GDP grew at an average rate of 5.9 percent while the debt grew at a measly pace, averaging 0.46 percent. By 1960, the debt-to-GDP ratio was 56 percent and headed down to the 30 percent range for the entire decade of the 1970s.

Table 2
Total Federal Debt and Percentage of GDP, After WWII to 1970[153]

End of Fiscal Year	Total Federal Debt, in $Millions	Total Federal Debt, % of GDP
1945	$260,123	117.5%
1946	$270,991	121.7%
1947	$257,149	110.3%
1948	$252,031	98.2%
1949	$252,610	93.1%
1950	$256,853	94.1%
1951	$255,288	79.7%
1952	$259,097	74.3%
1953	$265,963	71.4%
1954	$270,812	71.8%
1955	$274,366	69.3%
1956	$272,693	63.9%
1957	$272,252	60.4%
1958	$279,666	60.8%
1959	$287,465	58.6%
1960	$290,525	56.0%
1961	$292,648	55.2%
1962	$302,928	53.4%
1963	$310,324	51.8%
1964	$316,059	49.3%
1965	$322,318	46.9%
1966	$328,498	43.5%
1967	$340,445	42.0%

1968	$368,685	42.5%
1969	$365,769	38.6%
1970	$380,921	37.6%

This is where we need to be! We need to get from a debt-to-GDP ratio of 106 percent in 2013, to a ratio of about 40 percent. Note how America extracted itself from the high debt-to-GDP ratio after World War II. The country was in a growing economy so that the rate at which the GDP was growing was higher than the rate at which the debt was growing, so the debt-to-GDP ratio went down. (When economists start talking about rates, some people's eyes glaze over. It is not the actual amount of debt or GDP we have, but the rate or speed at which they are changing. Since it's a ratio, if the top number - the debt, is changing at a slower pace that the bottom number - the GDP, the ratio will decrease and in time, get to an acceptable level. The key is the rate, or speed, the numbers are changing, not the actual values. (A debt of $16 trillion sounds like a tremendous burden but it's not if the GDP were $32 trillion.) Note too, how long it took. Fifteen years to get to a ratio of 56 percent and another ten years to get to the high 30 percent range. You can't change the direction of a moving ocean liner on a dime. If you could, the Titanic would have avoided the iceberg and been cruising the oceans for fifty years. Today (in early 2020) the Gross Domestic Product according to the Bureau of Economic Analysis is $21.54 trillion and the national debt is $22 trillion, a ratio of $22T/21.54T = 1.02. The national debt is the largest it has even been and is growing. We are not in great shape, but we've been here before and survived. Now is the time to take action.

How do we get out of this mess? The Republican way.

The question now is how do we get out of our debt situation? Republicans believe that the industrial giants control industry: the J.P. Morgans, John D. Rockefellers, Andrew Carnegies and Cornelius Vanderbilts of today. They argue that *lowering* taxes on the wealthy— along with reduced government regulations on businesses—will result in economic growth, creation of jobs and *increased* tax revenues. You might think that lowering taxes would lower the tax revenues, not increase them. However, some Republicans and Tea Partiers theorize that if the taxes are too high, at some point the industrialists and entrepreneurs lose their incentive to make more money and, consequently, to build the economy. By lowering taxes, the entrepreneur's incentive will be restored and the economy and tax revenues will flourish. Lowering taxes on rich businessmen will provide more money to invest. That will spur the economy, bring in more profit and the tax revenues will actually *increase*. This philosophy of heavy dependency on production is known as "Supply-side Economics" and is the keystone of Republican economy philosophy. Supply-side Economics has come to be known as the "trickle down economy." Humorist Will Rogers is quoted as saying, "The money was all appropriated for the top in the hopes it would trickle down to the needy," when supply-side economics was used during the Great Depression in the 1920s. But the big question is does it work?

Consider yourself to be a "Big Business Man," a captain of industry. You make "Double Barreled Slingshots." You're Don Dunker, President of the Double Barreled Slingshots (DBS) Company. Now all of a sudden the country goes into a recession and Congress says that they're going to reduce your taxes to encourage business production and stimulate the economy. They reduce your taxes from 30 percent to 20 percent. You have a multi-state operation and are producing about a thousand DBS per month. However, suppose you're not selling them all. You only sell about 90 percent of production. What are the chances that you're going to hire new employees? I'd say close to zero. You might invest that money in another company's common stock to grow your own wealth or you might invest the money in advertisement for your slingshots but you're not going to hire new employees.

In fact, you might lay off a worker since you're only selling 90 percent of your product or you might investigate having the slingshots made in China or Indonesia. As a businessman, your job is to keep the cost of making the slingshots as low as possible and to sell them as high as the market can bear.

Now let's consider another scenario. Let's say that you're producing your slingshots and they're selling like "hotcakes," you sell all that you produce. Do you think you will hire new employees to help make more? Do you think you might even add a new production line to increase production to two thousand slingshots a month? If the demand is high and you're selling all you make, you could sell more if you made more. You probably would increase production and increase your employees. So we see that the demand for products plays a huge role in determining the economy level. We saw that after World War II. When all the troops came home, they were hungry for new cars and new homes. The demand for products significantly increased above the demand that existed during the war and the economic level and GDP grew.

So let's look at how tax rates have influenced economic growth and the deficit in the United States. First let's look at the tax rates on the wealthy. Table 3 below presents examples of the highest tax bracket for those wealthy people filing as "Married Filing Jointly."

Year	Table 3 Highest Personal Income Tax Bracket for "Married Filing Jointly" for various years[154]	President
1941	81% for income over $5,000,000	Roosevelt
1942	88% for income over $200,000	Roosevelt
1944	94% for income over $200,000	Roosevelt
1949	91% for income over $400,000	Truman
1963	91% for income over $400,000	Johnson
1964	77% for income over $400,000	Johnson
1965	70% for income over $200,000	Johnson
1981	70% for income over $215,400	Reagan
1982	50% for income over $85,600	Reagan
1987	38.5% for income over $90,000	Reagan
1988	28% for income over $29,750	Reagan
1991	31% for income over $82,150	George H.W. Bush
1993	39.6% for income over $250,000	Clinton
2003	35% for income over $319,100	George W. Bush
2013	39.6% for income over $450,000	Obama

At the beginning of World War II, the tax rates were increased to help pay for the war and the Great Depression At the end of the war in 1944, the highest tax rate for "Married Filing Jointly" was 94 percent of all income over $200,000. Can you believe that! I remember when I was in high school someone told me that the highest tax levels were in the 90 percent range; I remember it because I was shocked. Although I knew little about paying taxes, since I hadn't earned enough to pay any yet, I knew that paying 94 percent in taxes is draconian and ridiculous! Who wants to work if the government takes 94 percent of everything you earn above $200,000 (about $2.6 million in present day dollars) away from you? The fact of the matter is, for twenty years—from 1944 through 1963—the tax rate on the highest tax bracket was over 90 percent. Up through 1981, the highest tax rate was still above 70 percent. "Supply side" theorists would predict that high taxes would reduce earnings, depress the economy and GDP and reduce tax receipts. But this is NOT what happened! Look at table 4 below of federal receipts from personal income taxes and the nation's GDP from 1941 to the end of 1981. The GDP during this period rose at an average rate of 8.36 percent per year (much higher than the nominal 3 to 4 percent) and the tax receipts rose at an even higher average rate of 14.40 percent per year.

Table 4: Income Taxes Received and GDP, 1941 to 1981[155]

Year	Receipts from Personal Income Taxes in Millions of Dollars[1]	GDP[1] in Millions of Dollars	Year	Receipts from Personal Income Taxes in Millions of Dollars[1]	GDP[1] in Millions of Dollars
1941	$1,314	$129,400	1961	$41,338	$563,300
1942	$3,263	$166,000	1962	$45,571	$605,100
1943	$6,505	$203,100	1963	$47,588	$638,600
1944	$19,705	$224,600	1964	$48,697	$685,800
1945	$18,372	$228,200	1965	$48,792	$743,700
1946	$16,098	$227,800	1966	$55,446	$815,000
1947	$17,935	$249,900	1967	$61,526	$861,700
1948	$19,315	$274,800	1968	$68,726	$942,500
1949	$15,552	$272,800	1969	$87,249	$1,019,900
1950	$15,755	$300,200	1970	$90,412	$1,075,900
1951	$21,616	$347,300	1971	$86,230	$1,167,800
1952	$27,934	$376,700	1972	$94,737	$1,282,400
1953	$29,816	$389,700	1973	$103,246	$1,428,500
1954	$29,542	$391,100	1974	$118,952	$1,548,800
1955	$28,747	$426,200	1975	$122,386	$1,688,900
1956	$32,188	$450,100	1976	$131,603	$1,877,600
1957	$35,620	$474,900	1977	$157,626	$2,086,000
1958	$34,724	$482,000	1978	$180,988	$2,356,600
1959	$36,719	$522,500	1979	$217,841	$2,632,100
1960	$40,715	$543,300	1980	$244,069	$2,862,500
			1981	$285,917	$3,210,900

			Avg Rate for 40 yrs	14.40% (9.52% in 2009 dollars)	8.36%
			(3.80% in 2009 dollars)		

[1]) Dollars are in "then year" or "current" dollars, i.e. not adjusted for inflation

These percentages do not include the effects of inflation. If the inflation rate increases, as it almost always does, the cost of items people and the government buy also increase. So to get the same quantity of items you must pay more, i.e. taxes revenues must increase. If the inflation rate and tax revenues were the same, you couldn't buy any more items than you did before. The "real" value of your money would be the same. So you must remove the effects of inflation to determine the value your money really has. Accounting for inflation, using 2009 as the reference year for the dollar value, the "real" growth in GDP from 1941 to 1981 is 3.80 percent and in tax revenues is 9.52 percent, both very healthy numbers. The difference is the average annual rate of inflation, 4.40 percent.

Even though a 90 percent tax rate is awful, the personal income tax receipts actually grew at a very rapid pace. This is exactly the opposite of what "supply-side" would predict. "Supply side" would predict that with high taxes on the rich, the tax receipts would fall and the economy would perform poorly. What we see is the tax receipts rapidly increasing and the GDP growing at a healthy rate right alongside it.

To test "supply-side economics" further, I have summarized in table 5 the average annual change in personal income tax receipts and average change in GDP over a number of years. Starting first with years 1941 to 1981 as shown in table 4 and then in succeeding years whenever the tax rate on the wealthy changed significantly. This table compares how changes in tax rates on the wealthiest taxpayers affect the rate of tax receipts and economic growth on the country as indicated by the GDP. (Please don't slam this book on the ground and run away as fast as you can, the mathematics here is not complicated. For those who are interested, an appendix to this chapter presents the details of the table.)

Year Span	Tax rate of the highest tax bracket	Average annual % change in Personal Income Tax Receipts during the years span	Average annual % change in GDP during the years span	Average annual % change in taxes constant 2009 dollars	Average annual % change in GDP constant 2009 dollars	Comments
1941 to 1981	tax rate remained above 70% for 40 years, above 90% for 19 of those years	14.40%	8.36%	9.52%	3.80%	40 years following World War II.
1982 to 1990	tax rates of 70% reduced to 28% over 6yrs	5.78%	7.53%	2.32%	4.01%	Reagan tax cuts, George H. W. Bush increased taxes in 1991 & 1992 to 31%.
1993 to 2000	tax rates increased from 31% to 39.6%	10.18%	5.92%	8.23%	4.06%	Clinton increased taxes by 8.6%, which remained until 2000.

Table 5: Summary of Federal Tax Receipts and GDP Growth Resulting from Changes in Tax Rates on the Wealthy

2001 to 2008	tax rates reduced from 39.6% to 35% over 3 years	2.05%	4.77%	-0.53%	2.26%	George W. Bush reduced taxes to 35%, which remained in place until 2012. Recession starts in 2008.
2009 to 2012	tax rates remain at 35%	7.35%	4.06%	5.60%	2.38%	End of recession. Obama institutes stimulus spending.

For those less mathematically inclined, in the discussion below I'll refer to rate of growth, specifically the average rate of growth each year or average annual growth rate. What I'm talking about is not the actual numerical value of the tax receipt or GDP but how fast it is growing or declining. Consider this. Suppose you have $1.00 invested and it accumulates interest at a rate of 5.0 percent each year. I've prepared a brief table so you can see how the initial dollar you invested will grow.

Beginning	$1.00
End of year 1	$1.05 ($1.00 x 5% or $1.00 x 1.05)
End of year 2	$1.1025 (NOT just $1.05 + $1.05 = $1.1000 because the interest is compounded. It is $1.05 x 1.05 = $1.1025)
End of year 3	$1.1576 ($1.1025 x 1.05)
End of year 4	$1.2155 ($1.1576 x 1.05)
End of year 5	$1.2763 ($1.2155 x 1.05)

In this example, the average annual growth rate is 5.0 percent. In the real world of tax receipts and GDP, the growth rate is NOT the same each year; it changes. But not to worry, I can figure out what the average annual rate (i.e. the average rate over many years) must be. So that's what I'm talking about, the average rate of change over several years. That wasn't too bad, was it?

Notice the following from the summary table:

1. The average annual rate of growth for income tax receipts between 1941 and 1981, a time when tax rates on the rich were draconian and higher than any other time, was 14.4 percent (9.52 percent in terms of constant 2009 dollars). And note that the GDP grew at an average rate of 8.36 percent (3.80 percent in constant 2009 dollars), a very respectable increase. Supply side would predict a low GDP because of the high taxes but this is not what happened.

2. When Reagan reduced taxes by 42 percent on the wealthiest Americans between 1982 and 1990, income tax revenue rates declined from 9.52 percent to 2.32 percent (in terms of constant year dollars) while the GDP grew slightly from 3.80 percent to 4.01 percent. Supply-side theory would predict that GDP growth would increase and it did. However, the theory also requires that by lowering the taxes on the rich, the rate of taxes receipts would rise because more money was being investigated in the economy.. This is definitely not what happened; they fell from an average of 9.52 percent increase per year to an average of 2.32 percent increase per year.

3. However, in the 1990s (from 1993 to 2000), when Clinton again increased taxes on the rich, both annual rates of tax receipts and GDP growth rates grew, 8.23

percent and 4.06 percent respectively, in terms of constant 2009 dollars. Again, not what the supply-side theory would predict.

4. When George W. Bush again reduced taxes on the rich by 8.6 percent between 2001 and 2008, the annual rate of tax receipts were actually decreasing by 0.5 percent each year in terms of constant 2009 dollars. The real economic growth dropped from 4.06 percent to a sluggish 2.26 percent.

5. Between 2009 and 2012, the financial stimulus effort was in play. During this period, the tax rates on the rich remained unchanged at 35 percent. In spite of the high unemployment and depressed economy during these recession burdened years, the tax receipts and GDP did manage small increases in real terms, to a 5.60 percent growth rate in tax receipts and 2.38 percent growth rate in GDP. This growth could not be due to tax policy since taxes on all brackets remained constant during this period. Based on the tax receipts results we've observed in previous years, had Obama increased taxes on the wealthy in 2008 from 35 percent to say 40 percent, (possible since the Senate and House were controlled by the Democrats) our growth rate, tax receipts and debt would have been in far better condition.

The conclusion reached by this discussion is that:
- High taxes on the wealthiest—as exhibited after WWII and the Clinton tax increase—does not necessarily result in lower federal tax revenues or economic growth.
- Low taxes on the wealthiest—as shown by Reagan and George W. Bush's tax cuts—does not necessarily result

in higher revenues or growth. In fact, it seems that high taxes result in higher revenues and higher growth.

The analysis above shows that in only one case did the economy grow after a tax rate reduction on the rich, 1982 to 1988, when the real GDP rate grew a small amount from 3.80 percent to 4.01 percent. In every other case, for the past fifty years, when tax rates on the wealthy increased, the tax revenues and GDP increased at a higher rate than before and when the tax rate decreased, the tax receipts and GDP rates declined. By "Supply Side" theory, the taxes and GDP should increase.

Another way, Keynesian Economics.
There is another way to increase employment, grow the economy and increase tax revenues. In 1936, John Maynard Keynes, a British economist, published a theory that championed raising "aggregate demand" to grow the economy. In other words, implement policies that will encourage people to buy products. Rather than trying to drive the economy from the top down by supplying more products whether the demand exists or not; drive the economy from the bottom, up. How do you spur demand? The classic example is construction projects. The government encourages highways, airports, waste treatment facilities, power generation plants, and all types of municipal projects by giving tax incentives and lower interest loans to construction companies. These projects put people to work, deducting unemployment and putting more money into middle class working people's pocket which they then go out and spend. Thus the demand increases, the economy increases, the GDP increases and with people having more money, the tax receipts increases. As we saw in the chapter on the "Financial Crisis," this is exactly what President Roosevelt did to help stem the tide of the Great Depression. He implemented the Work Progress Administration, the Civil Conservation Corps and the Tennessee Valley Authority to put people back to work in order to increase the demand.

In more modern times, the government has developed a more flexible array of alternatives to increase demand. President Bush, for example, used the "Economic Stimulus Act" that provided tax rebates worth about $152 billion to put money in people's hands to increase demand. President Obama instituted the American Recovery and Reinvestment Act worth $787 billion, which provided stimulus funds for student loans, tax credits, extended unemployment, infrastructure projects, scientific research and many other projects. Additionally, the government has provided extended unemployment benefits for those chronically unemployed and has provided "tax holidays" from payroll deductions for social security and Medicare to provide more "bring home pay" for workers.

These stimulus efforts, however, cost money; the government is providing funds to the citizens to help growth in the economy. This is what part of Keynesian economics requires; during a recession the government purposefully runs deficit budgets to get the economy going. Then when times are better, the debt is paid down, just as we did after WWII. It's the deficit spending part of this theory, though, that drives the Republicans bonkers. At least until the time of President Trump.

There's a good reason that Keynesian (aggregate demand) Economics works better than Supply-side Economics.

One of the main reasons that government spending and stimulus money is more effective at increasing the economy and raising employment than tax reductions on the wealthy is contained in the concept of "fiscal multipliers." When the government extends the eligibility period for unemployment insurance, for example, it provides funds to the unemployed to help with food and housing. These unemployed people spend that money, almost all of it. Some of the money that goes to the grocery store or landlord also gets spent on more grocery stock, on employee paychecks and on electric bills. In turn, the grocery supplier and the electric company spend some of that money. The effect of this process is that a dollar spent by the unemployed is actually spent over and over again and effectively has a multiplied result, multiplying the original dollar by an additional percentage increase. The fact that the same dollar can actually increase its economic worth above $1.00 (or below $1.00) is called the "fiscal multiplier." The "fiscal multiplier" is determined by the increase in the GDP resulting from a specific amount of government spending or tax reduction. The multiplier is dependent on the consumer's desire to either spend the money or to save it. If the consumer spends the money such as those on welfare and the unemployed, the multiplier is above 1.0. If the consumer saves the money or if the government policies actually encourage the consumer to save, such as tax cuts, or if the deficit spending creates uncertainty in the consumer, the "multiplier" can be less than 1.0.

There have been many studies—both for the U.S. and for other countries—to determine the magnitude of the "fiscal multiplier" and to determine what government economic policies best suit an economic condition. A good example was developed by Mark Zandi, chief economist of Moody's Analytics.[156] Here are the results:

- Tax rebate　　　　　　　　　　　　　　　　1.0/1.3
- Payroll tax holiday (social security, Medicare)　1.3
- Extension of unemployment insurance　1.6' benefits

(The U.S. Department of Labor estimates a factor of 2 for unemployment insurance.)

- Temporary increase in food stamps payment　1.7
- General aid to states　　　　　　　　　　　1.4
- Infrastructure spending　　　　　　　　　　1.6
- Tax cuts　　　　　　　　　　　　　　　　　1.0
- Accelerated depreciation　　　　　　　　　0.3
- Extension of alternative minimum tax　　　0.5

- Bush's income tax cuts 0.3
- Dividend/capital gains tax cut 0.4
- Cut in corporate income tax rate 0.3

Note that every stimulus type action taken by the government, such as tax rebates, extending unemployment insurance and increasing food stamps has a multiplier at 1.0 or above. For every dollar spent, there is at least one dollar or more increased in the economy, i.e. GDP. For every tax reduction, the people tend to save their higher tax refund and there is a multiplier of one or less. This general conclusion, that deficit spending and stimulus money usually have a multiplier greater than one while tax reductions generally have a multiplier less than one, has been found in many studies.

This small analysis is somewhat mathematical I know, but the bottom line is that tax reductions are ineffective at increasing the economy of a nation. This agrees with the comparison between taxes and GDP in the paragraphs above. Tax reductions are ineffective because many people tend to save additional money they receive from their tax refund. This is only common sense. People with lower incomes will spend any additional funds they receive while middle income and wealthy people tend to save any tax refund. And this is especially true of the wealthy. After all, they already have everything they want, so why spend it? Invest it and make more money. From the eyes of the wealthy, you can never have too much money.

Money policy and quantitative easing.

In addition to using financial methods, i.e. tax policy and spending measures, to encourage growth, Keynesian Economics also depends on monetary policies to help growth. In other words, by using the Federal Reserve Bank, the government can adjust interest rates to increase economic growth. First, the Federal Reserve can lower the *short-term* interest rate it charges commercial banks to borrow money. (This is the Federal Fund Rate we discussed in the chapter on Financial Crisis.) So when the commercial bank borrows a billion dollars from the Fed, the bank only pays 1.0 percent on the loan instead of 1.25 percent interest. Furthermore, the long-term loans, used by corporations for long-term investments and people for mortgages, are tied to the short-term loans. Long-term loans are riskier, so the interest paid for a long-term loan is higher. However, the interest rate for long-term loans starts with the short-term rate and then increases the short-term rate based on supply and demand in the bond market and what the bond buyers expect the additional rate should be. So, lower short-term rates will indirectly result in a lower long-term rate. The commercial banks can then pass along this lower interest to its borrowers. This obviously encourages companies to borrow money for new investments and encourages homebuyers to buy new homes at a lower interest or refinance their homes. These investments and loans, in turn, help the economy to grow.

However, you can only lower interest rates so far; they cannot get below 0.0 percent interest. When the interest rate nears 0.0 percent, there is another monetary policy that can be used called "quantitative easing." This is exactly what Ben Bernanke, chairman of the Federal Reserve, has been doing since 2008. Here's how that works. The Federal Reserve buys large quantities of long-term securities, mostly government bonds and mortgage backed securities, from banks. By large quantities, I mean billions of dollars worth. In 2013, the Fed was buying $85 billion of securities *each month*. Buying these securities does two things. First, it increases banks liquidity (the money they have on hand) and allows them to make more loans. The money goes into the economy and increases the money supply. If people have more money, they spend it and that helps increase economic growth. Also, a larger money supply helps makes the cost of American goods cheaper in foreign countries. (If there are more dollars, then Germans can get more dollars for his/her Deutsche Mark, which makes it cheaper for Germans.) This helps the American economy.

Second, by buying large amounts of securities (mortgage backed securities or treasury bonds), it drives the demand for these securities upward. When the demand increases, the costs of the securities increase. When the costs of the securities increase, the yield (i.e. interest rate the bond pays) decreases. Here's why: Suppose you buy a 10-year, $10,000 bond with a 5 percent yield, i.e. interest rate. At 5 percent, the $10,000 will pay $500 per year and at the end of the ten years, the $10,000 will be returned to you. However, you don't have to wait for the entire ten years to sell the bond. You can sell it at any time. So suppose before the bond matures (i.e. the 10-year period) the demand for bonds has increased and the value of the bond is now

$11,000. However, the annual dividend will still be only $500. So your effective yield is $500/$11,000 or 4.5 percent. The yield has gone down. Because the bond is a fixed income security, if the bond price goes up, the yield goes down; if the bond price goes down, the yield goes up. So, with lower yields, companies can now issue new bonds at lower rates and people wanting to buy homes can get lower rates on mortgages. Also, it encourages people who have invested in bonds to dump the bonds because of their low yields, and invest in corporate stocks and corporate bonds and therefore boost the economy.

Although "quantitative easing" seems like it might work in theory, it has its risks. Most important is that putting large quantities of money into the economy encourages inflation. So far, inflation has not been a problem; inflation for November 2013 was 1.2 percent while the historic average inflation rate is 3 percent to 4 percent. However, with the economy gaining ground, the Fed announced at the end of 2013 that the quantitative easing program would be scaled back. When this happens, bond prices will decline and yields will increase and people holding bonds will see the value of their bonds decline.

Effects of economic policies and wealth inequality.

Since the early 1980s, the inequality in wealth and income between the middle class and the wealthy has increased significantly. The wealthy has gained tremendous riches during this period while the middle class has fallen behind. This increase in wealth inequality is partly due to tax policies favoring the wealthy.

In terms of income, i.e. periodic payments that people receive through work plus dividends, interest, rent, etc.

- In 1976, the top 1 percent of earners received about 9 percent of the income.
- By 2007, however, the top 1 percent earned 23.5 percent (a 260 percent increase) of the income in the U.S.

Since 1979, the average pre-tax income for the bottom 90 percent of households has actually declined by $900 in terms of inflation adjusted dollars, while the average income of the top 1 percent in 2009 was $960,000.[157]

In terms of net wealth, i.e. stocks, bonds, financial securities, houses, etc.

- In 1976, the top 1 percent of Americans processed about 20 percent of the wealth.[158]
- In 2007, the richest 1 percent of Americans owned 34.6 percent of the wealth and the next 19 percent owned the next 50.5 percent. So the top 20 percent of the wealthiest Americans own 85 percent of the entire wealth of the country. The remaining 80 percent own only 15 percent.[159]

IF U.S. LAND MASS WERE DIVIDED LIKE U.S. WEALTH

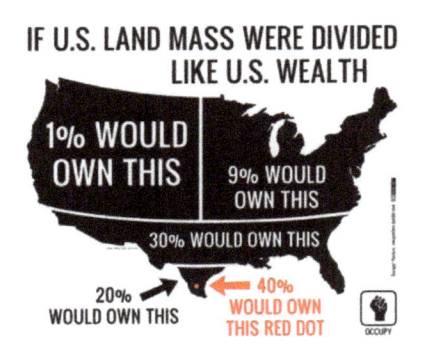

1% WOULD OWN THIS
9% WOULD OWN THIS
30% WOULD OWN THIS
20% WOULD OWN THIS
40% WOULD OWN THIS RED DOT

This graphic was created by Stephen Ewen and licensed under GNU Free Documentation, published here with permission from Stephen Ewen.

This inequality is largely due to unequal access to wealth and to government policies that favor the increase in wealth of the rich at the expense of the middle class.

All Americans should be upset by this tremendous disparity in income and wealth. Not only is it unfair but it is bad for the country; a true democracy depends on a thriving and healthy middle class and requires that no group of individuals possess more influence on the government than any other group. However, American citizens—both liberals and conservatives—seem numb to the situation. We don't seem to care that we've been cheated and robbed of our deserved rewards for hard work. In fact, many of us seem to support the tremendous prosperity of the wealthy.

APPENDIX: How the Tax Rate on the Rich Affect Tax Receipts and Economic Growth, 1982 to 2012

In 1982, President Reagan, a big proponent of "supply-side economics" (hence the name Reagonomics) passed the Economic Recovery Tax Act (ERTA). The tax reduction affected all taxpayers. The middle class got a 2 percent to 4 percent tax decrease and the top bracket received a 20 percent tax reduction, from

70 percent to 50 percent. In 1987, Reagan produced his second round of tax cuts, from 50 percent to 38.5 percent for the top income bracket (above $90,000) and then to a simple two-tier system in 1988: 15 percent below $29,750 and 28 percent above $29,750 ($57,735 in 2012 dollars). The 28 percent, two-tier system remained in effect until 1991 when taxes under George H.W. Bush increased to 31 percent and then 39.6 percent in 1993.

So during Reaganomics, the tax rate on the highest tax bracket decreased from 70 percent to 28 percent, a 42 percentage point drop in tax rate. This is a significant tax reduction on the wealthy and according to "supply-side," the tax receipts and economy should grow by significant proportions. So how did the government tax receipts and the economy do during this eight-year period, 1982 to 1990, when the tax rates decreased?

\multicolumn{4}{c}{Receipts and GDP, 1982 to 1990}
Year	Receipts from Personal Income Taxes in Million of Dollars[1]	GDP[1]) in Million of Dollars	
1982	$297,744	$3,345,000	Reagan's 1st tax cut, 70% to 50%
1983	$288,938	$3,638,100	
1984	$298,415	$4,040,700	
1985	$334,531	$4,367,000	
1986	$348,959	$4,590,100	
1987	$392,557	$4,870,200	Reagan's 2nd tax cut, 50% to 38.5%
1988	$401,181	$5,252,600	Reagan's 3rd tax cut, 38.5% to 28%
1989	$445,690	$5,657,700	George H.W. Bush President

1990	$466,884	$5,979,600	H.W. Bush increased rate to 31% in 1991
Avg Rate for 8 years	5.78% (2.32% in 2009 dollars)	7.53% (4.01% in 2009 dollars)	

[1] Dollars are in "then year" dollars, i.e. not adjusted for inflation

As you can see from the table above, tax receipts fell during the first year of Reagan's tax cut but then picked up for an average growth rate of 5.78 percent during the eight years (accounting for inflation, a "real" increase of 2.32 percent in 2009 dollars). The GDP grew at an average rate of 7.53 percent (4.01 percent "real" growth, 2009 dollars). These are respectable growth rates but represent a significant decrease from the 9.52 percent (real) average tax receipts rate following WWII. Meanwhile, the economic growth rate did increase to 4.01 percent from 3.80 percent following the war.

In 1991 and 1992, the tax rate on the upper tax bracket remained at 31 percent under President George H. W. Bush. When Clinton took office in 1993, Congress increased taxes on the top bracket to 39.6 percent, an 8.6 percentage point increase, which remained in place until 2000. So let's look at what happened to tax revenues and the GDP between 1993 and 2000, seven years, when taxes on the rich were 39.6 percent.

Receipts and GDP, 1993 to 2000			
Year	Receipts from Personal Income Taxes in Million of Dollars[1]	GDP[1] in Million of Dollars	
1993	$509,680	$6,878,700	Clinton Presidency, top bracket increase to 39.6%
1994	$543,055	$7,308,700	
1995	$590,244	$7,664,000	
1996	$656,417	$8,100,200	
1997	$737,466	$8,608,500	
1998	$828,586	$9,089,100	
1999	$879,480	$9,665,700	
2000	$1,004,462	$10,289,700	
Avg Rate for 7 years	10.18% (8.23% in 2009 dollars)	5.92% (4.06% in 2009 dollars)	

Under Clinton's tax increases, the tax receipts increased to a real rate of 8.23 percent while the GDP rate increased 4.06 percent. So giving a large tax *reduction* of 42 percent on the wealthiest Americans under Reagan, the tax revenues increased at a "real" rate of 2.32 percent. Meanwhile, given only an 8.6 percent *increase* on the same Americans under Clinton, the "real" tax receipts increased to 8.23 percent. The economic growth rate (GDP) under both administrations held constant at a little over 4 percent.

In 2001, George W. Bush resumed tax reductions until they reached 35 percent in 2003 and remained at that level until 2012. In 2008, the financial crisis and recession recovery started. From the table below, the tax reduction in 2001, 2002 and 2003 actually resulted in the decrease in receipts even though the economy was advancing. The average rate of tax receipts during these seven years actually decreased in real dollars (-0.53 percent, because inflation rate was higher than tax revenue rate) while the economy increased at an average rate of 2.26 percent.

Receipts and GDP, 2001 to 2008			
Year	Receipts from Personal Income Taxes in Million of Dollars[1]	GDP[1] in Million of Dollars	
2001	$994,339	$10,625,300	Bush President, 1st tax cut, top bracket 39.1%
2002	$858,345	$10,980,200	Bush President, 2nd tax cut, top bracket 38.6%
2003	$793,699	$11,512,200	Bush tax cut fully implemented, top bracket 35%
2004	$808,959	$12,277,000	
2005	$927,222	$13,095,400	
2006	$1,043,908	$13,857,900	
2007	$1,163,472	$14,480,300	
2008	$1,145,747	$14,720,300	Financial Crisis starts
Avg Rate for 7 yrs	2.05% (-0.53% in 2009 dollars)	4.77% (2.26% in 2009 dollars)	

When Obama took the Presidency in 2008, he initiated the American Recovery and Reinvestment Act, which funded the economy with $878 billion dollars. During this time the tax rate on the rich remained at 35 percent. Even though the tax receipts declined from 2007 to 2010 because 10 percent of the people were without work, the GDP, after declining from 2008 to 2009, increased steadily from 2009 to 2012 at an average real rate of 2.38 percent.

\multicolumn{4}{c}{**Receipts and GDP, 2001 to 2008**}
Year	**Receipts from Personal Income Taxes in Million of Dollars1)**	**GDP1) in Million of Dollars**	
2009	$915,308	$14,417,900	Obama President, ARRA initiated
2010	$898,549	$14,958,300	
2011	$1,091,473	$15,533,800	
2012	$1,132,206	$16,244,600	
	7.35% (5.60% in 2009 dollars)	4.06% (2.38% in 2009 dollars)	

BIBLIOGRAPHY

"2012 Presidential Campaign Financial Explorer." *The Washington* Post, December 7, 2012. http://www.washingtonpost.com/wp-srv/special/politics/campaign-finance/. (accessed October14, 2013).

Alter, Jonathan. "Obama HasToo Much Faith in Meritocrats." *Newsweek*, May 22, 2009. http://www.newsweek.com/alter-obama- has-too-much-faith-meritocrats-80051.

Alter, Jonathan. "Obama Must Make Insurers Compete." *Newsweek*, June 19, 2009. http://www.newsweek.com/alter-obama-must-make-insurers-compete-80429.

Amadeo, Kimberley. USeconomy.about.com, "FY 2012 U.S. Federal Government Budget." Last modified October 24, 2013. Accessed November 20, 2013. http://useconomy.about.com/od/usfederalbudget/p/US-Government-Federal- Budget-FY2012-Summary.htm.

Amadeo, Kimberley. USeconomy.about.com, "How Do Bonds Affect Mortgage Interest Rates." Last modified August 22, 2013. Accessed August 6, 2013. http://useconomy.about.com/od/ bondsfaq/f/Bonds_Mortgages.htm.

American Lung Association, "General Smoking Facts." Last modified June 2011. Accessed August 16, 2012. http://

www.lung.org/stop-smoking/about-smoking/facts-figures/general-smoking-facts.html.

Armstrong, Karen. *Islam: A Short History*. New York: Random House, 2000.

"The Asbestos Epidemic in America." *Environmental Working Group*. http://www.ewg.org/asbestos/facts/fact1.php (accessed August 13, 2012).

"Asbestos Litigation-History." *USLegal.com*. http://asbestoslitigation.uslegal.com/asbestos-litigation-history/ (accessed July 24, 2012).

Barry, Patricia. "Retooling Medicare." *AARP Bulletin*, June 2012, p.8. http://assets.aarp.org/rgcenter/general/52412_june_bulletin_retooling_medicare.pdf.

Begala, Paul. "Supreme Arrogance: Five Supreme Court Justices Put Our Health Care On The Line." *Newsweek*, April 2, 2012. http://www.newsweek.com/five-supreme-court-justices-put-our-health-care-line-63973.

Begley, Sharon. "The Five Biggest Lies in the Health Care Debate." *Newsweek*, September 2, 2009. http://www.sharonlbegley.com/the-top-5-lies-about-obama-s-health-care-reform-1 (accessed August 28, 2009).

Begley, Sharon. "The Truth About Obama's Health Plan." *Newsweek*, August 14, 2009. http://www.newsweek.com/truth-about-obamas-health-plan-79089.

Bergen, Peter L. *HolyWar, Inc. Inside the Secret World of Osama Bin Laden*. NewYork: Simon & Schuster, 2002.

Bleeker, Eric. The Motley Fool, "The Tragedy of Facebook: How Wall Street Robbed Main Street America." Last modified May 25, 2012. http://www.fool.com/investing/general/2012/05/25/the-tragedy-of-facebook-how-wall-street-robbed-ma.aspx.

"A brief history of tobacco." *CNN*. http://edition.cnn.com/US/9705/ tobacco/history/ (accessed January 24, 2009).

"Brief Summary of the Dodd-Frank Wall Street Reform and Consumer Protection Act." *Senate Committee on Banking,*

Housing and Urban Affairs, Chairman Chris Dodd (D-CT). http://www.banking.senate.gov/public/_files/070110_Dodd_Frank_Wall_Street_Reform_comprehensive_summary_Final.pdf.

Brill, Steven. "Bitter Pill: Why Medical Bills are Killing Us." *Time Magazine*, April 4, 2013. http://time.com/198/bitter-pill-why-medical-bills-are-killing-us/.

Brown, Paul. *Notes From a Dying Planet, 2002-2006*. Lincoln: iUniverse, 2006.

"The Budget and Economic Outlook: Fiscal Years 2013 to 2023." *Congressional Budget Office.* pp. 8-32. http://www.cbo.gov/sites/default/files/cbofiles/attachments/43907-BudgetOutlook.pdf.

"The Campaign Legal Center Guide to the Current Rules for Federal Elections." *The Campaign Legal Center*, 2012. http://www.campaignlegalcenter.org/images/THE_CAMPAIGN_LEGAL_CENTER_GUIDE_TO_THE_CURRENT_RULES_FOR_FEDERAL_ELECTIONS_10-25-12.pdf.

Center for Disease Control and Prevention, "Facts on Second Hand Smoke." Last modified April 11, 2014. http://www.cdc.gov/tobacco/data_statistics/fact_sheets/secondhand_smoke/general_facts/.

Chait, Jonathan. "War on the Weak." *Newsweek*, April 10, 2011. http://www.newsweek.com/war-weak-66573 (accessed April 18, 2011).

Clinton, Bill. "It's still the Economy, Stupid." *Newsweek*, June 19, 2011. http://www.newsweek.com/its-still-economy-stupid-67899.

Colliver, Victoria. "Misconception over key issues at core of debate." *SF Gate*, August 17, 2009. http://www.sfgate.com/health/article/Misconception-over-key-issues-at-core-of-debate-3289037.php (accessed August 29, 2009).

Congressional Budget Office, "CBO's Estimate of ARRA's Economic Impact." Last modified February 22, 2012. http://www.cbo.gov/publication/43014.

-----Congressional Budget Office, "Estimated Impact of the American Recovery and ReinvestmentAct on Employment and Economic Output from April 2011 Through June 2011." Last modified August 24, 2011. http://www.cbo.gov/publication/41147.

-----Congressional Budget Office, "Letter to Nancy Pelosi, Speaker of the House Effect of ACA of Federal Deficit." Last modified March 20, 2010. https://www.cbo.gov/sites/default/files/cbofiles/ftpdocs/113xx/doc11379/amendreconprop.pdf.

-----Congressional Budget Office, "The Budget and the Economic Outlook: Fiscal Years 2013 to 2023." Last modified February 5, 2013. Accessed February 18, 2014. http://www.cbo.gov/publication/43907.

"Contribution Limits for 2013-2014 Chart." *Federal Election Commission.* http://www.fec.gov/pages/brochures/contriblimits.shtml (accessed March 21, 2014).

Coppins, McKay, and Ian Yarrett. "Pyramid of Profiteers." *Newsweek*, April 18, 2011. http://www.newsweek.com/pyramid-profiteers-66535.

CoverageforAll.org, "2012 Federal Poverty Level." Last modified January 22, 2014. Accessed January 26, 2012. http://www.bds-corp.com/wp-content/uploads/2012/07/NY_Matrix-Health-Care-Options.pdf.

Cox, Jeff. "Fed Keeps Interest Rates Low, Continues Bond Buying Program." *CNBC*, May 1, 2013. http://www.cnbc.com id/100695681.

"Current-Dollar and "Real" Gross Domestic Product." *Bureau of Economic Analysis.* https://www.bea.gov/national/xls/gdplev.xls (accessed December 20, 2013).

Davidson, Paul. "Federal Reserve keeps stimulus going full speed." *USA Today*, May 1, 2013. http://www.usatoday.com/story/money/business/2013/05/01/fed-maintains-stimulus/2126381/.

DeNavas-Walt, Carmen, Bernadette D. Proctor, and Jessica C. Smith, U.S. Census Bureau, Current Population Reports,

P60-239, *Income, Poverty, and Health Insurance Coverage in the United States: 2010*, U.S. Government Printing Office, Washington, DC, 2011.

Dennis, Vanessa, and Jason Kane. "Health Care Reform by the Numbers." *PBS*, March 23, 2012. http://www.pbs.org/newshour/rundown/health-reform-by-the-numbers/ (accessed March 25, 2012).

Dickman, Sam, David Himmelstein, Danny McCormick, and Steffie Woolhandler. "Opting Out of Medicaid Expansion: The Health and Financial Impacts." *Health Affairs* (blog), January 30, 2014. http://healthaffairs.org/blog/2014/01/30/opting-out-of-medicaid-expansion-the-health-and-financial-impacts/ (accessed May 7, 2014).

Dorell, Oren. "Report blames Massey for W.Va. mine explosion." *USA Today*, May 19, 2011. http://usatoday30.usatoday.com/news/nation/2011-05-19-Massey-Energy-mine-explosion-West-Virginia-report_n.htm (accessed November 6, 2012).

Emerole, Obi. "Closing the Medicaid expansion gap: Why Middle Georgia needs Medicaid expansion." *The Macon Telegraph*, February 9, 2014. http://www.macon.com/2014/27/09/3219275/closing-the-medicaid-expansion-gap.html (accessed February 10, 2014).

"FACTBOX-US healthcare bill would provide immediate benefits." *Reuters*, March 19, 2010. http://www.reuters.com/article/2010/03/19/usa-healthcare-timeline-idUSN1914020220100319 (accessed MAY 8, 2012).

"Feds fine Wells Fargo over Discrimination Claims." *CBS News*, July 12, 2012. http://www.cbsnews.com/news/feds-fine-wells-fargo-over-discrimination-claims/ (accessed July 19, 2012).

"The Fed's QE3: how does it work and what are the risks?." *Reuters*, September 13, 2012. http://www.reuters.com/article/2012/09/13/us-usa-fed-easing-idUSBRE88C1CT20120913 (accessed January 13, 2014).

Flock, Elizabeth. "196 People Control 80 Percent of Super PAC Money: Who are They?" *U.S. News*, July 27, 2012. http://www.usnews.com/news/blogs/washington-whispers/2012/07/27/196-people-control-80-percent-of-super-pac-money-who-are-they (accessed October 20, 2013).

Follman, Mark. "Opinion flashback: NRA's gun-free zone myth." *USA Today*, September 18, 2013. http://www.usatoday.com/story/opinion/2013/03/24/nras-gun-free-zone-myth--column/2015657/.

Frank, Thomas. *What's the Matter with Kansas: How Conservatives Won the Heart of America*. NewYork: Picador, 2004.

Freudenrich, Ph.D., Craig, and Jonathan Strickland. "How Oil Drilling Works." *HowStuffWorks.com*, April 12, 2001. http://science.howstuffworks.com/environmental/energy/oil-drilling.htm (accessed October 30, 2012).

Friedman, Thomas L. *From Beirut to Jerusalem*. New York: Random House, 1995.

Friedman, Thomas L. *Longitudes and Attitudes: Exploring the World after September 11*. NewYork: Farrar, Straus and Giroux, 2002.

Frum, David. "How We Need to Learn to Say No to the Elderly." *Newsweek*, June 25, 2012. http://www.newsweek.com/david-frum-how-we-need-learn-say-no-elderly-65093 (accessed July 2, 2012).

Geraghty, Jim. "The Difference Between Super PACs and 501c4 nonprofits." *National Review Online*, July 5, 2012. http://www.nationalreview.com/campaign-spot/304808/difference-between-superpacs-and-501c4-nonprofits.

Gold, Dore. *Hatred's Kingdom: How Saudi Arabia Supports the New Global Terrorism*. Washington: Regnery Publishing, Inc., 2003.

Gore, Al. *Earth in the Balance*. NewYork: Penguin Books, 1992.
Gore, Al. *The Assault on Reason*. NewYork: Penguin Books, 2007.

Grondahl, Mika, Haeyoun Park, Graham Roberts, and Archie Tse. "Investigating the Cause of the Deepwater Horizon Blowout." *The New York Times*, June 21, 2010. http://www.nytimes.com/interactive/2010/06/21/us/20100621-bop.html.

Gross, Daniel. "Bankruptcy for Billionaires." *Newsweek*, September 10, 2012. http://www.newsweek.com/bankruptcy-filing-bain-owned-firm-shows-inequity-system-64721.

"Gross Domestic Product Percent change from preceding period." *Bureau of Economic Analysis*. https://www.bea.gov/national/ xls/gdpchg.xls (accessed August 4, 2014).

"Gun control, 5 common-ground steps: Our view." *USA Today*, January 30, 2013. http://www.usatoday.com/story/opinion/2013/01/29/gun-control-violence-hearings/1875975/.

Hampson, Rich. "Poll: Washington to blame more than Wall Street for economy." *USA Today*, October 18, 2011. http://usatoday30. usatoday.com/news/nation/2011-10-17-poll-wall-street-protests.htm.

Hanson, Rick. *Election Law* (blog), http://electionlawblog.org.

Harper, David. "Interest Rates and Your Bond Investments." *Investopedia*, 2012. http://www.investopedia.com/articles/03/122203.asp (accessed June 6, 2013).

Hartmann, Thom. *The Last Hours of Ancient Sunlight*. New York: Three Rivers Press, 1998.

Heakal, Reem. "Economics Basics: Supply and Demand." *Investopedia*, 2013. http://www.investopedia.com/university/economics/economics3.asp (accessed November 21, 2013).

"Health Insurance Costs." *The National Coalition on Health Care*, March 10, 2009. http://nchc.org/new-massachussetts-california-initiatives-could-help-curb-costs-nationwide/cost/.

HealthCare.gov, "Medicaid Expansion & What It Means for You." Accessed April 10, 2014. https://www.healthcare.gov/what-if-my-state-is-not-expanding-medicaid/.

Heath, Brad, and Blake Morrison. "Air tests reveal elevated levels of toxins around schools." *USA Today*, December 9, 2008. http://usatoday30.usatoday.com/news/nation/environment/school-air-monitoring1.htm (accessed September 11, 2012).

Henson, Robert. *The Rough Guide to Climate Change, 3rd Edition*. New York: Penguin Books, 2011.

Himmelstein, David, Deborah Thorne, Elizabeth Warren, and Steffie Woolhandler. "Medical Bankruptcy in the United States, 2007: Results of National Study." *The American Journal of Medicine*. no. 8 (2009): 741-746.

"History of Asbestos Litigation." *The Mesothelioma Center*. http://www.asbestos.com/mesothelioma-lawyer/lawsuit.php (accessed July 24, 2012).

"The History of Health-Care Reform in America." *Governing.com*, March 26, 2012. http://www.governing.com/news/federal/ap-history-health-care-reform-america.html (accessed March 26, 2012).

"How Much Does Single Payer National Health Care Cost?." *ThirdWorldTraveler.com*, October 1999. http://www.thirdworldtraveler.com/Health/HowMuchSPCost.html (accessed August 12, 2009).

Hulse, Carl. "House Approves Republicans Budget Plan to Cut Trillions." *The New York Times*, April 15, 2011. http://www.nytimes.com/2011/04/16/us/politics/16congress.html?_r=0.

"Infant Mortality Rates by State: National Vital Statistics Report." *Center for Disease Control and Prevention*. (2011). http://www.cdc.gov/nchs/deaths.htm.

"Insuring America's Health: Principles and Recommendations." *Institute of Medicine of the National Academies*, January 13, 2004. http://books.nap.edu/openbook.php?record_id=10874 (accessed May 6, 2014).

Jackson, David, and Aamer Madhani. "Line Drawn on Guns." *USA Today*, January 17, 2013. http://www.usatoday.com/story/news/politics/2013/01/16/line-drawn-on-guns/1566406/.

Jervis, Rick. "Judge OKs $4B BP oil spill criminal settlement." *USA Today*, January 29, 2013. http://www.usatoday.com/story/money/business/2013/01/29/bp-oil-spill-criminal-settlement/1874545/.

Johnston, David Cay. "Danger! Exploding pipelines, bursting dams. Massive Blackouts. This is what awaits America in the coming infrastructure crisis." *Newsweek*, September 10, 2012. http://www.newsweek.com/americas-coming-infrastructure-disaster-64729.

Jones, Del, and Pallavi Gogoi. "Obama limits exec pay to $500000 for bailed-out firms." *USA Today*, February 2, 2009. http://usatoday30.usatoday.com/news/washington/2009-02-04-obama-executives-cap_N.htm.

"Key Features of the Affordable Care Act, By Year." U.S. *Department of Health and Human Services*, March 26, 2012. http://www.hhs.gov/healthcare/facts/timeline/timeline-text.html (accessed March 26, 2012).

Klaidman, Daniel, James Warren, and Eleanor Clift. "Hey Buddy, Can You Spare $20 Million?." *Newsweek*, July 16, 2012, Vol. 160, Issue 3, p. 38.

Kogan, Richard. "How the Across-the-Board Cuts in the Budget Control Act Will Work." *Center on Budget and Policy Priorities*, April 27, 2012. http://www.cbpp.org/cms/?fa=view&id=3635 (accessed December 1, 2013).

Kramer, Mattea. "Top 5 Things to Know About President Obama's 2014 Budget." *NationalPriorities.org*, April 10, 2013. https://www.nationalpriorities.org/blog/2013/04/10/president-obamas-2014-budget-top-5-things-know/.

Krantz, Matt. "Gun stocks pop on Obama plans." *USA Today*, January 6, 2013. http://www.usatoday.com/story/money/markets/2013/01/16/obama-gun-control-gun-stocks/1839653/.

Kristof, Nicholas. "Looking for Lessons in Newtown." *The New York Times*, December 19, 2012. http://www.nytimes.com/2012/12/20/opinion/kristof-looking-for-lessons-in-newtown.html (accessed August 4, 2014).

Lanman, Scott, and Steve Matthews. "Greenspan Concedes to 'Flaw' in His Market Ideology." *Bloomberg.com*, October 23, 2008. http://www.bloomberg.com/apps/news?pid=newsarchive&sid=ah5qh9Up4rIg.

Light, Donald W., and Hagop kantarjian. "Cancer Rx: The $100,000 Myth." *AARP Bulletin*, May 2014, p. 22. http://pubs.aarp.org/aarpbulletin/201405_DC/?pg=22&pm=2&u1=friend.

Liptak, Adam. "Supreme Court Upholds Health Care Law, 5-4, in Victory for Obama." *The New York Times*, June 28, 2012. http://www.nytimes.com/2012/06/29/us/supreme-court-lets-health-law-largely-stand.html?pagewanted=all&_r=0 (accessed July 9, 2012).

"The Long Demise of Glass-Steagall." *Frontline: PBS*, May 8, 2003. http://www.pbs.org/wgbh/pages/frontline/shows/wallstreet/weill/demise.html (accessed February 14, 2012).

"Love Canal." *Environmental Protection Agency*. http://www.epa.gov/region2/superfund/npl/lovecanal/ (accessed January 30, 2009).

Luhby, Tami. "Who are the 1 percent?." *CNN Money*, October 29, 2011. http://money.cnn.com/2011/10/20/news/economy/occupy_wall_street_income/ (accessed October 6, 2012).

Manuel, Dave. "History of Surpluses and Deficits in the United States." *DaveManuel.com* (blog), October 6, 2012. http://www.davemanuel.com/history-of-deficits-and-surpluses-in-the-united-states.php (accessed October 6, 2012).

"The Many Roles of the Fed." *The Federal Reserve Bank of San Francisco*. http://www.frbsf.org/education/teacher-resources/what-is-the-fed (accessed February 16, 2012).

"Matthews Electroplating." *Environmental Protection Agency*, October 2005. http://www.epa.gov/reg3hscd/super/sites/VAD980712970/ (accessed May 8, 2014).

McGrath, Jane. "How Trickle-Down Economics Works." *HowStuffWorks.com*, December 9, 2008. http://money.howstuffworks.com/trickle-down-economics.htm (accessed October 27, 2012).

McKibben, Bill. *Eaarth*. New York: St. Martin's Press, 2010.

McKibben, Bill. *The End of Nature*. New York: Random House, 1989.

McKibben, Bill. *The Global Warming Reader*. New York: Penguin Books, 2011.

Mercer, Marsha. "Health Insurance Marketplace - What You Need to Know." *AARP Bulletin*, December 2013. http://www.aarp.org/health/health-insurance/info-10-2013/health-insurance-marketplace.html.

Morrison, Blake, and Brad Heath. "Health risks stack up for school kids near industry." *USA Today*, December 8, 2008. http://usatoday30.usatoday.com/news/nation/environment/school-air1.htm.

Morrissey, Ed. "Great news: "Too big to fail" banks even bigger now." *HotAir.com*, April 16, 2012. http://hotair.com/archives/2012/04/16/great-news-too-big-to-fail-banks-even-bigger-now/.

"Mothers Know Best: Myths and Facts about Healthcare Reform." *MomsRising.org*. http://www.momsrising.org/page/moms/HealthcareTruthSquad_Facts (accessed August 29, 2009).

"National Priorities Project: Democratizing the Federal Budget." *National Priorities*. https://www.nationalpriorities.org/about/mission/ (accessed November 20, 2013).

Nielson, Barry. "Fannie Mae and Freddie Mac, Boon or Boom?." *Investopedia*, December 10, 2007. http://www.investopedia.com/articles/07/fannie-freddie.asp (accessed June 12, 2011).

"Obama Firm on Bush Tax Expiry, Despite Biden Remarks." *Newsmax*, October 12, 2012. http://www.newsmax.com/

Newsfront/Biden-Bush-tax-cuts/2012/10/12/id/459803/ (accessed October 13, 2012).

OpenSecrets.org, "Super PACs." Last modified July 21, 2014. https://www.opensecrets.org/pacs/superpacs.php.

Park, Alice. "America's Health Checkup." *Time Magazine*, November 19, 2008. http://content.time.com/time/specials/packages/article/0,28804,1860289_1860561_1860562,00.html (accessed December 1, 2008).

Peterson, Jonathan. "Time for a Tune-up." *AARP Bulletin*, June 1, 2012. http://www.aarp.org/work/social-security/info-06-2012/ future-of-social-security.html.

Pfeffer, Jeffrey. "The Case Against Layoffs: They Often Backfire." *Newsweek*, February 4, 2010. http://www.newsweek.com/case-against-layoffs-they-often-backfire-75039 (accessed February 15, 2010).

Qutb, Sayyid. *Milestones*. Translated by S. Badrul Hasan. Kuwait: International Islamic Federation of Student Organizations, 1978.

Raum, Thom. "Bipartisan road to $14 trillion debt." *Yahoo News*, April 15, 2011. https://sg.news.yahoo.com/both-parties-helped-run-us-14-trillion-debt-20110413-150753-249.html.

Richardson, Owen. "List of Tax Brackets for Small Businesses." *Chron.com*. http://smallbusiness.chron.com/list-tax-brackets-small-businesses-4084.html (accessed April 3, 2012).

"The Road to Livability." *AARP Bulletin*, August 2012. http://www.aarp.org/home-family/livable-communities/info-05-2013/oregon-livable-communities-survey.html.

Robertson, Lori. "Medicare's 'Piggy Bank'." *FactCheck.org*, August 24, 2012. http://www.factcheck.org/2012/08/medicares-piggy-bank/ (accessed September 4, 2012).

Rohrlich, Justin. "Extended Unemployment Benefits: Will the Multiplier Effect Have an Impact." *Minyanville.com*, July 27, 2010. http://www.minyanville.com/businessmarkets/articles/unemployment-unemployment-extended-benefits-christine-owens/7/27/2010/id/29331 (accessed October 16, 2012).

Romano, Andrew P., and Daniel Klaidman. "President Obama's Executive Power Grab." *Newsweek*, October 22, 2012. http://www.newsweek.com/president-obamas-executive-power- grab-65287 (accessed October 29, 2012).

Romano, Andrew P., and Pat Wingert. "2,405 Shot Dead Since Tucson." *Newsweek*, March 13, 2011. http://www.newsweek. com/2405-shot-dead-tucson-66191 (accessed March 21, 2011).

Rubin, Robert. "Robert Rubin On How To Make Capitalism Work Again." *Newsweek*, December 28, 2009. http://www.newsweek.com/robert-rubin-how-make-capitalism-work-again-75809 (accessed June 30, 2011).

Salant, Johnathan D. "Spending Doubled as Obama Led First Billion-Dollar Race in 2008." *Bloomberg.com*, December 26, 2008. http://www.bloomberg.com/apps/news?sid=aerix-76GvmRM&pid=newsarchive (accessed October 14, 2013).

Samuelson, Robert J. "Obama's Budget Avoids Hard Choices (Again)." *Newsweek*, February 4, 2010. http://www.newsweek.com/obamas-budget-avoids-hard-choices-again-75079 (accessed February 15, 2010).

Samuelson, Robert J. "We Like Big Government, But We Hate Taxes." *Newsweek*, July 10, 2009. http://www.newsweek.com/we-big-government-we-hate-taxes-81905.

Schmlt, Julie. "Feds, states, banks agree to mortgage settlement." *USA Today*, February 9, 2012. http://usatoday30.usatoday.com/money/story/2012-02-08/states-mortgage-settlement/53016420/1.

Schneider, Andrew. "Triangle Shirtwaist Fire Lessons May Be Lost 100 Years Later." *HuffingtonPost*, March 25, 2011. http://www.huffingtonpost.com/2011/03/25/triangle-shirtwaist-fire-_n_840634.html.

Schoen, JohnW. "Bank of America former employees:'We were told to lie'." *NBC News*, June 17, 2013. http://www.nbcnews.com/business/business-news/bank-america-former-employees-we-were-told-lie-f6C10351458 (accessed June 17, 2013).

Sells, Michael. *Approaching the Qur'an: The Early Revelations.* Ashland, OR: White Cloud Press, 2001.

Senate Committee on Banking, Housing and Urban Affairs, Chairman Chris Dodd (D-CT), "Summary: Restoring American Financial Stability." March 16, 2010. http://www.banking.senate.gov/public/_files/FinancialReformSummary231510FINAL.pdf.

Shaw, Hannah, and Chad Stone. "Tax Data Show Richest 1 Percent Took a hit in 2008, But Income Remains Highly Concentrated." *Center on Budget and Policy Priorities*, May 25, 2011. http:// www.cbpp.org/cms/?fa=view&id=3309 (accessed October 6, 2012).

Shea-Porter, Carol. "The Truth about Medicare." *Daily Kos* (blog), August 30, 2012. http://www.dailykos.com/story/2012/08/30/1125863/-The-Truth-about-Medicare (accessed September 4, 2012).

Shear, Michael D. "Obama Vows Fast Action in New Push for Gun Control." *The New York Times*, December 19, 2012. http://www.nytimes.com/2012/12/20/us/politics/obama-to-give-congress-plan-on-gun-control-within-weeks.html?pagewanted=all (accessed December 20, 2012).

Skocpol, Theda, and Vanessa Williamson. *The Tea Party and the Remaking of Republican Conservatism.* Oxford, UK: Oxford University Press, 2012.

Spilimbergo, Antonio, Steve Symansky, and Martin Schindler. "Fiscal Multipliers." *International Monetary Fund*, May 20, 2009. http://www.imf.org/external/pubs/ft/spn/2009/spn0911.pdf.

Stauber, John, and Sheldon Rampton. "Smoking'! How the America tobacco industry employs PR scum to continue its murderous assault on human lives." *Tucson Weekly*,

November 22, 1995. http://www.tucsonweekly.com/tw/11-22-95/cover.htm.

Stockman, David. "Mitt Romney and the Brain Drain." *Newsweek*, October 15, 2012. http://www.newsweek.com/david-stockman-mitt-romney-and-bain-drain-65439 (accessed October 22, 2012).

Suskind, Ron. *The Price of Loyalty George W. Bush, the White House and the Education of Paul O'Neill.* New York: Simon & Schuster, 2004.

Szabo, Liz, and Julie Appleby. "21% of Americans scramble to cover medical, drug bills." *USA Today*, March 11, 2009. http://usatoday30.usatoday.com/news/health/2009-03-10-gallup- medical-bills_N.htm.

Taibbi, Matt. "How Wall Street Killed Financial Reform." *Rolling Stone*, May 10, 2012. http://www.rollingstone.com/politics/news/how-wall-street-killed-financial-reform-20120510 (accessed May 24, 2012).

Taibbi, Matt. "The Great American Bubble Machine." *Rolling Stone*, April 5, 2012. http://www.rollingstone.com/politics/news/the-great-american-bubble-machine-20100405 (accessed June 9, 2012).

Tavernise, Sabrina. "Report Faults Mine Owner for Explosion That Killed 29." *The New York Times*, May 19, 2011. http://www.nytimes.com/2011/05/20/us/20mine.html?pagewanted=all&_r=0 (accessed November 6, 2012).

Thomas, Evan. "We Need to Talk About Death." *Newsweek*, September 11, 2009. http://www.newsweek.com/we-need-talk-about-death-79221 (accessed September 21, 2009).

Touryalai, Halah. "Obama's Consumer Protection Agency Strikes: $210M Fine for Capital One." *Forbes*, July 18, 2012. http://www.forbes.com/sites/halahtouryalai/2012/07/18/obamas-consumer-protection-agency-strikes-210m-fine-for-capital-one/ (accessed July 19, 2012).

U.S. Department of Labor, "Summary: The Role of Unemployment as an Automatic Stabilizer During a Recession." http://www.

dol.gov/opa/media/press/eta/eta20101615fs.htm (accessed October 16, 2012).

U.S. Government Printing Office, "Table 2.1- Receipts by Source, 1934-2018." http://www.gpo.gov/fdsys/granule/ BUDGET- 2014-TAB/BUDGET-2014-TAB-2-1.

"The U.S. Health Care System: Best in the World, or Just the Most Expensive." *Bureau of Labor Education, University of Maine*, 2001. http://umaine.edu/ble/files/2011/01/US-healthcare-system.pdf.

"Universal Health Care May Cost $1.5 Trillion." *Fox News*, March 18, 2009. http://www.foxnews.com/politics/2009/03/18/universal-health-care-cost-trillion/ (accessed August 12, 2009).

Wagand, Jeffrey. "Testimony of the 7 CEOs of Big Tobacco." *JeffreyWagand.com* (blog), http://www.jeffreywigand.com/7ceos.php (accessed January 24, 2009).

Walsh, Bryan. *TIME Global Warming: The Causes, The Perils, The Solution*. NewYork: Time, 2012.

"War Costs." *Afghanistan Study Group*, February 26, 2013. http://www.afghanistanstudygroup.org/tag/war-costs/.

Weisbert, Jacob. "Why the Public Is to Blame for the Political Mess." *Newsweek*, February 4, 2010. http://www.newsweek.com/why-public-blame-political-mess-75055 (accessed February 15, 2010).

Weisman, Alan. *TheWorldWithout Us*. NewYork: Picador, 2007.

White, Jonathan R. *Terrorism: An Introduction*. Stamford, CT: Thomson Learning, 2003.

WhiteHouse.gov, "Federal Debt at the End of the Year: 1940-2017." *WhiteHouse.Gov: Office of Management and Budget*, April 13, 2012. http://www.whitehouse.gov/sites/default/files/ omb/budget/fy2013/assets/hist07z1.xls.

------"Table 1.3 Summary of Receipts, Outlays and Surplus or Deficits in Current Dollars, Constant (2005) Dollars and as a Percentage of GDP: 1940 to 2018." Last modified May 7,

2013. http://www.whitehouse.gov/sites/default/files/ omb/budget/fy2014/assets/hist01z3.xls.

Wikimedia Commons, "Leverage Ratios for Major Investment Banks." Last modified February 7, 2014. Accessed October 16, 2008. http://commons.wikimedia.org/wiki/File:Leverage_ Ratios.png.

Wikipedia, "2012 United States federal budget." Last modified June 25, 2014. Accessed October 8, 2012. http://en.wikipedia. org/wiki/2012_United_States_federal_budget.

------"2013 United States federal budget." Last modified June 17, 2014. Accessed October 6, 2012. http://en.wikipedia.org/wiki/2012_United_States_federal_budget.

------"American Recovery and Reinvestment Act of 2009." Last modified July 30, 2014. Accessed November 1, 2011. http://en.wikipedia.org/wiki/American_Recovery_and_Reinvestment_Act_of_2009.

------"ARRA Unemployment Rate Graph 2011." Last modified June 4, 2011. Accessed October 26, 2011. http://commons.wikimedia.org/wiki/File:ARRA_Unemployment_Rate_Graph_2011-05.jpg.

------"Asbestos." Last modified July 31, 2014. Accessed July 24, 2012. http://en.wikipedia.org/wiki/Asbestos.

------"Asbestos and the Law." Last modified May 24, 2014. Accessed January 28, 2009. http://en.wikipedia.org/wiki/Asbestos_ and_the_law.

------"Budget Sequestration in 2013." Last modified July 16, 2014. Accessed November 20, 2013. http://en.wikipedia.org/wiki/Budget_sequestration_in_2013.

------"Bush tax cuts." Last modified May 6, 2014. Accessed October 13, 2012. http://en.wikipedia.org/wiki/Bush_tax_cuts.

------"Charitable Organizations, 501c organizations." Last modified August 3, 2014. Accessed June 4, 2013. http://en.wikipedia. org/wiki/501(c)_organization.

Bibliography

------"Citizens United v Federal Election Commission." Last modified July 31, 2014. http://en.wikipedia.org/wiki/Budget_sequestration_in_2013.

------"Commodity Market." Last modified July 31, 2014. Accessed June 25, 2011. http://en.wikipedia.org/wiki/Commodity_market.

------"Community Reinvestment Act." Last modified July 29, 2014. Accessed February 29, 2009. http://en.wikipedia.org/wiki/ Community_Reinvestment_Act.

------"Deepwater Horizon." Last modified July 23, 2014. Accessed September 10, 2012. http://en.wikipedia.org/wiki/Deepwater_Horizon.

------"Distribution of Wealth." Last modified June 15, 2014. Accessed October 10, 2012. http://en.wikipedia.org/wiki/Distribution_of_wealth.

------"Dodd-Frank Wall Street Reform and Consumer Protection Act." Last modified June 8, 2014. Accessed December 5, 2011. http://en.wikipedia.org/wiki/Dodd–Frank_Wall_Street_Reform_and_Consumer_Protection_Act.

------"Economic Growth and Tax Relief Reconciliation Act of 2001." Last modified June 7, 2014. Accessed October 13, 2012. http://en.wikipedia.org/wiki/Economic_Growth_and_ Tax_Relief_Reconciliation_Act_of_2001.

------"Glass-Steagall Act." Last modified July 21, 2014. Accessed June 6, 2011. http://en.wikipedia.org/wiki/Glass–Steagall_Legislation.

------"Health care in the United States." Last modified August 1, 2014. Accessed May 1, 2014. http://en.wikipedia.org/wiki/Health_care_in_the_United_States.

------"International Comparison - Healthcare spending as % of GDP." Last modified July 30, 2014.Accessed March 26, 2012. http://en.wikipedia.org/wiki/Health_system#International_ comparisons.

------"Jobs and Growth Tax Relief Reconciliation Act of 2003." Last modified February 12, 2014. Accessed October 13,

2012. http://en.wikipedia.org/wiki/Jobs_and_Growth_ Tax_Relief_Reconciliation_Act_of_2003.

------"Laffer curve." Last modified June 27, 2014. Accessed October 6, 2012. http://en.wikipedia.org/wiki/Laffer_curve.

------"List of countries by life expectancy." Last modified August 3, 2014. Accessed April 11, 2012. http://en.wikipedia.org/wiki/List_of_countries_by_life_expectancy.

------"List of countries by total health expenditure (PPP) per capita." Last modified January 21, 2014. Accessed May 5, 2014. http://en.wikipedia.org/wiki/List_of_countries_by_total_health_expenditure_(PPP)_per_capita.

------"Medicaid." Last modified May 28, 2014. Accessed February 5, 2009. http://en.wikipedia.org/wiki/Medicaid.

------"Medicare." Last modified July 23, 2014. Accessed February 2, 2009. http://en.wikipedia.org/wiki/Medicare_(United_States).

------"National debt of the United States." Last modified August 3, 2014. Accessed November 29, 2012. http://en.wikipedia.org/wiki/National_debt_of_the_United_States.

------"Patient Protection and Affordable Care Act." Last modified August 3, 2014. Accessed March 26, 2012. http://en.wikipedia.org/wiki/Patient_Protection_and_Affordable_Care_Act.

------"Provisions of the Patient Protection and Affordable Care Act." Last modified June 31, 2014. Accessed July 16, 2014. http://en.wikipedia.org/wiki/Patient_Protection_and_Affordable_Care_Act.

------"Robert Rubin." Last modified June 26, 2014. Accessed June 30, 2011. http://en.wikipedia.org/wiki/Robert_Rubin.

------"Second Amendment to the United States Constitution." Last modified June 27, 2014. http://en.wikipedia.org/wiki/Second_Amendment_to_the_United_States_Constitution.

------"Strict liability." Last modified July 22, 2014. Accessed January 28, 2009. http://en.wikipedia.org/wiki/Strict_liability.

------"Subprime mortgage crisis." Last modified June 29, 2014. Accessed August 8, 2011. http://en.wikipedia.org/wiki/Subprime_mortgage_crisis.

------"Superfund." Last modified June 27, 2014. Accessed January 30, 2009. http://en.wikipedia.org/wiki/Superfund.

------"Supply and Demand." Last modified July 29, 2014. Accessed October 27, 2012. http://en.wikipedia.org/wiki/Supply_and_demand.

------"Tobacco Industry." Last modified June 30, 2014. Accessed August 16, 2012. http://en.wikipedia.org/wiki/Tobacco_industry.

------"U. S. Property with Foreclosure Activity." Last modified May 13, 2014. Accessed July 24, 2011. http://en.wikipedia.org/wiki/File:U.S._Properties_with_Foreclosure_Activity.png.

------"United States federal budget." Last modified June 23, 2014. Accessed October 6, 2012. http://en.wikipedia.org/wiki/United_States_federal_budget.

------"Upper Big Branch Mine disaster." Last modified May 14, 2014. Accessed November 6, 2012. http://en.wikipedia.org/wiki/Upper_Big_Branch_Mine_disaster.

------"Wellhead." Last modified April 30, 2014. Accessed October 28, 2012. http://en.wikipedia.org/wiki/Wellhead.

Wilper, Andrew P., Steffie Woolhandler, Karen E. Lasser, Danny McCormick, David H. Bor, and David U. Himmelstein. "Health Insurance and Mortality in US Adults." *American Journal of Public Health*. no. 12 (2009): 2289-2295. http://www.pnhp.org/excessdeaths/health-insurance-and-mortality-in-US-adults.pdf.

Woodward, Bob. *State of Denial: Bush at War, Part III*. New York: Simon & Schuster, 2006.

Zakaria, Fareed. "A Lonely Success." *Newsweek*, September 19, 2010. http://www.newsweek.com/zakaria-dont-forget-bailouts-worked-71933 (accessed September 27, 2010).

ENDNOTES

Chapter 1
Citizens United, Super PACs and Nonprofits

1. Federal Election Commission report, "2008 Presidential Campaign Financial Activity, Summary: Receipts Nearly Double 2004 Total" www.fec.gov/press2009/20090608PresStat.shtml
2. Washington Post, "2012 Presidential Campaign Finance Explorer," www.washingtonpost.com
3. www.opensecrets.org/PACS/superu7pacs.php, (opensecrets is a national website tracking the influence of money on U.S. politics.}
4. op. cit, Washington Post
5. op. cit, Washington Post
6. U.S. News & World Report, "Washington Whispers" by Elizabeth Fleck, July 27, 2012, reported that the top 196 contributed 80 percent of the Super PAC funds
7. Wikipedia, "Political Action Committee" indicates that the Center for Responsive Politics reported that only 100 contributors accounted for 80 percent of super PAC donations, http:// en.wikipedia.org/wiki/Political_Action_Committee.
8. op. cit. www.opensecrets.org

Endnotes

9   "A Guide to the Current Rules for Federal Elections," the Campaign Legal Center. www.campaignlegalcenter.org

Chapter 2
Gun Control in America

10   "There are more guns than people in the United States according to a new Study of Global Firearm Ownership,"Washington Post, June 19, 2018

11   Wikipedia: Estimated number of civilian guns per capita by country, Map of civilian guns per 100 people by country from the Small Arms Survey, 2017

12   Gallup, "What percentage of Americans own guns?" Lydia Saad, Aug 14, 2019

13   Pew Research Center, Factank News in the Numbers, "What the data says about gun deaths in the U. S." by John Gramlech, August 29, 2019

14   Pew Research Center, Ibid

15   USA Today, March 25, 2013: "'Opinion flashback, NRA's Gun-Free Zone Myth" by Mark Follman

16   https://en.wikipedia.org Universal Background Checks and www. factcheck.org/2013/03/guns-acquired-without-background-checks: Mareh 21, 2013

17   WSB-TV Atlanta, Georgia, "Where does Georgia rank in Gun Violence deaths?" Feb 1, 2018

Chapter 3
Global Warming and the Environment

18   Al Gore, Earth in the Balance (Penguin Books, NewYork, 1992)

19   TIME, Special Climate Issue. September 23, 2019

20   The Week, December 14, 2018

21   NewYork Magazine, July 10-23, 2017

22   Paul Brown, PhD., Notes From a Dying Planet, 2002-2006 (iUniverse, Lincoln, NE 2006)

23　Wikipedia
24　Wikipedia
25　Robert Henson, The Rough Guide to Climate Change, 3rd Edition (Rough Guides 2011)
26　Ibid
27　Paul Brown, Ph.D., Notes From a Dying Planet, 2002-2006 (iUniverse, Lincoln, NE 2006
28　Wikipedia
29　Bryan Walsh, "Global Warming, The Causes, The Perils. The Solutions", TIME, (Collector's Edition, 2012, Time Home Entertainment Inc.)
30　TIME, Special Climate Issue. September 23, 2019
31　Thom Hartmann, The Last Hours of Ancient Sunlight (Three Rivers Press, NewYork 1998
32　Paul Brown, Ph.D. Notes From a Dying Planet, 2002-2006 (iUniverse, Lincoln, NE 2006)
33　Thom Hartman, The Last Hours of Ancient Sunlight (Three Rivers Press, NewYork 1998
34　Ibid - Introduction
35　Al Gore, Earth in the Balance the the Balance (Penguin Books, NewYork, 1992)
36　Paul Brown, Ph.D. Notes From a Dying Planet, 2002-2006 (iUniverse, Lincoln, NE 2006)
37　Ibid
38　Thom Hartmann, The Last Hours of Ancient Sunlight (Three Rivers Press, NewYork 1998)
39　Ibid
40　TIME, Special Climate Issue. September 23, 2009
41　Bryan Walsh, "Global Warming, The Causes, The Perils, The Solutions", TIME, (Collector's Edition, 2012, Time Home Entertainment Inc.)
42　Paul Brown, PhD. Notes From a Dying Planet, 2002-2006 (iUniverse, Lincoln, NE 2006)

Endnotes

43 Bryan Walsh, "Global Warming, The Causes, The Perils, The Solutions"Time (Collector's Edition, 2012, Time Home Entertainment Inc.
44 Ibid
45 Thom Hartman, The Last Hours of Ancient Sunlight (Three Rivers Press, NewYork 1998)
46 truthdig, September 23, 2019
47 Bill McKibben, Eaarth (St. Martins Press, NewYork, 2010)
48 Wikipedia
49 Paul Brown, Ph.D. Notes From a Dying Planet, 2002-2006 (iUniverse, Lincoln, NE 2006)
50 Alan Weisman, The World Without Us (Picador, NewYork, 2007)
51 Paul Brown, Ph.D. Notes From a Dying Planet, 2002-2006 (iUniverse, Lincoln, NE 2006)
52 Thom Hartman, The Last Hours of Ancient Sunlight (Three Rivers Press, NewYork 1998)
53 Paul Brown, Ph.D. Notes From a Dying Planet, 2002-2006 (iUniverse, Lincoln, NE 2006)
54 Ibid
55 Ibid
56 Ibid
57 Ibid
58 Bill McKibben, The End of Nature (Random House 1989)
59 Paul Brown, Ph.D. Notes From a Dying Planet, 2002-2006 (iUniverse, Lincoln, NE 2006)
60 Ibid
61 New York Magazine, July 10-23
62 Paul Brown, Ph.D. Notes From a Dying Planet, 2002-2006 (iUniverse, Lincoln, NE 2006)
63 Bill McKibben, Eaarth (St. Martin's Press,NewYork, 2010)
64 Ibid
65 Paul Brown, PhD, Notes From a Dying Planet, 2002-2006 (iUniverse, Lincoln, NE 2006)
66 Ibid

67 Bill McKibben, Eaarth (St. Martin's Press, NewYork, 2010)
68 Wikipedia
69 Wikipedia
70 Ibid
71 Ibid
72 Paul Brown, Ph.D. Notes From a Dying Planet, 2002-2006 (iUniverse, Lincoln, NE 2006)
73 Ibid
74 Ibid
75 Bryan Walsh, "Global Warming, The Causes. The Perils. The Solutions", TIME, (Collector's Edition, 2012, Time Home Entertainment Inc.)
76 Paul Brown, PhD, Notes From a Dying Planet, 2002-2006 (iUniverse, Lincoln, NE 2006)
77 Ibid
78 Ibid
79 Ibid
80 Bill McKibben, Editor, The Global Warming Reader (Penguin Books, 2001)

Chapter 4
Health Care in America

81 National Health Expenditures Data, www.cms.gov, Center for Medicare and Medicaid Services, 12/11/2018.
82 "Income, Poverty, and Health Insurance Coverage in the United States: 2007." U.S. Census Bureau. Issued August 2008.
83 Newsweek magazine, "Supreme Arrogance, Five Justices put our Lives on the Line," by Paul Begala, April 9, 2012.
84 Investopedia, What Country Spends the Most on Healthcare? Sept 28, 2019 and Healthcare Administrative Costs will tally nearly $500B this year by Rebacca Pifer April 9, 2019.

85 Institute of Medicine of the National Academies, "Insuring Americas Health: Principle and Recommendations", January 13, 2004, http://en.wikipedia.org/wiki/Health_care_in_the_United_ States

86 CIA Factbook, Life expectancy by country. https://www.cia.gov/library/publications/the-world-factbook/rankorder/2102rank.html

87 World Atlas, Infant Mortality Rate by Country, Aug 19, 2018.

88 New Medicines for Better Health, European Federation of Pharmaceutical Industries and Associations, EFPIA, updated June 1, 2012.

89 New Study Finds 45,000 Deaths Annually Linked to Lack of Health Coverage, Health & Medicine, The Harvard Gazette, Sept, 17, 2009

90 EPA Infant Mortality, https://cfpub.epa.gov/roe/indicator_pdf

91 The American Journal of Medicine, August 2009, Volume 122, issue.

92 The Future of Freedom, Illiberal Democracy at Home and Aboard, Fareed Zakaria, W.W. Norman and Co., 2004.

93 Congressional Budget Office, Cost Estimates for H.R. 4872, Reconciliation Act of 2010 (Final Health Care Legislation) (March 20, 2010).

94 Wikipedia, Efforts to Repeal the Patient Protection Affordable Care Act

95 Dubay L., Holahan J. and Cook A., The Uninsured and the Affordability of Health Insurance Coverage, Health Affairs (Web Exclusive), November 2006.

96 Times.com, The Final Obamacare Tally is in. About 400,000 fewer people signed up for this year NY

97 Requirements of Medicaid in Georgia, Jeannine Mancini, www. E-How.com.

98 Sam Dickman, et. al., Health Affairs Blog, "Opting Out of Medicaid Expansion: The Health and Financial

Impact", January 30, 2014, http://healthaffairs.org/blog/2014/01/30/opting-out-of-medicaid-expansion-the-health-and-financial-impacts/

Chapter 5
Business in America

Triangle Shirtwaist Factory fire

99 "Eyewitness at the Triangle" by William G. Shephard. From Leon Stein, ed., *Out of the Sweatshop: The Struggle for Industrial Democracy* (New York: Quadrangle/New Times Book Company, 1977). Originally published in the Milwaukee Journal, March 27, 1911.

Asbestos

100 Environmental Working Group website, www.erg.org/sites/asbestos/facts/fact3.php.
101 www.ringsurf.com/online/2161-asbestos_litigation_history.html.
102 op. cit. Environmental Working Group.

Tobacco

103 "Smokin'!, How the American Tobacco Industry Employs PR Scam to Continue Its Murderous Assault on Human Lives", published in Tucson Weekly, 11/22/95.
104 "Facts on Second Hand Smoke," Centers for Disease Control and Prevention, cdcinfo@cdc.gov.
105 op. cit. "Smokin'!."
106 Testimony before House Subcommittee on Health and the Environment, April 14, 1994.
107 Haines v Liggett Group, Inc., 818 F Supp 414, 421 (DNJ 1993), quoted in Daynard et al. 2000.

108 American Lung Association, "Who is Really Benefiting from the Tobacco Settlement Money?" February 3, 2016, updated Nov 19, 2018.
109 www.cdc.gov/tobacco/data-statistics/fact_sheet/fast_facts, Center for Disease Control and Prevention, "Smoking and Tobacco Use, Fast Facts" 2019
110 American Lung Association, General Smoking Facts, Centers for Disease Control and Prevention. Smoking-Attributable Mortality, Years of Potential Life Lost, and Productivity Losses—United States, 2000–2004. Morbidity and Mortality Weekly Report. November 14, 2008; 57(45):1226–28.
111 Ibid.

Environmental pollution

112 Blum, Elizabeth D. (2008). *Love Canal Revisited : Race, Class, and Gender in Environmental Activism*. Kansas: University Press of Kansas. ISBN 978-0-7006-1560-5. http://books.google.com/ books?id=ZDkSAQAAIAAJ,

Air Pollution

113 "National Priorities List". United States Environmental Protection Agency. Retrieved March 5, 2014, http://en.wikipedia.org/wiki/List_of_Superfund_sites_in_the_United_States
114 USA TODAY December 8, 2009, "Toxic air and America's Schools, Health risks stack up for school kids near industry," by Blake Morrison and Brad Health. The results of the entire USA Today analysis can be found at www.usatoday.com/news/nation/environment/school-air-monitoring1.htm.

Deep Water Horizon

115 http://www.epa.gov/airtrends/aqtrends.html. *[pg.130]*

Massey Mining in West Virginia

116 Rascoe, Ayesha, 5 January 2011, "BP Firm Made Risky Decisions before Spill, Report," Reuters.
117 Sabrina Tavernise, New York Times, "Report Faults Mine Owner for Explosion that Killed 29," May 19, 2011.
118 Ibid.

The Opioid Crisis

119 www.statnews.com/2019/09/22/abbott-oxycontin-crusade
120 Ibid
121 Ibid
122 Tracking the Flow of Opioids across America, PBS News Hour, Aug 15, 2019
123 Purdue Pharma: Sackler Family's Personal Wealth offered in Opioid Deal, September 9, 2019.
124 https://www.NPR.org/2019/05/27/72409309, "This case will set a Precedent: 1st Major Opioid Trail Opens in Oklahoma", May 27, 2019

Chapter 6
The Financial Crisis

125 "Fannie Mae and Freddie Mac, Boon or Boom" by Barry Nielsen, Dec 10, 2007, www.investopedia.com/article/07/barrynielsen Dec 10, 2007
126 "CARPE DIEM: The Rise and Fall of the Subprime Mortgage Market". Mjperry.blogspot.com. 2008-07-17. http://mjperry.blogspot.com/2008/07/rise-and-fall-of-subprime-mortgage.html. Retrieved 2009-02-27. and a b "Harvard Report" (PDF). http:// www.jchs.harvard.edu/publications/markets/son2008/son2008.pdf
127 Wikipedia.org/wiki/subprime_mortgage_crisis
128 *Wall Street Journal* Oct. 11, 2008,

129 U.S. FORECLOSURE ACTIVITY INCREASES 75 PERCENT IN 2007". RealtyTrac. 2008-01-29. http://www.realtytrac.com/ContentManagement/pressrelease.aspx? ChannelID=9&ItemID=3988&accnt=64847.
RealtyTrac Press Release 2008FY". Realtytrac.com. 2009-01-15. http://www.realtytrac.com/ContentManagement/pressrelease.aspx?ChannelID=9&ItemID=5681&accnt=64847. Retrieved 2009-02-27
Realty Trac-2009Year End Report". Realtytrac.com. http://www.realtytrac.com/contentmanagement/press-release.aspx?channelid=9&accnt=0&itemid=8333. Retrieved 2010-10-03

130 Wells Fargo Economic Research-Weekly Economic and Financial Commentary-September 17, 2010

131 American Social History Project. Center for Media and Learning, "Graph of U.S. Unemployment Date 1930 to 1945", source: Bureau of Labor Statistics, http://herb.ashp.cuny.edu/items/slow/1510

132 "CBO, Estimated Impact of the American Recovery and Reinvestment Act on Employment and Economic Output from April 2011 through June 2011" and included "Table 1, Estimate Macroeconomic Impact of the American Recovery and Reinvestment Act, 2009 to 2012", August 2011

133 U.S. Labor Department, "Summary: The Role of Unemployment as an Automatic Stabilizer During a Recession", http://www.dol.gov/opa/media/press/eta/eta20101615fs.htm

134 Bureau of Economic Analysis, National Economic Accounts at www.bea.gov/national/index.htm#gdp.Data as of 9/17/2012.

135 Bureau of Labor Statistics of the U.S. Department of Labor, October 14, 2012, "Databases, Tables & Calculators by Subject", available at http://data.bls.gov/timeseries/LNS14000000

136 Winston-Salem Journal, "Five Big Banks larger than before Crisis, Bailout", April 22, 2012, http://www2.journalnow.com/business/2012/apr/22/wssunbiz01-big-five-banks-larger-than-before-crisi-ar-2188584/
137 Ibid
138 Forbes, "Obama's Consumer Protection Agency Strikes: $210 million Fine for Capital One", 7/18/2012, http://www.forbes.com/sites/halahtouryalai/2012/07/18/obamas-consumer-protection-agency-strikes-210m-fine-for-capital-one/
139 CBS News, "CBS News Moneywatch", "Feds fine Wells Fargo over discrimination claims", July 12, 2012, http://www.cbsnews.com/8301-505123_162-57471109/feds-fine-wells-fargo-over-discrimination-claims/
140 Moneybeat, "Live Blog: J P Morgan's $13 billion Settlement Agreement", Nov 19, 2013.

Chapter 7
The Tea Party, A Comedy of Contradictions

141 "Rick Santelli and the Rant of the Year", February 19, 2009, www.youtube.com
142 "The Tea Party and the Remaking of Republican Conservatism" by Theda Skocpol and Vanessa Williamson, Oxford University Press, 2012
143 Wikipedia, "Distribution of Wealth"/
144 "Tax Data Show Richest 1 Percent Took a Hit in 2008, but Income Remained Highly Concentrated at the Top, Recent Gains of Bottom 90 Percent Wiped Out," by Hannah Shaw and Chad Stone, Center on Budget and Policy Priorities, May 5, 2011
145 "Who are the 1 percent?", CNNMoney, October 29, 2011.
146 Wall Street Journal, January 4, 2011
147 For more information about immigration identification see the Migration Information Source website. www.migrationinformation.org/feature/display.cfm?846

Chapter 8
Debt and the Economy

148 A New Way Forward, Rethinking U. S. Strategy in Afghanistan, Report of the Afghanistan Study Group, "War Costs: Cut Wasteful Pentagon Spending, Starting with the War Budget" Jan 28, 2013.

149 Wikipedia, "Casualties of the Iraq War" with notes taken from the Iraq Body Count Project.

150 Wikipedia, "Financial Cost of Iraq War", for Brown University Cost of War Project, Crawford, Neta and Catherine Lutz. "Economic and Budgetary Costs of the Wars in Afghanistan, Iraq and Pakistan to the United States: A Summary."

151 Extracted from the Office of Management and Budget, Historic Tables, Table 7.1. www.whitehouse.gov/omb/budget/historicals.

152 Ibid

153 Ibid

154 from taxfoundation.org/article/us-federal-individual-income-tax-history

155 Personal income tax is from the Office of Management and Budget, whitehouse.gov/ obm/budget/historicals table 2.1. The GDP is from the Bureau of Econonic Analysis, bea.gov/ national/index.htm

156 "Fiscal Multipliers", International Monetary Fund, Antorio Spilimbergo, Steve Symansky and Martin Schindler, Survey of Fiscal Multipliers in the Literature, May 20, 2009, last section by Mark Zandi

157 Who are the 1 percent?, CNN, October 29, 2011

158 Wealth, Income, and Power by G. William Domhoff of the UC- Santa Barbara Sociology Department

159 Wikipedia, Wealth Inequality in the United States,^ Jump up to:[a] [b] Occupy Wall Street And The Rhetoric of Equality Forbes November 1, 2011 by Deborah L. Jacobs

INDEX

Adjustable Rate Mortgages, 147, 150
AFL-CIO, 2, 11, 14
Agencies enacted from the Great Depression, 145
Air pollution, 122
America ranking in gun homicides, 29
America's preoccupation with guns, 30
American Recovery and Reinvestment Act, 157
American Tax Payers Relief Act of 2012, 13
Americans are dying from lack of health care, 79
Asbestos, 109, 110, 113
asbestosis, 110, 111
Bear Stearns was sold to JP Morgan Chase, 150, 155
Biofuel production, 66
Bipartisan Campaign Reform Act, 3
Brooksley Born, 141
Californians for Statewide Smoking Restrictions, 115
Canadian tar sands, 49
Cap and Trade, 63
CEOs of tobacco companies, 113, 116
Citizens United, 1, 4, 5, 8, 14, 18, 19
Deforestation, 50, 51
Coal, 65, 190
Collateralized Debt Obligations, 144
Columbine High School, 23, 24
Commodity Futures Trading Commission, 141, 164
Companies' asbestos manufacturing, 111

Index

Comprehensive Environmental Response, Compensation, and Liability Act, (CERCLA), 120
Consumer Financial Protection Bureau, 172, 173
Creating jobs during the Great Depression, 139
Debt to GDP ratio, 197-200 Deep Water Horizon, 190
Dodd-Frank Wall Street Reform and Consumer Protection Act, 164
Donation in Presidential election, Economic Stimulus Act, 157, 212
economic recovery, 156, 157
Expanded Medicaid, 98, 101
Exxon-Mobil, 60
Fannie Mae, 145, 146, 148
FDIC, 140, 142, 146, 169, 171, 189
Federal Election Commission, 1, 3, 5, 8, 15
Federal Fund Rate, 159, 215
fiscal multipliers, 213 five financial banks, 163 Fox News, 180, 181, 187
Glass-Steagall Act, 140, 141, 142, 164, 166, 188
global warming, 45, 46, 47, 49, 50, 52, 53, 56, 57, 58, 60, 61, 62, 63, 64, 66, 69
Gramm-Leach-Bliley Act, 147, 148
Great Depression, 64, 139, 153, 161, 164, 202, 204, 212
greenhouse gas, 46, 48, 50, 51, 58, 192
gun ownership to other industrialized countries, 28
caused by smoking, 108
highest health care costs, 73, 75, 78 history of tobacco in America,
Hobby Lobby, 97, 98
Hooker Chemical Company, 118
independent expenditure only committee, 4, 5
individual mandate, 72, 76, 85, 88, 90, 94, 95, 96
IPCC, 46, 47, 63
Johns-Manville, 111, 112
Joseph Ricketts, 13
Justice Anthony Kennedy, 5
Justice John Paul Stevens, 6
Lehman Brothers', 151
liberty and health care, 83
Love canal, 118
Massey Mining, 130
McCain-Feingold Act, 3, 4, 5, 19
Mesothelioma, 110
Methane, 48

Mortgage Backed Securities, 144, 145, 150, 196
Net Capital Ratio, 149, 169
NINA-no income, no asset, 147
Nuclear energy, 65
number without health care insurance, 73, 77, 79, 101
Obamacare, 72, 76, 83, 84, 93, 96, 99,101, 181. 182, 190, 191
Tar Sands oil, 49, 65
OMB and CBO, Orderly Liquidation Fund, 169
overview of derivatives, 165
Overview of the Financial Industry, 168
paying for those who are not insured, 76
Franklin D. Roosevelt, 75
President Jimmy Carter, 119
President Lyndon Johnson, 75
President Reagan, 80, 104
President Richard Nixon, 75
President Teddy Roosevelt, 75
preventive care, 77, 86
privately owned guns, 28
Provisions of the ACA, 72
quantitative easing, 215, 216, 217
Keynesian Economics, 212, 215
Rating agencies, 165

regulations on mortgage loan approval, 164, 166
Resource Conservation and Recovery Act, 121
Results of the recession, 155 Robert Rubin, 141, 150, 165, 188
Sandy Hook Elementary School, 26, 43
Second Amendment, 31-34 District of Columbia v. Heller, 32
Senator Bernie Sanders, 62
Senator James Inhofe, 60
Sheldon Adelson, 9, 12
Solar power, 67
SpeechNow.org, 5
Subprime mortgages, 143, 196
Superfund Act, 120
Supply Side Economics, 140, 141, 163, 188
Surgeon General's report on tobacco smoking, 114
tax rate vs tax receipts
Glenn Beck, 180
Rick Santelli, 178
Sarah Palin, 180
Tillman Act, 2, 4
Tobacco Industry Research Council, 114, 115
Triangle Shirtwaist Factory, 106, 108
wealth inequality, 217
Who are the Tea Partiers, 180

Why are health care
    costs so high, 73
William Koch, 13
Wind energy, 66

Lightning Source UK Ltd.
Milton Keynes UK
UKHW050411180920
369953UK00008BA/211